Communications
in Computer and Information Science   1398

T0171862

More information about this series at http://www.springer.com/series/7899

Mitra Baratchi · Lu Cao ·
Walter A. Kosters · Jefrey Lijffijt ·
Jan N. van Rijn · Frank W. Takes (Eds.)

Artificial Intelligence and Machine Learning

32nd Benelux Conference, BNAIC/Benelearn 2020
Leiden, The Netherlands, November 19–20, 2020
Revised Selected Papers

 Springer

Editors
Mitra Baratchi (iD)
LIACS, Leiden University
Leiden, The Netherlands

Walter A. Kosters (iD)
LIACS, Leiden University
Leiden, The Netherlands

Jan N. van Rijn (iD)
LIACS, Leiden University
Leiden, The Netherlands

Lu Cao
LIACS, Leiden University
Leiden, The Netherlands

Jefrey Lijffijt (iD)
Ghent University
Ghent, Belgium

Frank W. Takes (iD)
LIACS, Leiden University
Leiden, The Netherlands

ISSN 1865-0929   ISSN 1865-0937 (electronic)
Communications in Computer and Information Science
ISBN 978-3-030-76639-9   ISBN 978-3-030-76640-5 (eBook)
https://doi.org/10.1007/978-3-030-76640-5

This Springer imprint is published by the registered company Springer Nature Switzerland AG
The registered company address is: Gewerbestrasse 11, 6330 Cham, Switzerland

Preface

Artificial intelligence and machine learning are two thriving fields of research at the heart of countless modern day technological innovations. The BeNelux Conference on Artificial Intelligence (BNAIC) and the Belgian-Dutch Conference on Machine Learning (Benelearn) traditionally bring together these communities for an annual conference, and have done so jointly since 2018.

In 2020, the 32nd BNAIC/Benelearn conference was organized by Leiden University, under the auspices of the Benelux Association for Artificial Intelligence (BNVKI). It took place in a fully online format as a direct result of the COVID-19 pandemic. During November 19–20, 2020, researchers and practitioners were welcomed to discuss and exchange novel scientific findings, as well as new developments and applications in business and industry. The conference was a great success, with interesting keynote talks by Joost Batenburg (Leiden University), Gabriele Gramelsberger (Aachen University) and Tom Schaul (Google Deepmind), and invited talks by Luc de Raedt (KU Leuven), Nico Roos (Maastricht University) and Yingqian Zhang (Eindhoven University of Technology). In addition, lively contributed sessions and a succesful "industry and society" afternoon were organized.

This volume contains the postproceedings of the BNAIC/Belenearn 2020 conference. Authors were invited to submit papers on all aspects of artificial intelligence and machine learning. Out of the 41 full papers submitted to the conference, 12 papers (29%) were invited to contribute to the postproceedings. All papers were subject to a single-blind review by at least three Program Committee members.

We want to express our gratitude towards all those who contributed to organizing and running the conference and its postproceedings. This includes the Program Committee, additional reviewers, conference chairs, local organizers, students, conference sponsors, Leiden University and the Leiden Institute of Advanced Computer Science.

February 2021

M. Baratchi
L. Cao
W. A. Kosters
J. Lijffijt
J. N. van Rijn
F. W. Takes

Organization

Program Committee

Martin Atzmueller	Tilburg University, Netherlands
Bernard de Baets	Ghent University, Belgium
Henning Basold	Leiden University, Netherlands
Mitra Baratchi	Leiden University, Netherlands
Souhaib Ben Taieb	Université de Mons, Belgium
Floris Bex	Utrecht University, Netherlands
Hendrik Blockeel	Katholieke Universiteit Leuven, Belgium
Koen van der Blom	Leiden University, Netherlands
Bart Bogaerts	Vrije Universiteit Brussel, Belgium
Tibor Bosse	Vrije Universiteit Amsterdam, Netherlands
Bert Bredeweg	University of Amsterdam, Netherlands
Egon L. van den Broek	Utrecht University, Netherlands
Lu Cao	Leiden University, Netherlands
Tom Claassen	Radboud University, Netherlands
Walter Daelemans	University of Antwerp, Netherlands
Mehdi Dastani	Utrecht University, Netherlands
Kurt Driessens	Maastricht University, Netherlands
Tim van Erven	Leiden University, Netherlands
Ad Feelders	Utrecht University, Netherlands
George H. L. Fletcher	Eindhoven University of Technology, Netherlands
Benoît Frénay	Université de Namur, Belgium
Lieke Gelderloos	Tilburg University, Netherlands
Pierre Geurts	University of Liège, Belgium
Nicolas Gillis	Université de Mons, Belgium
Nick Harley	Vrije Universiteit Brussel, Belgium
Frank van Harmelen	Vrije Universiteit Amsterdam, Netherlands
Andrew Hendrickson	Tilburg University, Netherlands
Tom Heskes	Radboud University, Netherlands
Arjen Hommersom	Open University, Netherlands
Mark Hoogendoorn	Vrije Universiteit Amsterdam, Netherlands
Anna V. Kononova	Leiden University, Netherlands
Walter Kosters	Leiden University, Netherlands
Johan Kwisthout	Radboud University, Netherlands
Bertrand Lebichot	Université Libre de Bruxelles, Belgium
John Lee	Université Catholique de Louvain, Belgium
Jan Lemeire	Vrije Universiteit Brussel, Belgium
Tom Lenaerts	Université Libre de Bruxelles, Belgium
Jefrey Lijffijt	Ghent University, Belgium

Gilles Louppe	University of Liège, Belgium
Peter Lucas	Leiden University, Netherlands
Bernd Ludwig	University of Regensburg, Germany
Elena Marchiori	Radboud University, Netherlands
Wannes Meert	Katholieke Universiteit Leuven, Belgium
Vlado Menkovski	Eindhoven University of Technology, Netherlands
John-Jules Meyer	Utrecht University, Netherlands
Arno Moonens	Vrije Universiteit Brussel, Belgium
Nanne van Noord	University of Amsterdam, Netherlands
Frans Oliehoek	Delft University of Technology, Netherlands
Aske Plaat	Leiden University, Netherlands
Eric Postma	Tilburg University, Netherlands
Henry Prakken	Utrecht University and University of Groningen, Netherlands
Mike Preuss	Leiden University, Netherlands
Peter van der Putten	Leiden University and Pegasystems, Netherlands
Jan N. van Rijn	Leiden University, Netherlands
Yvan Saeys	Ghent University, Belgium
Chiara F. Sironi	Maastricht University, Netherlands
Evgueni Smirnov	Maastricht University, Netherlands
Gerasimos Spanakis	Maastricht University, Netherlands
Jennifer Spenader	University of Groningen, Netherlands
Johan Suykens	Katholieke Universiteit Leuven, Belgium
Frank Takes	Leiden University, Netherlands
Dirk Thierens	Utrecht University, Netherlands
Leon van der Torre	University of Luxembourg, Luxembourg
Remco Veltkamp	Utrecht University, Netherlands
Joost Vennekens	Katholieke Universiteit Leuven, Belgium
Jonathan K. Vis	Leiden University, Netherlands
Arnoud Visser	University of Amsterdam, Netherlands
Marieke van Vugt	University of Groningen, Netherlands
Willem Waegeman	Ghent University, Belgium
Hui Wang	Leiden University, Netherlands
Gerhard Weiss	University Maastricht, Netherlands
Marco Wiering	University of Groningen, Netherlands
Jef Wijsen	Université de Mons, Belgium
Mark H. M. Winands	Maastricht University, Netherlands
Marcel Worring	University of Amsterdam, Netherlands
Menno van Zaanen	Centre for Digital Language Resources, South Africa
Yingqian Zhang	Eindhoven University of Technology, Netherlands

Contents

Evaluating the Robustness of Question-Answering Models to Paraphrased Questions

Paulo Alting von Geusau$^{(\boxtimes)}$ (iD) and Peter Bloem (iD)

Vrije Universiteit Amsterdam, De Boelelaan 1105,
1081 Amsterdam, HV, The Netherlands
`vu@peterbloem.nl`

Abstract. Understanding questions expressed in natural language is a fundamental challenge studied under different applications such as question answering (QA). We explore whether recent state-of-the-art models are capable of recognizing two paraphrased questions using unsupervised learning. Firstly, we test QA models' performance on an existing paraphrased dataset (Dev-Para). Secondly, we create a new paraphrased evaluation set (Para-SQuAD) containing multiple paraphrased question pairs from the SQuAD dataset. We describe qualitative investigations on these models and how they present paraphrased questions in continuous space. The results demonstrate that the paraphrased dataset confuses the QA models and decreases their performance. Visualizing the sentence embeddings of Para-SQuAD by the QA models suggests that all models, except BERT, struggle to recognize paraphrased questions effectively.

Keywords: Natural language · Transformers · Question answering · Embeddings

1 Introduction

Question answering (QA) is a challenging research topic. Small variations in semantically similar questions may confuse current state-of-the-art QA models and result in giving different answers. For example, the questions "Who founded IBM?" and "Who created the company IBM?" should be recognised as having the same meaning by a QA model. QA models need to understand the meaning behind the words and their relationships. Those words can be ambiguous, implicit, and highly contextual.

The motivation for writing this paper springs from the observation that QA models can provide a wrong answer to a question that is phrased slightly different compared to a previous question [15]. Despite the questions being semantically similar. This sensitivity to question paraphrases needs to be improved to provide more robust QA models. Modern QA models need to recognise paraphrases effectively and provide the same answers to paraphrased questions.

© Springer Nature Switzerland AG 2021
M. Baratchi et al. (Eds.): BNAIC/Benelearn 2020, CCIS 1398, pp. 1–14, 2021.
https://doi.org/10.1007/978-3-030-76640-5_1

Despite the release of high-quality QA datasets, test sets are typically a random subset of the whole dataset, following the same distribution as the development and training sets. We need datasets to test the QA models' ability to recognise paraphrased questions and analyse their performance. Therefore, we use two datasets, based on SQuAD [28], to conduct two separate experiments on BERT [7], GPT-2 [26] and XLNet [34].

The first dataset we use is an existing paraphrased test set (Dev-Para). Dev-Para is publicly available,[1] and we use it to evaluate the models' over-sensitivity to paraphrased questions. Dev-Para is created from SQuAD development questions and consists of newly generated paraphrases. Dev-Para evaluates the models' performance on unseen test data to better indicate their generalisation ability. We hypothesise that adding new paraphrases to the test set will result in the models suffering a drop in performance. This paper will search for properties that the models learn in an unsupervised way, as a side effect of the original data, setup, and training objective.

In addition, we introduce a new paraphrased evaluation set (Para-SQuAD) to test the QA models' ability in recognizing the semantics of a question in an unsupervised manner. Para-SQuAD is a subset of the SQuAD 1.1 development set, whereas Dev-Para is much larger and consists of newly added paraphrases. Para-SQuAD consists of question pairs that are semantically similar but have a different syntactic structure. The first author manually selected all the paraphrased question pairs from the SQuAD 1.1 development set to create Para-SQuAD. We analyze all sentence embeddings of Para-SQuAD in an embedding space with the help of t-SNE visualization. For each model, we calculate the average cosine similarity of all question pairs to gain an understanding of the semantic similarity between paraphrased questions.

The contributions of this paper are threefold:

1. We test the QA models' performance on an existing paraphrased test set (Dev-Para) to evaluate their robustness to question paraphrases.
2. We create a new paraphrased evaluation set (Para-SQuAD) that consists of question pairs from the original SQuAD 1.1 development set, the question pairs are semantically similar but have a different syntactic structure.
3. We create and visualize useful sentence embeddings of Para-SQuAD by the QA models, and calculate the average cosine similarity between the sentence embeddings for each QA model.

The paper is organized as follows. Section 2 describes the models, sentence embeddings, and the datasets used in this paper. Section 3 presents two experiments. The first experiment measures the performance of the QA models on Dev-Para and the second experiment visualizes the sentence embeddings of Para-SQuAD for each QA model. In Sect. 4, we present the related work, before concluding in Sect. 5.

---

[1] https://github.com/nusnlp/paraphrasing-squad.

2 Methodology

This section describes the models and sentence embeddings used in this paper, and we introduce our method to create Para-SQuAD.

2.1 BERT, GPT-2 and XLNet

We use QA models based on the transformer architecture from Vaswani et al. [32]. The models have been pre-trained on enormous corpora of unlabelled text, including Books Corpus and Wikipedia, and only require task-specific fine-tuning. The first model we use is Google's BERT. BERT is bidirectional because its self-attention layer performs self-attention in both directions; each token in the sentence has self-attention with all other tokens in the sentence. The model learns information from both the left and right sides during the training phase. BERT's input is a sequence of provided tokens, and the output is a sequence of generated vectors. These output vectors are referred to as 'context embeddings' since they contain information about the tokens' context. BERT uses a stack of transformer encoder blocks and has two self-supervised training objectives: masked language modelling and next-sentence prediction.

The second model used in this paper is OpenAI's GPT-2. GPT-2 is also a transformer model and has a similar architecture to BERT; however, it only handles context on the left and uses masked self-attention. GPT-2 is built using transformer decoder blocks and was trained to predict the next word. The model is auto-regressive, just like Google's XLNet.

XLNet, the third model used in this paper, has an alternative technique that brings back the merits of auto-regression while still incorporating the context on both sides. XLNet uses the Transformer-XL as its base architecture. The Transformer-XL extends the transformer architecture by adding recurrence at a segment level. XLNet already achieves impressive results for numerous supervised tasks; however, it is unknown if the model generates useful embeddings for unsupervised tasks. We explore this question further in this paper.

We use the small GPT-2, BERT-Base, and XLNet-Base, all consisting of 12 layers. The larger versions of BERT and XLNet have 24 layers; the larger version of GPT-2 has 36 layers.

2.2 Embeddings

Classic word embeddings are static and word-level; this means that each word receives exactly one pre-computed embedding. Embedding is a method that produces continuous vectors for given discrete variables. Word embeddings have demonstrated to improve various NLP tasks, such as question answering [4]. These traditional word embedding methods have several limitations in modelling the contextual awareness effectively. Firstly, they cannot handle polysemy. Secondly, they are unable to grasp a real understanding of a word based on its surrounding context.

Advances in unsupervised pre-training techniques, together with large amounts of data, have improved contextual awareness of models such as BERT, GPT-2, and XLNet. Contextually aware embeddings are embeddings that not only contain information about the represented word, but also information about the surrounding words. The state-of-the-art transformer models create embeddings that depend on the surrounding context instead of an embedding for a single word.

Sentence embeddings are different from word embeddings because they provide embeddings for the entire sentence. We aim to extract the numerical representation of a question to encapsulate its meaning. Semantically meaningful means that semantically similar sentences are clustered with each other in vector space.

The network structures of the transformer models compute no independent sentence embeddings. Therefore, we modify and adapt the transformer networks to obtain sentence embeddings that are semantically meaningful and used for visualization. We use QA models that are deep unsupervised language representations. Moreover, all QA models are pre-trained with unlabelled data.

Feeding individual sentences to the models will result in fixed-size sentence embeddings. A conventional approach to retrieve a fixed size sentence embedding is to average the output layer, also called mean pooling. Another common approach for models like BERT and XLNet is to use the first [CLS] token.

2.3 SQuAD

To create Para-SQuAD, we use the Stanford Question Answering Dataset [28], which consists of over 100.000 natural question and answer sets retrieved from over 500 Wikipedia articles by crowd-workers. The SQuAD dataset is widely used as a popular benchmark for QA models. The QA models take a question and context as input to predict the correct answer. The two metrics used for evaluation are the exact match (EM) and the F1 score. The SQuAD dataset is a closed dataset; this means that the answer to a question exists in the context. Figure 1 illustrates an example from the SQuAD development set.

SQuAD treats question answering as a reading comprehension task where the question refers to a Wikipedia paragraph. The answer to a question has to be a span of the presented context; therefore, the starting token and ending token of the substring is calculated.

2.4 Para-SQuAD

To evaluate the models' robustness in recognising paraphrased questions, we create a new dataset called Para-SQuAD, using existing question pairs from the SQuAD 1.1 development set. The SQuAD development set uses at least two additional answers for each question to make the evaluation more reliable. The human performance score on the SQuAD 1.1 development set is 82.3% for the exact match and 91.2% for F1.[2]

---

[2] https://rajpurkar.github.io/SQuAD-explorer/.

> The Broncos took an early lead in Super Bowl 50 and never trailed. Newton was limited by Denver's defense, which sacked him seven times and forced him into three turnovers, including a fumble which they recovered for a touchdown. Denver linebacker Von Miller was named Super Bowl MVP, recording five solo tackles, 2.5 sacks, and two forced fumbles.

> **Who was the Super Bowl 50 MVP?**

> *Ground Truth Answers:* Von Miller, Miller

Fig. 1. Example of the SQuAD 1.1 development set with context, question, and answers.

To create Para-SQuAD, we manually search SQuAD for any two questions that are paraphrases of one another (this annotation was performed solely by the first author). We did not introduce any new questions, only annotation on the existing data. As a result, all paraphrased question pairs in Para-SQuAD are selected from the SQuAD 1.1 development set, without creating additional paraphrases. Humans have a consistent intuition for "good" paraphrases in general [19]. The key method for creating paraphrases in this paper is the manipulation of syntactic structure. To be specific, we consider questions as paraphrases if they yield the same answer and have the same intention. Moreover, word substitution is sufficient to count as a paraphrase.

Questions in the SQuAD development set relate to specific Wikipedia paragraphs and are grouped together. The first author merely selected existing paraphrased question pairs from the SQuAD 1.1 development set to create Para-SQuAD, without creating new questions. This method ensures that Para-SQuAD is a subset of the SQuAD development set without inducing dataset bias. Moreover, the data distribution and dataset bias in Para-SQuAD and the SQuAD development set remains identical. Para-SQuAD consists of 700 questions, 350 paraphrased question pairs, and 12 different topic categories.

After paraphrase collection, we perform post-processing to check for any mistakes. We check the paraphrased questions on English fluency using context-free grammar concepts.[3] Furthermore, we use spaCy[4] to conduct a sanity check after manually collecting all paraphrased questions. SpaCy is an industrial-strength natural language processing tool and provides sentence similarity scores of the question pairs using word embedding vectors.

Using Para-SQuAD for visualisation has a significant advantage compared to using Dev-Para. Namely, the data distribution of Dev-Para changes after the addition of new paraphrases. On the contrary, the data distribution of Para-SQuAD remains the same because we do not add new paraphrases; we only select the existing paraphrases in the SQuAD 1.1 development set.

---

[3] https://www.nltk.org/.
[4] https://spacy.io/.

2.5   Para-SQuAD Sentence Embeddings

We present a proof-of-concept visualization of the models' capability to represent semantically similar sentences closely in vector space. Previous research by Coenen et al. [3] reveals that much of the semantic information, of BERT and related transformer models, is visible and encoded in a low-dimensional space. Therefore, we map all the paraphrased questions from Para-SQuAD to a sentence embedding space for every pre-trained model. Distance in the vector space can be interpreted roughly as sentence similarity according to the model in question.

We calculate the fixed-length vectors for each question using the Flair framework,[5] with mean pooling, to receive the final token representation. Mean pooling uses the average of all word embeddings to obtain an embedding for the whole sentence.

All transformer models produce 768-dimensional vectors for every question, and t-SNE [20] is applied to transform the high-dimensional space to a low-dimensional space in a local and non-linear way. The dimensionality is first reduced to 50 using Principal Component Analysis (PCA) [22] to ensure scalability, before feeding into t-SNE.

We use a perplexity of 50 for all models, after tuning the 'perplexity' parameter, to capture the clusters. Perplexity deals with the balance between global and local aspects of the data. We tested diverse perplexity values to ensure robustness. We also explore the traditional word-based model GloVe [23] and compare its sentence embeddings to the state-of-the-art transformer models. We investigate if GloVe captures the nuances of the meaning of sentences more effectively as compared to the transformer models.

3   Results

In this section, we evaluate the two experiments. The first experiment measures the performance of the QA models on Dev-Para. The second experiment visualizes the sentence embeddings of Para-SQuAD for each QA model.

3.1   Experiments on QA Models

We conduct experiments on three pre-trained models: BERT, GPT-2, and XLNet. The training code of the models is based on the Hugging Face implementation, which is publicly available.[6] We fine-tune the models on the SQuAD 1.1 training set in addition to using the pre-trained models directly. We first measure the performance of the pre-trained models on Dev-Para. Secondly, we use the three pre-trained models and GloVe to visualize the sentence embeddings of Para-SQuAD in an embeddings space. Both experiments are performed in an unsupervised manner.

---

[5] https://github.com/flairNLP/flair.
[6] https://github.com/huggingface/transformers.

3.2   Dev-Para Performance

We evaluate the performance of all three pre-trained QA models on Dev-Para. Dev-Para consists of the original set and the paraphrased set. The original set contains more than 1.000 questions from the SQuAD development set; the paraphrased set contains between 2 and 3 generated paraphrased questions for each question from the original set [16].

We present the QA models' performance on Dev-Para in Table 1. Although Dev-Para's original set is semantically similar to the paraphrased set, we see a drop in performance of all three models. Especially GPT-2 and XLNet are suffering a significant drop in performance.

Table 1. Performance of the QA models on Dev-Para.

Model	EM score		F1 score	
	Original	Paraphrased	Original	Paraphrased
BERT	82.2	78.7	89.2	86.2
GPT-2	71.6	62.9	80.4	72.7
XLNet	89.4	82.6	93.7	85.3

The drop in performance is unexpected since the meaning of the questions did not change between the original set and the paraphrased set of Dev-Para. One possible explanation is that the models exploit surface details in the original set that are not reproduced by the protocol used to create Dev-Para. If true, this demonstrates a lack of robustness in the models. Moreover, the added questions could be more complicated, therefore allowing for more variability in the syntactic structure, and those questions for which there are paraphrases are variants of more frequent questions.

3.3   Visualization of Para-SQuAD

For the following continuous space exploration of Para-SQuAD, we focus on the BERT, GPT-2, XLNet, and GloVe sentence embeddings. Each point in the space represents a question; the 12 colours in Fig. 2, 3, 4 and 5 represent the different categories. Moreover, the lines in Fig. 6, 7, 8 and 9 illustrate the distance between the paraphrased question pairs.

Figure 6, 7, 8 and 9 all consist of the same number of lines; however, some lines are difficult to see if both paraphrased question pairs appear close to each other in the embedding space. Paraphrased question pairs representing the same location in the embedding space appear as a single dot without lines. As a result, it seems that Fig. 6 contains fewer lines compared to Fig. 8, which is a false assumption.

Using visualization as a key evaluation method has important risks to consider. Relative sizes of clusters cannot be seen in a t-SNE plot as dense clusters are expanded, and spare clusters are shrunk. Furthermore, distances between the separated clusters in the t-SNE plot may mean nothing. Lastly, clumps of points in the t-SNE plot might be noise coming from small perplexity values.

The visualization of Para-SQuAD consists of all 350 paraphrased question pairs. We argue that the semantics of the questions occupy different locations in continuous space. This hypothesis is tested qualitatively by manually analyzing the t-SNE plots of the models. As a sanity check, we manually analyze all sample points in the plots with their corresponding sentences to check for mistakes (e.g., wrong colour or pairs).

We explore sample points within clusters to gain relevant insights. If two sample points are far from each other in the plot, it does not necessarily imply that they are far from each other in the embedding space. However, the number of long distances between paraphrased question pairs, coming from different clusters, can reveal information on the models' robustness to recognise paraphrased question pairs and their semantics.

Figure 2 illustrates that BERT creates clear and distinct clusters for every category; we only observe a few errors. Most paraphrased questions are within the same cluster and close to each other (see Fig. 6). Therefore, it seems that BERT can capture similar semantic sentences effectively.

GPT-2 has trouble clustering the different categories (see Fig. 3). After manually analysing the sentences in the different clusters, it seems that GPT-2 offers special attention to the first tokens in the sentence. The paraphrased question pairs are close to each other in vector space if they start with the same token. The starting token is often the 'question word' in Para-SQuAD. It seems that GPT-2 organises questions by their structure instead of their semantics.

XLNet forms one large cluster, with smaller clusters within (see Fig. 4). However, these clusters are not that clear when compared to BERT. The different categories are all spread out, and no apparent clusters are formed.

Figure 5 suggests that GloVe clusters the different categories more effectively than GPT-2 and XLNet, despite using static embeddings. This finding is interesting since contextualised embedding are thought to be superior compared to traditional static embeddings. At the same time, the paraphrased questions that appear close to each other in Fig. 9 have similar words in the sentence and can be considered as easy paraphrases. GloVe is unable to recognise more complex paraphrases, which can be explained by the model's architecture and not providing contextualised embeddings.

In this paper, we use the cosine similarity to measure the closeness between paraphrased question pairs. For each model, we calculate the average cosine similarity for all the paraphrased question pairs in Para-SQuAD to see if the fine-tuned models perform better than the pre-trained models (see Table 2). Calculating the average cosine similarity was only relevant for comparing the pre-trained BERT model and the fine-tuned BERT model. The cosine similarity of the fine-tuned BERT model increased with 7.3%. The plots of the fine-tuned models reveal no interesting findings; therefore, we only illustrate the sentence embeddings of the basic pre-trained models.

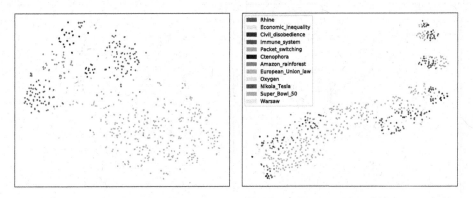

Fig. 2. BERT categories.   Fig. 3. GPT-2 categories.

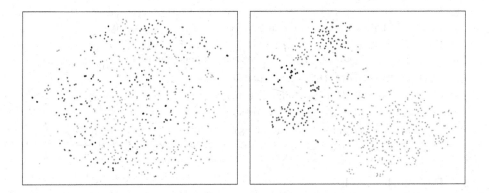

Fig. 4. XLNet categories.   Fig. 5. GloVe categories.

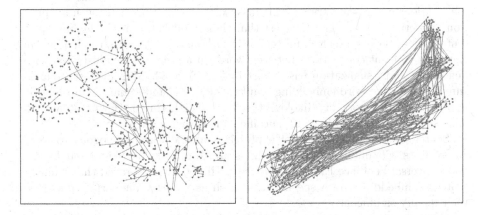

Fig. 6. BERT paraphrased question pairs. Fig. 7. GPT-2 paraphrased question pairs.

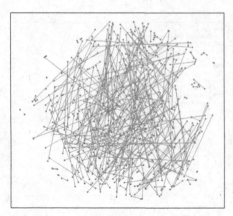 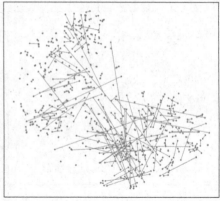

Fig. 8. XLNet paraphrased question pairs.   **Fig. 9.** GloVe paraphrased question pairs.

Table 2. Average cosine similarity of the QA models.

Model	Average cosine similarity
BERT	0.875
BERT (fine-tuned)	0.939
GPT-2	0.987
XLNet	0.981

4   Related Work

Recent research on deep language models and transformer architectures has demonstrated that context embeddings in transformer models contain sufficient information to perform various NLP tasks with simple classifiers, such as question answering [25,30]. They suggest that these models produce valuable representations of both syntactic and semantic information. Attention matrices can encode significant connections between words in a sentence, as illustrated with qualitative and visualization-based work by Jesse Vig [33]. Multiple tests to measure how effective word embeddings capture syntactic and semantic information is defined in the work of Mikolov et al. [21]. Furthermore, Hewitt et al. [12] analysed context embeddings for specific transformer models.

Sentence embeddings can be helpful in multiple ways, analogous to word embeddings. Common proposed methods are: InferSent [5], Skip-Thought [17] and Universal Sentence Encoder (USE) [1]. Hill et al. [13] proved that training sentence embeddings on a specific task, such as question answering, impacted their quality significantly.

Conneau et al. [6] presented probing tasks to evaluate sentence embeddings intrinsically. Evaluation of sentence embeddings happens most often in 'transfer learning' tasks, e.g., question type prediction tasks. The study measures to what degree linguistic features, like word order or sentence length, are accessible in a sentence embedding. This study was continued with SentEval [4], which serves as a toolkit to evaluate the quality of sentence embeddings. This quality is measured both intrinsically and extrinsically. SentEval proves that no sentence embedding technique is flawless across all tasks [24].

Recently, numerous QA datasets have been published (e.g., Rajpurkar et al. [27,28]). However, defining a suitable QA task and developing methodologies for annotation and evolution is still challenging [18]. Key issues include the metrics used for evaluation and the methods and sources used to obtain the questions.

Our analysis focuses on three specific transformer models; however, there are numerous transformer models available. Other notable transformer models are XLM [11] and ELECTRA [2].

Whether QA models are learning the task of question answering, instead of finding shortcuts in the dataset has been studied by Vakulenko et al. [31]. Moreover, recent papers have focused on generalisability of robust models with human-driven natural perturbations [16] and by evaluating different models on several datasets [29], but not for paraphrasing specifically.

5   Conclusion

This paper presents an initial exploration of how QA models handle paraphrased questions. We used two different datasets and performed tests on each dataset. Firstly, we used an existing paraphrased test set (Dev-Para) to test the QA models' robustness to paraphrased questions. The results demonstrate that all three QA models drop in performance when exposed to more unseen paraphrased questions. The drop in performance could be explained by exposing the models to new paraphrased questions that deviate from the original SQuAD questions. The experiments underline the importance of improving QA models' robustness to question paraphrasing to generalise effectively. Moreover, improved robustness is necessary to increase the reliability and consistency of the QA models when tested on unseen questions in real-life world applications.

Secondly, we constructed a paraphrased evaluation set (Para-SQuAD) based on SQuAD to illustrate interesting insights into QA models handling paraphrased questions. The findings reveal that BERT creates the most promising and informative sentence embeddings and seems to capture semantic information effectively. The other models, however, seem to fail in recognising paraphrased question pairs effectively and lack robustness.

5.1   Discussion

The models' drop in performance on Dev-Para is unexpected. We hypothesise that the original SQuAD training set does not consist of enough diverse question paraphrases. This lack of variation leads to the QA models not learning to answer different questions, that have the same intention and meaning, correctly.

The QA models fail to recognise some questions that convey the same meaning using different wordings. Exposing the QA models to more diverse question phrases would be a logical step to improve the QA models' robustness to question paraphrasing.

Generating paraphrases and recognizing paraphrases are still critical challenges across multiple NLP tasks, including question answering. A relatively robust and diverse source for generating paraphrases is through neural machine translation. We can make larger datasets consisting of paraphrased questions with machine translation: the question is translated into a foreign language and then back-translated into English. This back-translation approach achieved remarkable results in diversity compared to paraphrases created by human experts [9].

5.2   Limitations

One limitation of the performed experiments is the small size of Para-SQuAD. Increasing Para-SQuAD with data augmentation could be achieved using neural machine translation to generate more paraphrases. Increasing the size of Para-SQuAD would lead to more reliable results, but we would lose the advantage of keeping the data distribution intact.

Another downside is the simplicity of Para-SQuAD. The paraphrases used are relatively simple and basic. Therefore, models achieving excellent results on the set does not guarantee their robustness to question paraphrases.

In general, there is no inter-annotator agreement measure to ensure consistent annotations because we only have one annotator. However, we consider this justified due to the simple task of selecting paraphrased question pairs in the SQuAD 1.1 development set.

Using visualization as the primary evaluation method has its risks. A common pitfall includes pareidolia; to see structures and patterns that we would like to see. As an example, we can see that BERT forms clear clusters that are known to us; however, other models could form divergent cluster structures to represent patterns. We could, therefore, easily overlook those cluster structures that are unfamiliar to us. Furthermore, clusters can disappear in the t-SNE transformation.

Lastly, it is hard to distinguish whether BERT recognizes the actual semantics of the questions or merely the Wikipedia extracts with the performed method. Further research is needed to investigate this distinction.

Acknowledgments. We thank the three anonymous reviewers for their constructive comments, and Michael Cochez for his feedback and helpful notes on the manuscript.

References

1. Cer, D., et al.: Universal sentence encoder. arXiv preprint arXiv:1803.11175 (2018)
2. Clark, K., Luong, M., Le, Q., Manning, C.: ELECTRA: pre-training text encoders as discriminators rather than generators. arXiv preprint arXiv:2003.10555 (2020)

3. Coenen, A., et al.: Visualizing and measuring the geometry of BERT. arXiv preprint arXiv:1906.02715 (2019)
4. Conneau, A., Kiela, D.: SentEval: an evaluation toolkit for universal sentence representations. arXiv preprint arXiv:1803.05449 (2018)
5. Conneau, A., Kiela, D., Schwenk, H., Barrault, L., Bordes, A.: Supervised learning of universal sentence representations from natural language inference data. arXiv preprint arXiv:1705.02364 (2018)
6. Conneau, A., Kruszewski, G., Lample, G., Barrault, L., Baroni, M.: What you can cram into a single vector: probing sentence embeddings for linguistic properties. arXiv preprint arXiv:1805.01070 (2018)
7. Devlin, J., Chang, M., Lee, K., Toutanova, K.: BERT: pre-training of deep bidirectional transformers for language understanding. arXiv preprint arXiv:1810.04805 (2019)
8. Ethayarajh, K.: How contextual are contextualized word representations? Comparing the Geometry of BERT, ELMo, and GPT-2 Embeddings. arXiv preprint arXiv:1909.00512 (2019)
9. Federmann, C., Elachqar, O., Quirk, C.: Multilingual whispers: generating paraphrases with translation. In: Proceedings of the 5th Workshop on Noisy User-Generated Text (W-NUT 2019), Hong Kong, China, pp. 17–26. Association for Computational Linguistics (2019). https://doi.org/10.18653/v1/D19-5503
10. Gan, W.C., Ng, H.T.: Improving the robustness of question answering systems to question paraphrasing. In: Proceedings of the 57th Annual Meeting of the Association for Computational Linguistics, Florence, Italy, pp. 6065–6075. Association for Computational Linguistics (2019). https://doi.org/10.18653/v1/P19-1610
11. Guillaume, L., Conneau, A.: Cross-lingual language model pretraining. arXiv preprint arXiv:1901.07291 (2019)
12. Hewitt, J., Manning, C.D.: A structural probe for finding syntax in word representations. In: Proceedings of the 2019 Conference of the North American Chapter of the Association for Computational Linguistics: Human Language Technologies, Volume 1 (Long and Short Papers), Minneapolis, Minnesota, pp. 4129–4138. Association for Computational Linguistics (2019). https://doi.org/10.18653/v1/N19-1419
13. Hill, F., Cho, K., Korhonen, A.: Learning distributed representations of sentences from unlabelled data. In: Proceedings of the 2016 Conference of the North American Chapter of the Association for Computational Linguistics: Human Language Technologies, San Diego, California, pp. 1367–1377. Association for Computational Linguistics (2016). https://doi.org/10.18653/v1/N16-1162
14. Howard, J., Ruder, S.: Fine-tuned language models for text classification. arXiv preprint arXiv:1801.06146 (2018)
15. Jia, R., Liang, P.: Adversarial examples for evaluating reading comprehension systems. arXiv preprint arXiv:1707.07328 (2017)
16. Khashabi, D., Khot, T., Sabharwal, A.: More bang for your buck: natural perturbation for robust question answering. In: Proceedings of the 2020 Conference on Empirical Methods in Natural Language Processing (EMNLP), pp. 163–170. Association for Computational Linguistics (2020). https://doi.org/10.18653/v1/2020.emnlp-main.12
17. Kiros, R., et al.: Skip-thought vectors. arXiv preprint arXiv:1506.06726 (2015)
18. Kwiatkowski, T., et al.: Natural questions: a benchmark for question answering research. In: Transactions of the Association of Computational Linguistics (2019)

19. Liu, C., Dahlmeier, D., Ng, H.T.: PEM: a paraphrase evaluation metric exploiting parallel texts. In: Proceedings of the 2010 Conference on Empirical Methods in Natural Language Processing, Cambridge, MA, pp. 923–932. Association for Computational Linguistics (2010)
20. Van Der Maaten, L., Hinton, G.: Visualizing data using t-SNE. J. Mach. Learn. Res. **9**, 2579–2605 (2008)
21. Mikolov, T., Chen, K., Corrado, G., Dean, J.: Efficient estimation of word representations in vector space. arXiv preprint arXiv:1301.3781 (2013)
22. Pearson, K.: LIII. On Lines and Planes of Closest Fit to Systems of Points in Space. The London, Edinburgh, and Dublin Philosophical Magazine and Journal of Science, vol. 2 (1901)
23. Pennington, J., Socher, R., Manning, C.D.: GloVe: global vectors for word representation. In: Empirical Methods in Natural Language Processing (EMNLP), Doha, Qatar, pp. 1532–1543. Association for Computational Linguistics (2014). https://doi.org/10.3115/v1/D14-1162
24. Perone, C.S., Silveira, R., Paula, T.S.: Evaluation of sentence embeddings in downstream and linguistic probing tasks. arXiv preprint arXiv:1806.06259 (2018)
25. Peters, M.E., Neumann, M., Iyyer, M., Gardner, M., Clark, C., Lee, K., Zettlemoyer, L.: Deep contextualized word representations. arXiv preprint arXiv:1802.05365 (2018)
26. Radford, A., Wu, J., Child, R., Luan, D., Amodei, D., Sutskever, I.: Language models are unsupervised multitask learners. OpenAI Blog (2019)
27. Rajpurkar, P., Jia, R., Liang, P.: Know what you don't know: unanswerable questions for SQuAD. In: Proceedings of the 56th Annual Meeting of the Association for Computational Linguistics, , Melbourne, Australia, pp. 784–789. Association for Computational Linguistics (2018). https://doi.org/10.18653/v1/P18-2124
28. Rajpurkar, P., Zhang, J., Lopyrev, K., Liang, P.: SQuAD: 100,000+ questions for machine comprehension of text. In: Proceedings of the 2016 Conference on Empirical Methods in Natural Language Processing, Austin, Texas, pp. 2383–2392. Association for Computational Linguistics (2016). https://doi.org/10.18653/v1/D16-1264
29. Sen, P., Saffari, A.: What do models learn from question answering datasets? arXiv preprint arXiv:2004.03490 (2020)
30. Tenney, I., et al.: What do you learn from context? probing for sentence structure in contextualized word representations. arXiv preprint arXiv:1905.06316 (2019)
31. Vakulenko, S., Longpre, S., Tu, Z., Anantha, R.: A wrong answer or a wrong question? An intricate relationship between question reformulation and answer selection in conversational question answering. arXiv preprint arXiv:2010.06835 (2020)
32. Vaswani, A., et al.: Attention is all you need. arXiv preprint arXiv:1706.03762 (2017)
33. Vig, J.: Visualizing attention in transformer-based language representation models. arXiv preprint arXiv:1904.02679 (2019)
34. Yang, Z., Dai, Z., Yang, Y., Carbonell, J., Salakhutdinov, R., Le, Q.V.: XLNet: generalized autoregressive pretraining for language understanding. arXiv preprint arXiv:1906.08237 (2019)

FlipOut: Uncovering Redundant Weights via Sign Flipping

Andrei C. Apostol[1,2(✉)], Maarten C. Stol[2], and Patrick Forré[1]

[1] Informatics Institute, University of Amsterdam, Amsterdam, The Netherlands
p.d.forre@uva.nl
[2] BrainCreators B.V., Amsterdam, The Netherlands
{apostol.andrei,maarten.stol}@braincreators.com

Abstract. We propose a novel pruning method which uses the oscillations around 0, i.e. sign flips, that a weight has undergone during training in order to determine its saliency. Our method can perform pruning before the network has converged, requires little tuning effort due to having good default values for its hyperparameters, and can directly target the level of sparsity desired by the user. Our experiments, performed on a variety of object classification architectures, show that it is competitive with existing methods and achieves state-of-the-art performance for levels of sparsity of 99.6% and above for 2 out of 3 of the architectures tested. For reproducibility, we release our code at https://github.com/AndreiXYZ/flipout.

Keywords: Deep learning · Network pruning · Computer vision

1 Introduction

The success of deep learning is motivated by competitive results on a wide range of tasks [3,9,24]. However, well-performing neural networks often come with the drawback of a large number of parameters, which increases the computational and memory requirements for training and inference. This poses a challenge for deployment on embedded devices, which are often resource-constrained, as well as for use in time sensitive applications, such as autonomous driving or crowd monitoring. Moreover, costs and carbon dioxide emissions associated with training these large networks have reached alarming rates [21]. To this end, pruning has been proven as an effective way of making neural networks run more efficiently [5,6,13,15,18].

Early works [6,13] have focused on using the second-order derivative to detect which weights to remove with minimal impact on performance. However, these methods either require strong assumptions about the properties of the Hessian, which are typically violated in practice, or are intractable to run on modern neural networks due to the computations involved.

Supported by BrainCreators B.V.

M. Baratchi et al. (Eds.): BNAIC/Benelearn 2020, CCIS 1398, pp. 15–29, 2021.
https://doi.org/10.1007/978-3-030-76640-5_2

One could instead prune the weights whose optimum lies at or close to 0 anyway. Building on this idea, the authors of [5] propose training a network until convergence, pruning the weights whose magnitudes are below a set threshold, and allowing the network to re-train, a process which can be repeated iteratively. This method is improved on in [4], whereby the authors additionally reset the remaining weights to their values at initialization after a pruning step. Yet, these methods require re-training the network until convergence multiple times, which can be a time consuming process.

Recent alternatives either rely on methods typically used for regularization [17,18,26] or introduce a learnable threshold, below which all weights are pruned [16]. All these methods, however, require extensive hyperparameter tuning in order to obtain a favorable accuracy-sparsity trade-off. Moreover, the final sparsity of the resulting network cannot be predicted given a particular choice of these hyperparameters. These two issues often translate into the fact that the practitioner has to run these methods multiple times when applying them to novel tasks.

To summarize, we have seen that the pruning methods presented so far suffer from one or more of the following problems: (1) computational intractability, (2) having to train the network to convergence multiple times, (3) requiring extensive hyperparameter tuning for optimal performance and (4) inability to target a specific final sparsity.

We note that by using a heuristic in order to determine during training whether a weight has a locally optimal value of low magnitude, pruning can be performed before the network reaches convergence, unlike the method proposed by the authors of [5]. We propose one such heuristic, coined *the aim test*, which determines whether a value represents a local optimum for a weight by monitoring the number of times that weight oscillates around it during training, while also taking into account the distance between the two. We then show that this can be applied to network pruning by applying this test at the value of 0 for all weights simultaneously, and framing it as a saliency criterion. By design, our method is tractable, allows the user to select a specific level of sparsity and can be applied during training.

Our experiments, conducted on a variety of object classification architectures, indicate that it is competitive with respect to relevant pruning methods from literature, and can outperform them for sparsity levels of 99.6% and above. Moreover, we empirically show that our method has default hyperparameter settings which consistently generate near optimal results, easing the burden of tuning.

2   Method

2.1   Motivation

Mini-batch stochastic gradient descent [2] is the most commonly used optimization method in machine learning. Given a mini-batch of B randomly sampled

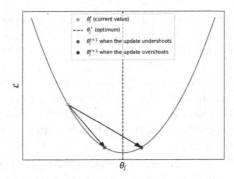

Fig. 1. Over- and under-shooting illustrated. The vertical line splits the x-axis into two regions relative to the (locally-)optimal value θ_j^*. Overshooting corresponds to when a weight gets updated such that its new value lies in the opposite region (blue dot), while undershooting occurs when the updated value is closer to the optimal value, but stays in the same region (green dot). (Color figure online)

training examples consisting of pairs of features and labels $\{(x_b, y_b)\}_{b=1}^B$, a neural network parameterised by a weight vector $\boldsymbol{\theta}$, a loss objective $\mathcal{L}(\boldsymbol{\theta}, \boldsymbol{x}, \boldsymbol{y})$ and a learning rate η, the update rule of stochastic gradient descent is as follows:

$$g^t = \frac{1}{B} \sum_{b=1}^{B} \nabla_{\theta^t} \mathcal{L}(\theta^t, x_b, y_b)$$

$$\boldsymbol{\theta}^{t+1} \leftarrow \boldsymbol{\theta}^t - \eta g^t$$

Given a weight θ_j^t, one could consider its possible values as being split into two regions, with a locally optimal value θ_j^* as the separation point. Depending on the value of the gradient and the learning rate, the updated weight θ_j^{t+1} will lie in one of the two regions. That is, it will either get closer to its optimal value while remaining in the same region as before or it will be updated past it and land in the opposite region. We term these two phenomena under- and over-shooting, and provide an illustration in Fig. 1. Mathematically, they correspond to $\eta|g_j^t| < |\theta_j^t - \theta_j^*|$ and $\eta|g_j^t| > |\theta_j^t - \theta_j^*|$, respectively.

With the behavior of under- and over-shooting, one could construct a heuristic-based test in order to evaluate whether a weight has a local optimum at a specific point without needing the network to have reached convergence:

1. For a weight θ_j, a value of ϕ_j is chosen for which the test is conducted.
2. Train the model regularly and record the occurrence of under- and over-shooting around ϕ_j after each step of SGD.
3. If the number of such occurrences exceeds a threshold κ, conclude that θ_j has a local optimum at ϕ_j, i.e. $\theta_j^* = \phi_j$.

We coin this method *the aim test*.

Previous works have demonstrated that neural networks can tolerate high levels of sparsity with negligible deterioration in performance [4,5,16,18]. It is then reasonable to assume that for a large number of weights, there exist local optima at exactly 0, i.e. $\theta_j^* = 0$. One could then use the aim test to detect these weights and prune them. Importantly, when using the aim test for $\phi_j = 0$, the two regions around the tested value are the set of negative and positive real numbers, respectively. Checking for over-shooting then becomes equivalent to testing whether the sign of θ_j has changed after a step of SGD, while under-shooting can be detected when a weight has been updated to a smaller absolute value and retained its sign, i.e. $(|\theta_j^{t+1}| < |\theta_j^t|) \wedge (\text{sgn}(\theta_j^t) = \text{sgn}(\theta_j^{t+1}))$.

However, under-shooting can be problematic; for instance, a weight could be updated to a lower magnitude, while at the same time being far from 0. This can happen when a weight is approaching a non-zero local optimum, an occurrence which should not contribute towards a positive outcome of the aim test. By positive outcome, we refer to determining that $\phi_j = 0$ is indeed a local optimum of θ_j. A similar problem can occur for over-shooting, where a weight receives a large update that causes it to change its sign but not lie in the vicinity of 0. These scenarios, which we will refer to as *deceitful shots* going forward, are illustrated in the general case, where ϕ_j can take any value, in Fig. 2a and Fig. 2b. Following, we make two observations which help circumvent this problem.

Firstly, one could reduce the impact of deceitful shots by also taking into account the distance of the weight to the hypothesised local optimum, i.e. $|\theta_j - \phi_j|$, when conducting the aim test. In other words, the number of occurrences of under- and over-shooting should be weighed inversely proportional to this quantity, even if they would otherwise exceed κ.

Our second observation is that by ignoring updates which are not in the vicinity of ϕ_j, the number of deceitful shots are reduced. In doing so, one could also simplify the aim test; with a sufficiently large perturbation to θ_j, an update that might otherwise cause under-shooting can be made to cause over-shooting. Adding a perturbation of $\pm\epsilon$ is, in effect, inducing a boundary around the tested value, $[\phi_j - \epsilon, \phi_j + \epsilon]$; all weights that get updated such that they fall into that boundary will be said to over-shoot around ϕ_j. With this framework, checking for over-shooting is sufficient; updates that under-shoot and are within ϵ of the tested value are made to over-shoot (Fig. 3a) and updates which under-shoot but are not in the vicinity of ϕ_j, i.e. a deceitful shot, are now not recorded at all (Fig. 3b). This can also be seen as restricting the aim test to only operate within a vicinity around ϕ_j.

2.2   FlipOut: Applying the Aim Test for Pruning

Determining Which Weights to Prune. Pruning weights that have local optima at or around 0 can obtain a high level of sparsity with minimal degradation in accuracy. The authors of [5] use the magnitude of the weights once the network is converged as a criterion; that is, the weights with the lowest absolute value, i.e. closest to 0, get pruned. The aim test can be used to detect whether a point represents a local optimum for a weight and can be applied before the

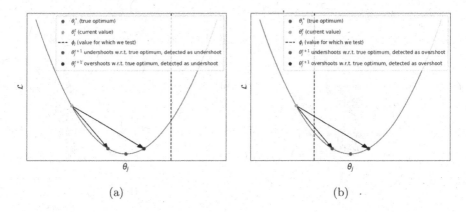

(a)   (b)

Fig. 2. In the plots above, the dotted vertical line represents the value at which the aim test is conducted, i.e. a value we would like to determine as a local optimum or not, while the red dot represents the value of a true local optimum. When testing for a value which is not a locally optimal value $\phi_j \neq \theta_j^*$, over- or under-shooting around ϕ_j can be merely a side-effect of that weight getting updated towards its true optimum θ_j^*. These observations would then contribute towards the aim test returning a false positive outcome, i.e. $\phi_j = \theta_j^*$. Whether we observe an over-shoot or an under-shoot in this case depends on the relationship between ϕ_j and θ_j^*. In (a), we have $\phi_j > \theta_j^*$, where if the hypothesised and true optimum are sufficiently far apart, we observe an under-shoot. Conversely, in (b), we have $\phi_j < \theta_j^*$ and observe over-shooting.

network reaches convergence, during training. For pruning, one could then apply the aim test simultaneously for all weights with $\phi = 0$. We propose framing this as a saliency score; at time step t, the saliency τ_j^t of a weight θ_j^t is:

$$\tau_j^t = \frac{|\theta_j^t|^p}{\text{flips}_j^t} \tag{1a}$$

$$\text{flips}_j^t = \sum_{i=0}^{t-1}[\text{sgn}(\theta_j^i) \neq \text{sgn}(\theta_j^{i+1})] \tag{1b}$$

With perturbation added into the weight vector, it is enough to check for over-shooting, which is equivalent to counting the number of sign flips a weight has undergone during the training process when $\phi_j = 0$ (Eq. 1b); a scheme for adding such perturbation is described in Sect. 2.2. In Eq. 1a, the denominator $|\theta_j^t|^p$ represents the proximity of the weight to the hypothesised local optimum, $|\theta_j^t - \phi_j|^p$ (which is equivalent to the weight's magnitude since we have $\phi_j = 0$ for all weights). The hyperparameter p controls how much this quantity is weighted relative to the number of sign flips.

When determining the amount of parameters to be pruned, we adopt the strategy from [4], i.e. pruning a percentage of the remaining weights each time, which allows us to target an exact level of sparsity. Given m, the number of times

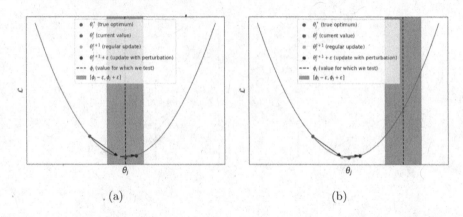

(a)   (b)

Fig. 3. (a) All weights that under-shoot but are within ϵ of ϕ_j will be made to over-shoot. (b) When testing at a value which is not a local optimum for θ_j, i.e. $\phi_j \neq \theta_j^*$, and adding a perturbation ϵ to θ_j, not taking under-shooting into account means that if the weight gets updated such that it does not lie in the boundary around ϕ_j induced by the perturbation, an event that would otherwise contribute to a false positive outcome for the aim test will not be recorded, so the likelihood of rejecting ϕ_j as an optimum increases.

pruning is performed, r the percentage of remaining weights which are removed at each pruning step, k the total number of training steps, d_θ the dimensionality of the weights and $\| \cdot \|_0$ the L_0-norm, the resulting sparsity s of the weight tensor after training the network is simply:

$$s = 1 - \frac{\|\theta^k\|_0}{d_\theta} = (1 - r)^m \tag{2}$$

This final sparsity can then be determined by setting m and r appropriately.

Perturbation Through Gradient Noise. Adding gradient noise has been shown to be effective for optimization [19,25] in that it can help lower the training loss and reduce overfitting by encouraging an exploration in the parameter space, thus effectively acting as a regularizer. While the benefits of this method are helpful, our motivation for its usage stems from allowing the aim test to be performed in a simpler manner; weights that get updated closer to 0 will occasionally pass over the axis due to the injected noise, thus making checking for over-shooting sufficient. We scale the variance of the noise distribution by the L_2 norm of the parameters θ, normalize it by the number of weights and introduce a hyperparameter λ which scales the amount of noise added into the gradients. For a layer l and d_l its dimensionality, the gradient for the weights in that layer used by SGD for updates will be:

$$\hat{g}^{t,l} \leftarrow g^{t,l} + \lambda \epsilon^{t,l} \tag{3a}$$

$$\epsilon^{t,l} \sim \mathcal{N}(0, \sigma_{t,l}^2) \tag{3b}$$

$$\sigma_{t,l}^2 = \frac{\|\theta^{t,l}\|_2^2}{d_l} \tag{3c}$$

As training is performed, it is desirable to reduce the amount of added noise so that the network can successfully converge. Previous works use annealing schedules by decaying the variance of the Gaussian distribution proportional to the current time step. Under our proposed formulation, however, explicitly using an annealing schema is not necessary. By pruning weights, the term in the numerator in Eq. 3c decreases, while the denominator remains constant. This ensures that annealing will be induced automatically through the pruning process, and there is no need for manually constructing a schedule.

Pruning periodically throughout training according to the saliency score in Eq. 1a in conjunction with adding gradient noise into the weights forms the *FlipOut* pruning method.

3   Related Work

3.1   Deep-R

In Deep-R [1], the authors split the weights of the neural network into two matrices, the connection parameter θ_k and a constant sign s_k with $s_k \in \{-1, +1\}$; the final weights of the network are then defined as $\theta \odot s$. The connections whose θ_k is negative are inactive; whenever a connection changes its sign, it is turned dormant and another randomly sampled connection is re-activated, ensuring the same sparsity level is maintained throughout training. Gaussian noise is also injected into the gradients during training.

Two similarities with our method can be observed here, namely the fact that the authors also use sign flipping as a signal for pruning a weight, and the addition of Gaussian noise. However, our methods differ in that we do not impose a set level of sparsity throughout training; instead, we use the number of sign flips of a weight in order to determine its saliency, while in Deep-R a single sign flip is required for a weight to be removed. Our method of injecting noise into the gradients also differs in that it does not explicitly encode an annealing scheme, allowing for the pruning process itself to reduce the noise throughout training. Finally, in Deep-R, the network is initialized with a specific level of sparsity which is maintained throughout training, while our method prunes gradually.

3.2   Magnitude and Uncertainty Pruning

The M&U pruning criterion is proposed in [11]. Given a weight θ_j, its uncertainty estimate $\tilde{\sigma}_{\theta_j}$ and a parameter λ controlling the trade-off between magnitude and uncertainty, the M&U criterion will evaluate the saliency of the weight as:

$$\tau_j = \frac{|\theta_j|}{\lambda + \tilde{\sigma}_{\theta_j}}$$

Uncertainty is estimated as the standard deviation across the previous n values of that weight, via a process called pseudo-bootstrapping. This criterion is a generalization of the Wald test, and is equivalent to it when $\lambda = 0$.

Our method is similar in that our saliency score also normalizes the weight's magnitude by a function of its past values. However, this method assumes asymptotic normality. While this is the case when using negative log-likelihood or an equivalent as the loss function, this property does not necessarily hold when using modified variants of the SGD estimator, such as Adam [10] or RMSprop [22]. In contrast, FlipOut is not derived from the Wald test and does not make any assumptions about the weight distribution at convergence.

4   Experiments

4.1   General Setup

Baselines. As baselines, we consider a slightly modified version of magnitude pruning [5] (Global magnitude), due to the similarity between its saliency criterion and that of our own method, SNIP [14] due to it being an easily applicable method which does not suffer from any of the issues that are commonly found in pruning methods (Sect. 1) and Hoyer-Square, as introduced in [26], for the state-of-the-art results that it has demonstrated. We also include random pruning (Random) as a control. For FlipOut, Global magnitude and Random, pruning is performed periodically throughout training. We compare these methods at five different compression ratios, chosen at regular log-intervals (Table 1); for Hoyer-square, the performance at those points is estimated by a sparsity-accuracy trade-off curve. Magnitude pruning, in its original formulation, performs pruning only once the network has reached convergence. However, employing this strategy can create a confounding variable: training time. Since we would like to compare all methods at equal training budgets, we have opted to simply perform pruning after a fixed number of epochs for these methods. Note that the training budget that we allocate allows all of the networks that we consider to reach convergence when trained without performing any pruning. We make an exception to this equal budget rule for Hoyer-Square, since it prunes after training and would otherwise not benefit from any SGD updates after sparsification. As such, we have performed an additional 150 epochs of fine-tuning without the regularizer, as per the original method, although we have observed negligible benefits to this. All baselines were modified to rank the weights globally when a pruning decision is made, as per the strategy from [4], in order to avoid creating bottleneck layers. The models that we test on are ResNet18 [7] and VGG19 [20] trained on the CIFAR-10 dataset [12], and DenseNet121 [9] trained on Imagenette [8].

Table 1. Compression ratios, resulting sparsity levels and prune frequencies (in epochs) used in the experiments, assuming 350 epochs of training and that 50% of the remaining weights are removed at each step.

Compression ratio ($\frac{d_\theta}{\|\theta\|_0}$)	Resulting sparsity ($1 - \frac{\|\theta\|_0}{d_\theta}$)	Pruning frequency
2^2	75%	117
2^4	93.75%	70
2^6	98.43%	50
2^8	99.61%	39
2^{10}	99.9%	32

Hyperparameters. The training parameters for all experiments are taken from [23]; specifically, we use a learning rate of 0.1, batch size of 128, 350 epochs of training and a weight decay penalty of $5e-4$. The learning rate is decayed by a factor of 10 at epochs 150 and 250. The networks are trained with the SGD optimizer with a momentum value of 0.9 [2]. For the methods that perform iterative pruning (Global magnitude, Random, FlipOut), we remove 50% of the remaining weights at each pruning step, with the pruning frequencies chosen such that the compression ratios from Table 1 are achieved; we use the same pruning rates and frequencies across all three methods. SNIP accepts a single hyperparameter, namely the desired final sparsity, which we have chosen such that it matches the aforementioned compression ratios. For Hoyer-Square, which does not allow for a specific level of sparsity to be chosen and, instead, relies on parameter tuning, we generate a sparsity-accuracy trade-off curve by using 15 different values for the regularization term, ranging from $1e-7$ to $6e-3$ with 3 values at each decimal point, e.g. $1e-7$, $3e-7$, $6e-7$, $1e-6$ etc., and a fixed pruning threshold of $1e-4$. Finally, for FlipOut, we use the values of $p = 2$ (Eq. 1) and $\lambda = 1$ (Eq. 3) for all experiments, a choice we motivate in Sect. 4.2.

4.2   Choosing the Hyperparameters for FlipOut

We have experimented with different values of the two hyperparameters and found that $p = 2$ (Eq. 1a) and $\lambda = 1$ (Eq. 3a) offer optimal or near optimal results in all scenarios. In the following paragraphs, we detail the procedure used in determining these values.

Choosing λ. For λ, we have run all networks at 15 different values, ranging from 0.75 to 1.5 in increments of 0.05. The value of $p = 2$ was used. The networks are evaluated on a validation set, created by removing a random subset of samples from the training set. The size of the validation set was 10000 for CIFAR10 and 2000 for Imagenette. For our subsequent experiments, (Sects. 4.3 and 4.4), the networks have been trained on the full training set. As a metric, we have used the accuracy of the networks at the end of training for the sparsity levels of 93.75% and 99.9%. We provide in Table 2 the accuracies generated by the optimal value of λ, as discovered through this process, and the ones generated

Table 2. Accuracies when using the best value of λ discovered by grid search and the value of $\lambda = 1$ at two levels of sparsity. The parantheses indicate the gain offered by the optimal parameter.

Model	Acc. at sparsity 93.75%		Acc. at sparsity 99.9%	
	λ^*	$\lambda = 1$	λ^*	$\lambda = 1$
ResNet18	94.58 (+0.02)	94.56	83.75 (+1.68)	82.07
VGG19	93.07 (+0.11)	92.96	87.72 (+0.48)	87.24
DenseNet121	89.75 (+0.0)	89.75	73.5 (+1.45)	72.05

Table 3. Table of results for different values of p at two levels of sparsity.

Model	Acc. at sparsity 93.75%					Acc. at sparsity 99.9%				
	$p=0$	$p=\frac{1}{2}$	$p=1$	$p=2$	$p=4$	$p=0$	$p=\frac{1}{2}$	$p=1$	$p=2$	$p=4$
ResNet18	93.71	88.39	94.18	**94.26**	94.11	72.69	77.08	79.83	82.07	**83.15**
VGG19	91.68	82.44	92.56	**92.96**	92.57	81.48	80.69	86.01	**87.24**	86.64
DenseNet121	10.35	77.40	88.9	**89.75**	88.86	10.35	10.35	70.85	**72.05**	60.55

at $\lambda = 1$. Notice that the differences are almost negligible at 93.75% sparsity. For the larger sparsity level the disparity increases, although the default value still remains within 2% points of the optimum value for all networks considered. The largest gap can be seen for ResNet18 and DenseNet121, at approximately 1.7 and 1.5% points, respectively. Since there are only two out of six cases in which optimizing λ has helped beyond a negligible amount, we have used the value of 1 for this hyperparameter throughout our experiments.

Choosing p. We perform similar experiments for p on five values, $p \in \{0, \frac{1}{2}, 1, 2, 4\}$ and λ set to 1. Note that the value of $p = 0$ corresponds to the case when the magnitudes of the weights are not taken into account; that is, the pruning decisions will be made solely based on the number of sign flips. As can be seen in Table 3, the value of $p = 2$ consistently outperforms all other tested values, with the exception of ResNet18 at 99.9% sparsity, for which the value of $p = 4$ achieves better results by approximately 1% point. Another interesting observation is that the values of 1, 2 and 4 tend to perform better than 0 and $\frac{1}{2}$; we conjecture that this is due to the fact that deceitful shots (Sect. 2.1) occur when not taking into account the distance between the weight and its hypothesised local optimum, which have a negative impact on the pruning decision. This can be especially observed at the higher sparsity level and in the case of DenseNet121, where pruning with $p = 0$ causes the network to not perform better than random guessing. Given that the value of $p = 2$ is favored in 5 out of 6 cases, we have decided to use it as a default value in our subsequent experiments.

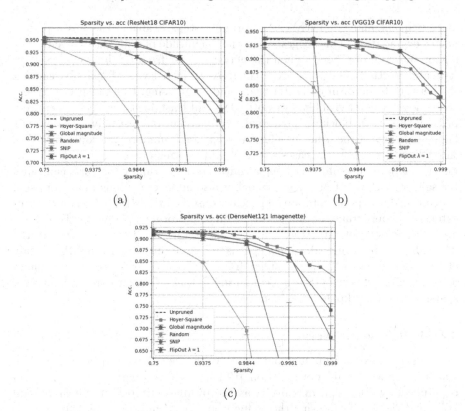

Fig. 4. Results of our pruning experiments on the 3 reference networks. Each point is averaged over 3 runs; error bars indicate standard deviation. (a) ResNet18 on CIFAR 10. (b) VGG19 on CIFAR10. (c) DenseNet121 on ImageNette.

4.3   Comparison to Baselines

The results for the three models tested are found in Fig. 4. FlipOut obtains state-of-the-art performance on ResNet18 and VGG19 for sparsity levels of 99.61% and beyond. For the highest tested sparsity level, it outperforms the second-best method by 1.9 and 4.5% points, respectively (Fig. 4a, 4b). Notably, when using FlipOut on VGG19 for this sparsity, the drop in accuracy compared to the unpruned model is only 6.2% points. At the same time, it remains competitive with other baselines for lower degrees of sparsity, staying within a 1% point difference compared to the best method and with a minimal drop relative to the unpruned model. For DenseNet121, however, Hoyer-Square dominates all other methods tested in most cases (Fig. 4c), with FlipOut as second best for the highest sparsity level.

Interestingly, the simple criterion of magnitude pruning, when modified to rank the weights globally instead of a layer-by-layer basis, is competitive with other, more recent, baselines, and even obtains state-of-the-art results for moderate levels of sparsity. However, at high levels of sparsity, which correspond to more frequent and implicitly earlier pruning steps (Table 1) there is a performance degradation. This suggests that the magnitude of a weight by itself is not a good measure of saliency when the network is far from reaching convergence. It is also worth noting that SNIP collapses at high levels of sparsity, causing the network to perform no better than random guessing. Upon inspecting these cases (not shown for visibility) we noticed that at least one layer has been entirely pruned, effectively blocking any signal from passing. Interestingly, this does not happen for any of the other baselines (except for Random). We conjecture that this collapse as well as the cases where SNIP performs worse than random pruning (Fig. 4b) are a result of pruning at initialization; pruning too early can cause the saliency criterion to be inaccurate, but also impedes training in and of itself.

During our experiments, we empirically observed that Hoyer-Square requires extensive hyperparameter tuning for optimal performance. Our method, however, has strong default values and can also target the final sparsity directly, while also not requiring additional epochs of fine-tuning. Finally, SNIP, the only other baseline which does not suffer from any of the issues commonly found among pruning methods (Sect. 1) compromises on performance for high levels of sparsity, whereas FlipOut does not.

4.4   Is It Just the Noise?

The performance of FlipOut could simply be a result of the noise addition, which is known to aid optimization [19,25]. To investigate this, we perform experiments with global magnitude as the pruning criterion in which we add noise into the gradients using the recipe from Eq. 3c and compare it to our own method. Notably, the saliency criterion of these two methods differ only in that FlipOut normalizes the magnitude by the number of sign flips (denominator in Eq. 1a). The hyperparameters were kept at their default values of $p = 2$ for FlipOut and $\lambda = 1$ for both methods. We also include runs of FlipOut where no noise was added, i.e. $\lambda = 0$. These serve as a control, decoupling the two novel components of our method: noise addition and scaling magnitudes by the number of sign flips. The same pruning rates and frequency of pruning steps have been used as before (Table 1). The results are illustrated in Fig. 5.

For sparsity levels up to 98.44%, adding gradient noise causes a slight deterioration on performance, as can be seen by the fact that both global magnitude and FlipOut with $\lambda = 0$ outperform their noisy counterparts. It can also be seen that FlipOut with $\lambda = 1$ performs comparably to noisy global magnitude, indicating that measuring saliency by sign flips does not benefit accuracy in these regimes compared to using only the magnitude, and the performance gap between the noisy and non-noisy methods is likely a result of noise addition. For sparsity levels of 99.61% and above, however, the opposite is true. It seems that gradient noise disproportionately benefits networks with a small number of remaining parameters; we conjecture that this is due to the fact that the exploration in parameter space induced by noise is more effective when that space is heavily constrained. Focusing on the highest level of sparsity, FlipOut outperforms noisy global magnitude on VGG19 (Fig. 5b) and DenseNet121 (Fig. 5c)

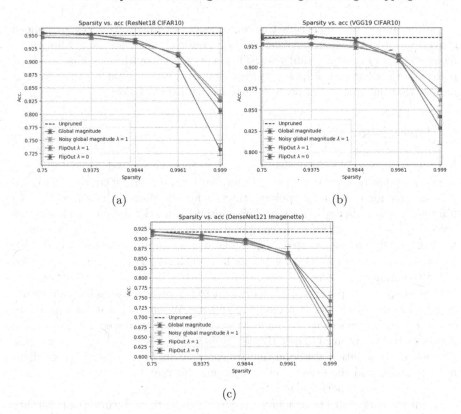

(a)   (b)

(c)

Fig. 5. Results of the ablation study on the noise. Global magnitude without noise addition is also shown for comparison. (a) ResNet18 on CIFAR 10. (b) VGG19 on CIFAR10. (c) DenseNet121 on ImageNette.

by 1.2 and 8.2% points, respectively, while being outperformed by 0.8% points on ResNet18 (Fig. 5a). The standard deviation of FlipOut at this point is lower than for noisy global magnitude for all networks tested, making it more robust to initial conditions and the noise sampling process. At this level, the addition of gradient noise to FlipOut also shows performance boosts compared to its non-noisy counterpart, namely 9.3% points for ResNet18, 3.2 for VGG19 and 3.7 for DenseNet121. The benefits caused by adding noise to global magnitude as compared to adding it to FlipOut are similar for VGG19; however, it is relatively small for ResNet18 at 2.6% points and even causes a 2% point drop in performance for DenseNet121.

Since FlipOut with $\lambda = 1$ outperforms noisy global magnitude in 2 out of 3 cases for the highest level of sparsity while maintaining similar performance in all other cases as well as being less sensitive to the choice of seed, we conclude that its results cannot be explained only by the addition of noise and is also caused by the sign flips being taken into account when computing saliency.

Additionally, we conjecture that occurrences of under-shooting are indeed converted into over-shooting when adding gradient noise, allowing FlipOut to more accurately compute saliencies. This is evidenced by the fact that gradient noise addition benefits FlipOut more so than it does global magnitude, and implies that our method of dealing with deceitful shots is sound.

5   Discussion

In this work, we introduce the aim test, a general method for determining whether a point represents a local optimum for a weight during training, and propose using it for pruning by applying the test for all weights simultaneously and framing it as a saliency criterion. This method, coined FlipOut, demonstrates several desirable qualities: it is computationally tractable, allows for an exact level of sparsity to be selected, requires a single training run and has default hyperparameter settings which generate near optimal results, easing the burden of hyperparameter search.

We compare the performance of FlipOut to relevant baselines from literature on a variety of object classification architectures. We show that it achieves state-of-the-art performance at the highest levels of sparsity tested for 2 out of 3 networks and maintains competitive performance in less sparse regimes. Finally, we conduct an ablation study on the two components of our algorithm, gradient noise addition and the saliency criterion, and find that both play an important role in yielding this performance.

A future work yet to be concluded is a more in-depth probe into the generality of our algorithm and its properties. This includes using larger scale datasets, different data modalities (e.g. natural language) as well as architectures other than convolutional neural networks.

References

1. Bellec, G., Kappel, D., Maass, W., Legenstein, R.: Deep rewiring: training very sparse deep networks. In: International Conference on Learning Representations (2018)
2. Bottou, L.: Online algorithms and stochastic approximations. In: Online Learning and Neural Networks. Cambridge University Press, Cambridge (1998). Revised, October 2012
3. Brock, A., Donahue, J., Simonyan, K.: Large scale GAN training for high fidelity natural image synthesis. In: International Conference on Learning Representations (2019)
4. Frankle, J., Carbin, M.: The lottery ticket hypothesis: finding sparse, trainable neural networks. In: International Conference on Learning Representations (2019)
5. Han, S., Pool, J., Tran, J., Dally, W.: Learning both weights and connections for efficient neural network. In: Advances in Neural Information Processing Systems (2015)
6. Hassibi, B., Stork, D.G.: Second order derivatives for network pruning: optimal brain surgeon. In: Advances in Neural Information Processing Systems (1993)

7. He, K., Zhang, X., Ren, S., Sun, J.: Deep residual learning for image recognition. In: 2016 IEEE Conference on Computer Vision and Pattern Recognition (CVPR) (2016). https://doi.org/10.1109/CVPR.2016.90

8. Howard, J.: Imagenette (2019). https://github.com/fastai/imagenette. Accessed 6 Apr 2020

9. Huang, G., Liu, Z., Van Der Maaten, L., Weinberger, K.Q.: Densely connected convolutional networks. In: 2017 IEEE Conference on Computer Vision and Pattern Recognition (CVPR) (2017). https://doi.org/10.1109/CVPR.2017.243

10. Kingma, D., Ba, J.: Adam: a method for stochastic optimization. In: International Conference on Learning Representations (2015)

11. Ko, V., Oehmcke, S., Gieseke, F.: Magnitude and uncertainty pruning criterion for neural networks. In: 2019 IEEE International Conference on Big Data (Big Data) (2019). https://doi.org/10.1109/BigData47090.2019.9005692

12. Krizhevsky, A.: Learning multiple layers of features from tiny images (2009)

13. LeCun, Y., Denker, J.S., Solla, S.A.: Optimal brain damage. In: Advances in Neural Information Processing Systems, vol. 2 (1990)

14. Lee, N., Ajanthan, T., Torr, P.: SNIP: single-shot network pruning based on connection sensitivity. In: International Conference on Learning Representations (2019)

15. Li, H., Kadav, A., Durdanovic, I., Samet, H., Graf, H.P.: Pruning filters for efficient convnets. In: International Conference on Learning Representations (2017)

16. Liu, J., Xu, Z., Shi, R., Cheung, R.C.C., So, H.K.: Dynamic sparse training: find efficient sparse network from scratch with trainable masked layers. In: International Conference on Learning Representations (2020)

17. Louizos, C., Welling, M., Kingma, D.P.: Learning sparse neural networks through l_0 regularization. In: International Conference on Learning Representations (2018)

18. Molchanov, D., Ashukha, A., Vetrov, D.: Variational dropout sparsifies deep neural networks. In: International Conference on Machine Learning (2017)

19. Neelakantan, A., et al.: Adding gradient noise improves learning for very deep networks. arXiv e-prints arXiv:1511.06807, November 2015

20. Simonyan, K., Zisserman, A.: Very deep convolutional networks for large-scale image recognition. In: International Conference on Learning Representations (2015)

21. Strubell, E., Ganesh, A., McCallum, A.: Energy and policy considerations for deep learning in NLP. In: Proceedings of the 57th Annual Meeting of the Association for Computational Linguistics (2019). https://doi.org/10.18653/v1/P19-1355

22. Tieleman, T., Hinton, G.: Lecture 6.5-rmsprop: divide the gradient by a running average of its recent magnitude. COURSERA: Neural Netw. Mach. Learn. 4, 26–31 (2012)

23. Train CIFAR10 with PyTorch (GitHub Repository): Pytorch CIFAR-10 GitHub repository (2017). https://github.com/kuangliu/pytorch-cifar/. Accessed 6 Apr 2020

24. Vaswani, A., et al.: Attention is all you need. In: Advances in Neural Information Processing Systems (2017)

25. Welling, M., Teh, Y.W.: Bayesian learning via stochastic gradient Langevin dynamics. In: International Conference on Machine Learning (2011)

26. Yang, H., Wen, W., Li, H.: DeepHoyer: learning sparser neural network with differentiable scale-invariant sparsity measures. In: International Conference on Learning Representations (2020)

Evolving Virtual Embodied Agents Using External Artifact Evaluations

Lesley van Hoek[✉], Rob Saunders, and Roy de Kleijn

Leiden Institute of Advanced Computer Science, Leiden University,
Leiden, The Netherlands
l.s.van.hoek@umail.leidenuniv.nl, r.saunders@liacs.leidenuniv.nl,
kleijnrde@fsw.leidenuniv.nl
http://www.cs.leiden.edu

Abstract. We present *neatures*, a computational art system exploring the potential of digitally evolving artificial organisms for generating aesthetically pleasing artifacts. Hexapedal agents act in a virtual environment, which they can sense and manipulate through painting. Their cognitive models are designed in accordance with theory of situated cognition. Two experimental setups are investigated: painting with a narrow- and wide perspective vision sensor. Populations of agents are optimized for the aesthetic quality of their work using a complexity-based fitness function that solely evaluates the artifact. We show that external evaluation of artifacts can evolve behaviors that produce fit artworks. Our results suggest that wide-perspective vision may be more suited for maximizing aesthetic fitness while narrow-perspective vision induces more behavioral complexity and artifact diversity. We recognize that both setups evolve distinct strategies with their own merits. We further discuss our findings and propose future directions for the current approach.

Keywords: Aesthetic evaluation · Artificial intelligence · Artificial life · Autonomous behavior · Computational creativity · Embodied agents · Evolutionary art · Neural networks · Situated action · Situated cognition

1 Introduction

Computational systems that produce artworks with high levels of autonomy have always provoked discussion about the definition of art and creativity. Researchers and artists working in the field of evolutionary and generative art cede control to autonomous systems that produce artworks, often intending to eliminate human intervention where possible [17]. Digital evolution is an established algorithmic process that has proven very capable of innovation [18]. In art and design, appropriate implementation of this technique can aid the generation of novel, valuable and surprising artifacts [2,4] that may be deemed creative by unbiased observers [8]. It has also been essential in the field of artificial life (a-life) [26] where researchers have been consistently surprised by creative solutions invented

© Springer Nature Switzerland AG 2021
M. Baratchi et al. (Eds.): BNAIC/Benelearn 2020, CCIS 1398, pp. 30–47, 2021.
https://doi.org/10.1007/978-3-030-76640-5_3

by artificial organisms evolving in computational environments [28]. Naturally, the process of digital evolution merely imitates life itself. The biological mechanism of natural selection is known to find and cause inventive adaptations that enhance the survival and reproduction of organisms [15]. Consequently, these may lead to the appearance of design without a designer [10]. Adaptations may include changes in behavior. We aim our attention at a particular behavior in some non-human organisms, namely the creation of artifacts.

Several species in the natural world are known to decorate and produce structures that resemble visual art in the sense that they are intended to be attractive to potential mates. This structure creation is an important behavioral characteristic of male bower birds [12] and white-spotted pufferfishes [31]. In this paper, we explore whether artificial organisms could adapt to similar, but digitally induced pressures as a consequence of constructing artifacts. The following sections briefly discuss some challenges related to building such a computational system.

1.1 Computational Aesthetic Evaluation

Early examples of evolutionary art include the highly influential work of Sims [41] and Latham [47], who used genetic algorithms to mutate symbolic expressions for the composition of unpredictable yet interesting visual shapes and patterns. Both adopted a top-down approach that relies on human aesthetic judgment for the evaluation of artifacts using an interactive genetic algorithm (IGA). This technique facilitates easy exploration of large parameter spaces [44] but suffers from significant limitations: (1) IGAs rely on human evaluation at every iteration and so suffer from the *fitness bottleneck* [46], and (2) human fatigue and inconsistency make it difficult to capture universal measures [44]. Attempts to overcome these limitations have included massively multi-user systems [39] and the application of machine learning to capture user preferences [33].

Challenges in IGA helped inspire the research field of computational aesthetic evaluation (CAE), where people seek computational solutions for the assessment of human aesthetics [23]. Machado and Cardoso [29] created *NEvAr*, an autonomous system that evolves Sims' symbolic expressions with an automated evaluation procedure for images that focuses exclusively on form. Here, a speculative fitness function inspired by the study of *information aesthetics* [35] was designed which favors images that are "simultaneously, visually complex and that can be processed (by our brains) easily". In the science of aesthetics, *NEvAr*'s fitness function indicates a *formalist theory* as it proposes aesthetic experience relies on the intrinsic beauty of the artifact. In contrast, a *conceptual theory* relies on other factors that may be more important for aesthetic preference like socio-cultural contexts of the work and the previous experience of the artists and observers [40]. In a more recent publication, Redies [36] proposes a model of visual aesthetic experience that unifies these two theories. Ultimately, there is currently no agreement on which paradigm offers the most effective computational framework of human aesthetics.

1.2 Embodiment

Theorists in situated cognition view the environment as highly significant to driving human cognitive processes. Clark and Chalmers [7] suggest that the environment directly influences an agent's behaviors as part of a two-way interaction between action and perception. Here, embodiment is key because it allows us to manipulate it to our needs. Biological brains have evolved to take advantage of the environment by offloading cognition to it through the body. Simultaneously, our visual systems evolved to rely on it more. This perspective supports the view of *externalism*, in which the cognitive process is considered something that occurs in- and outside of the mind [7]. In this context, embodiment is key to the creation of art and can be imagined as a feedback loop of action and perception occurring through a body. Brinck [5] states that the production (and consumption) of visual art can be accounted for by the theory of situated cognition [6]: "Artist and canvas form a coupled system. Artistic practice starts with gaze, and then comes the gesture that accomplishes itself when the artist is in touch with the piece [they are] working on" [5].

Experiments in the use of embodied artificial organisms and situated cognition for computational art and creativity have largely been unexplored. Thus, we present *neatures*: a prototype for an autonomous art system that simulates artificial organisms capable of producing visual art in their environment.

2 Related Work

There have been several interesting art and research projects involving the use of embodied agents to create visual art. Jean Tinguely experimented with mechanical drawing machines in the 50s, exploring notions of automated artists and artificial creative processes [13]. Influences to his work can be seen in the field of swarm painting, which involves the simulation of agents supplied with some form of cognition producing emergent artworks. *Robotic Action Painter* [34] is an autonomous abstract art system based on behavioral studies of ants and other social insects. An artwork is created by employing several small wheeled robots that leave colored lines (pheromone) as they travel. A color detection sensor on each robot recognizes these lines in the environment and triggers specified behaviors for particular colors–a process analogous to *stigmergy*; a form of self-organization [14]. The result is a painting with chaotic structures that are free from preconceptions and merely represent the actions themselves. McCormack developed similar experiments using biological processes of niche construction to enhance the diversity and variation of agents' behaviors in his art system [32].

Drawing machines that take a more anthropomorphic approach can be classified as robot painters. *eDavid* [11] is an industrial robot that simulates the human painting process using a visual feedback loop to explore painterly rendering on a real canvas. Explorations in expanding its artistic skill demonstrated the possibility of expressing a given collection of images in a different style [48]. With *neatures*, we take inspiration from the flexibility of robot painters and the emerging complexity of swarms to explore the effects of aesthetic selection pressures in an evolutionary art system.

3   Implementation

Neatures[1] is a prototype computational visual art system that was developed in an attempt to employ artificial organisms for the production of visual artifacts. The current implementation is heavily inspired by the seminal work of Sims (1994), Evolving Virtual Creatures, in which a genetic algorithm was used to guide the evolution of specific abilities such as locomotion and jumping. *Neatures'* artificial organisms 'live' in three-dimensional space and are subject to physically plausible simulation. This is achieved using the Bullet physics engine [9]. The software comprises of a controller server which stores the population and commands the complete evolutionary process. A simulator client can connect to a controller and receive queries for queued rollouts. This component features a graphical user interface, allowing the user to observe the virtual organisms in real-time. The following sections briefly cover the system implementation.

3.1   Agent Morphology

Virtual organisms situated in physically plausible environments are subject to strict laws of physics and, like real organisms, require an appropriate body to fulfill their purpose. Designing such a body is a difficult task, and perhaps best suited for an evolutionary process to solve. Sims [41] used a genotypic encoding of nodes and connections for the morphology of his creatures, and genetic operators, allowing for the evolution of morphology alongside control policy. In this system, a genotypic encoding scheme is used to generate a hexapod at the start of a simulation and remains fixed. The reason for this is that evolutionary optimization of morphology dramatically increases the complexity of the search landscape and is incompatible with fixed-topology neural network architectures.

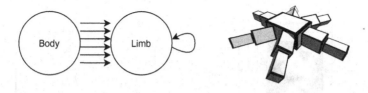

Fig. 1. Agent morphology genotype (left) and phenotype (right).

Each element stores some information about their phenotypic transformations such as size, attachment points, and node or joint type. A phenotype generation algorithm recursively traverses the graph and builds a hierarchical

---

[1] *Neatures* is open-source and available at https://github.com/lshoek/creative-evo-simulator.

structure of boxes connected to each other by joints. Figure 1 depicts the morphology encoding and phenotype of a hexapod. The algorithm in the current work was implemented after Krčah's example [25] with some alterations tailored to suit this work's purpose. One notable difference, for instance, is that we use a single degree of freedom per joint for simplicity.

3.2 Agent Control Policy

In every simulation rollout, agents are tasked to produce an artifact in their environment. In order to achieve this in *neatures*, we chose to implement a painting system. Each agent is equipped with a single brush-type node capable of applying virtual ink drops to the canvas; a specified surface area in the environment that the agent can sense and manipulate. Four invisible walls are located at a specified distance from the canvas edges to prevent agents from moving too far away from the center. Ink is only released under the conditions that the brush node is in contact with the canvas, and the agent has decided to activate it.

An agent's decision-making process and behavior are determined by its control policy. This is defined by a neural controller that continuously accepts sensory data as input, and based on this data, outputs a set of activation values. Agents sense their environment through two types of sensors: (1) a proprioceptive sensor, implemented by tracking the current joint angles and storing these in $a \in \mathbb{R}^j$, where j is equal to the number of joints in the agent's morphology and (2) a vision sensor capturing a 64×64 px grayscale bitmap representation of the current canvas' content. The data of both sensors is appended to form an observation to be fed to the neural controller at regular time intervals. The physics engine and control policy are updated 60 and 20 times per second of simulated time, respectively. Figure 2 presents the complete cognitive model of an agent.

The neural controller involves two cognitive modules; a vision model V for processing visual data inside the incoming observation, and an action model C to generate the agent's next action. V is a *convolutional variational autoencoder*

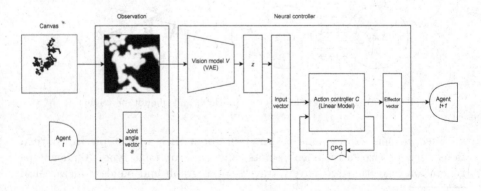

Fig. 2. Cognitive model of an agent.

(CVAE), pre-trained to compress the canvas data to a latent vector $z \in \mathbb{R}^{32}$. C is a simple linear model that takes as input a combination of latent vector z, a joint angle vector, and an additional value to stimulate continuous movement. Compression of the visual data allows the action controller to be kept small, which alleviates the credit assignment problem in difficult reinforcement learning (RL) tasks and tends to iterate faster [19]. The output layer of C uses a *tanh* activation function to output a vector of effector values, including target joint angles used to update the motor parameters of the agent's joints and a value indicating the stroke width of the brush. Finally, a stimulation output value connects to a central pattern generator (CPG) after which a feedback connection to the corresponding action model input is made for the next time the neural controller is queried [24]. This minimal recurrent network structure is set up this way to evoke changing joint angle outputs. Without it, the agent would cease to move in cases where its observations remain unchanged over multiple frames and its body incidentally has zero momentum. Additionally, as sensory input drives neural excitation, it grants C control over the agent's movement speed, which could bring about more interesting behaviors. Section 4.3 describes the training procedure for V and C.

4 Experiment

We carry out two experiments where an artificial organism is evolved by optimizing for the aesthetic quality of its artifacts. The artistic medium of expression chosen for this task is painting. The main reason for this is that there exists a multitude of interesting theories and evaluation techniques of visual human aesthetics–suitable for two-dimensional content–that could be pursued to design an acceptable fitness function [16].

Fig. 3. The *neatures* simulator showing an agent painting.

As stated in Sect. 3.1, we decided to exclude morphology from evolutionary optimization, meaning we must formulate an appropriate body design for the current experiment ourselves. We take inspiration from behavioral robotics research, where it has long been common practice to use biologically based robot designs to study artificial organisms [1]. As a matter of course, the insect-like hexapod was chosen for the current task. This design is a popular benchmark that we suppose will allow for an adequate degree of flexibility required to explore the possibilities of the virtual environment. Figure 3 shows a screenshot of the agent as it appears in the simulator client of the system.

4.1   Setup

The following is a brief description of the realized experiments. In the first setup, the agent is supplied with a wide-perspective vision sensor. This is defined as a 64×64 px grayscale bitmap representation of the environment that is equal to the size of the canvas. The orientation of this representation is at all times aligned with the facing direction of the agent and centered around the point where it last touched the canvas with its brush node. Figure 4a shows an example of how the canvas is sensed with this perspective. The second setup supplies the agent with a narrow-perspective vision sensor, encompassing 6.25% of the canvas area as shown in Fig. 4b.

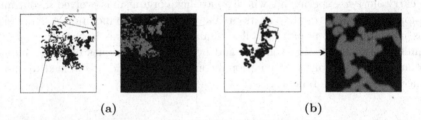

(a)   (b)

Fig. 4. The mapping from canvas (left) to visual field (right), marked in red, for wide-perspective (4a) and narrow-perspective (4b). (Color figure online)

The vision capabilities of the agent exist in a separate conceptual space from the one it is situated in. Agents' visual capabilities exist in *artifact space*, whereas their neural controllers output actions in *effector space*. The former is a two-dimensional representation of the environment, cultivated by the agent itself. The latter relates to objects in the three-dimensional virtual environment. Other than muscle memory (the action controller parameters), an agent has no other capabilities of memorization. As a result, the environment is the only cognitive resource to the agent by which an approximate model of situated cognition is realized. The key idea to this experiment is that, under the given conditions, a mapping between these two may be learned. If successful, the creature would be able to produce an aesthetically pleasing artifact in *artifact space* by means of its motor function in *effector space*.

4.2   Measuring Aesthetic Quality

After a rollout has ended, the resulting artifact is queued for fitness evaluation. In our computational environment, the fitness function is a proxy for natural selection pressures that cause the evolution of adaptations [15]. As outsiders to this virtual world, we can design this function externally, and observe what behaviors emerge from evolutionary optimization. Taking inspiration from some animal species' mate selection indicators that are attributed to external artifacts, we intentionally ignore any behavioral aspects of an agent's existence. Our fitness function is designed to evaluate images in accordance with speculative visual aesthetic theory, essentially assuming the role of an art critic.

To measure the aesthetic quality of an artifact, we use a metric closely related to Birkhoff's [3] formalist aesthetic measure, defining the formula $M = O/C$, where M is the aesthetic effectiveness, O is the degree of order and C is the degree of complexity. Birkhoff theorizes that aesthetic response to an object is stronger when the degree to which psychological effort is required to perceive it–induced by its complex features–is met with a higher degree of tension being released as the perception is realized–originating from orderly features such as symmetry and self-similarity. This formula has been disputed early and is generally regarded as inaccurate [49]. Scha and Bod [37], for instance, note that it penalizes complexity too considerably and is better suited as a measure of the degree of self-similarity. Galanter [16], however, notes that at least two aspects of Birkhoff's work remain legitimate today; the intuitive connection between aesthetic value and order/complexity relationships, and the search for a neurological base of aesthetic behavior. These aspects are reflected in the fitness function of Machado and Cardoso [29], defined in Eq. 1. Inspired by information aesthetics [35], Machado & Cardoso speculate an image's intrinsic aesthetic value to be equal to the ratio of image complexity IC to processing complexity PC.

$$reward_{aesthetic} = \frac{IC}{PC} \tag{1}$$

PC is measured at two temporal instances ($t0$ and $t1$) in the time it takes to perceive an image and provide Eq. 2. The processing complexity is maximized as PC_{t1} and PC_{t0} approach each other.

$$PC = (PC_{t0}PC_{t1})^a \left(\frac{PC_{t1} - PC_{t0}}{PC_{t1}} \right)^b \tag{2}$$

In order to find PC_{t0} and PC_{t1}, we calculate the inverse of the root mean square error (RMSE) between the original image i, and the same image after fractal compression $Fractal(i)$, as shown in Eq. 3.

$$PC_{tn} = \frac{1}{RMSE(Fractal(i),\ i)} \tag{3}$$

Machado et al. [30] compared several complexity measures with human ratings across a selected set of images in five distinct stylistic categories. Among the results of their feature extraction experiments, their JPEG-Sobel method was found to correlate the most with human ratings, especially those related to the abstract artistic category. We calculate IC following this method as shown in Eq. 4. First, the Sobel [42] edge detection operator is applied to i horizontal and vertical directions, after which the resulting gradients are averaged. Then, JPEG compression is performed on the edges. In the dividend, size defines the total number of bytes required to store the image data.

$$IC = \frac{RMSE(Sobel(i),\ JPEG(Sobel(i)))}{size(Sobel(i))size(JPEG(Sobel(i)))} \tag{4}$$

Taylor et al. [45] note the fractal qualities of late-period action paintings by Jackson Pollock and suggests their fractal dimensions are correlated with their aesthetic qualities. Therefore, we decided to parameterize Eq. 2 using $a = 0.6$ and $b = 0.3$, increasing bias towards artifacts with more orderly features with respect to the reference implementation [29]. We argue that this suits the current experimental setup by countering excessive levels of image complexity in the artifacts due to the generally chaotic nature of agents' behaviors that generate complex and incidental painting patterns by default.

In early experiments, we found that additional encouragement to act through an easily attainable coverage reward could help agents to advance faster in early generations. This has the added benefit that a minimum specified amount of content is imposed on the artifacts. Equation 5 defines $reward_{coverage}(x)$, where x is the mean of all normalized pixel intensities of the artifact and p is the peak coverage rate. It is essentially a smooth interpolation between x and p, ensuring a result of 1 when $x \geq p$.

$$reward_{coverage}(x) = 1 - \sin\left(\pi \frac{\frac{1}{p}x + 1}{2}\right)^4 \tag{5}$$

with initial condition

$$x = \min(x,\ p) \tag{6}$$

In our experiments, we use $p = 0.0625$, meaning that the maximum coverage reward is already reached when 6.25% of the canvas area is painted. Finally, the total artifact fitness is calculated as defined in Eq. 7. This shows the aesthetic reward is proportional to the coverage reward until peak reward p is reached, thus penalizing paintings that have little content. Table 1 presents a set of images and their fitness values.

$$fitness = 100\, reward_{coverage} + reward_{aesthetic} \times reward_{coverage} \tag{7}$$

We find these results to be satisfactory for our purposes. Although the fitness function is arguably too generous on Gaussian noise (Table 1d), such an artifact is practically impossible for an agent to produce. The Pollock-snippet (Table 1e) is evaluated far more positively and represents a more plausible result.

Table 1. A set of images and their fitness: (a) perfect symmetry, (b) an early-generation artifact with little variability in stroke width, (c) an early-generation artifact with high variability in stroke width, (d) Gaussian noise, (e) a contrast-enhanced snippet of No. 26A: Black and White by Jackson Pollock (1948).

	(a)	(b)	(c)	(d)	(e)
Fitness	101.2	116.2	145.9	399.5	871.5
Coverage	27.7%	15.5%	12.4%	18.2%	46.0%
IC	0.0697	0.4042	0.8046	44.269	48.443
PC	0.0561	0.0250	0.0175	0.0148	0.0063

4.3   Training Procedure

Before any control policies can be evolved, visual model V must be pre-trained to discern between visual observations. First, 20,000 artifact samples (256×256 grayscale bitmaps) were collected in a preliminary run using an untrained visual model V. Then, a new dataset was generated by applying random affine transformations to each collected sample. This new dataset is more representative of an agent's visual observations. Finally, using the updated dataset, V was trained to encode visual observations into latent vector $z \in \mathbb{R}^{32}$ for 200 epochs.

Agents' control policies are optimized through evaluation of the quality of their work, rather than the means by which it was achieved. This indirect correspondence between goal and action may reduce credit assignment accuracy of gradient-based numerical optimization algorithms as adaptations to action controller C could have unanticipated effects on an artifact's fitness. Therefore, gradient-free methods such as evolution strategies [38] might be best suited for solving this problem. *Neuroevolution* methods have a long history of success with evolutionary robotics and have recently increased in popularity as they have been found to perform considerably well on deep RL tasks [43]. With this in consideration, we chose *covariance matrix adaptation evolution strategy* (CMA-ES) [20] for the optimization of C's parameters. Evidence shows that the algorithm performs relatively well on deceptive landscapes or sparse-reward functions up to a couple of thousands of parameters [22]. We use an open-source Python implementation of the algorithm by Hansen [21].

At the start of every evolution process, the weights of every action controller C in the population are randomly initialized with $\mu = 0$ and $\sigma = 0.1$. A population size of 32 is used, where each candidate's behavior is determined by their corresponding C, comprising 658 trainable parameters each. Every generation, one rollout is performed per agent and results in 32 artifacts. A rollout is defined as 240 s of simulated time an agent spends in the environment. Evaluations occur immediately after each rollout in a separate process. After all rollouts and evaluations are finished, CMA-ES uses the collected fitness values to update each candidate's action controller parameters for the next generation. Both experiments are performed using an evolutionary process of 350 generations.

Our training setup marks several notable limitations. Foremost, the experiments are carried out separately on two mid-range laptops (i7-7700HQ/GTX1050 and i7-8750H/GTX1070), each running a single simulator client and controller server at the same time. The most significant bottleneck comes from the fractal compression procedure required for each artifact evaluation. In the current setup, we simulate two populations of 32 candidates for 350 generations and takes about 40 h to complete. More reliable results could be collected by increasing the population size and averaging fitness over multiple rollouts for a more representative metric of the agent's general painting strategy. This is however outside of the scope of this research.

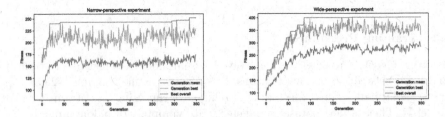

Fig. 5. Fitnesses of the narrow- (left) and wide-perspective populations (right).

5   Results

Figure 5 presents the fitness results of the narrow- and wide-perspective vision experiments. Here, we see that the narrow-perspective population's mean fitness starts with a steep positive trend and converges towards a local optimum before the 50th generation. The wide-perspective population's mean fitness improves gradually up to around the 100th generation before a local optimum is reached. We also see that the wide-perspective population is generally about 150 points ahead of the narrow-perspective population. From these results, it is evident that the wide-perspective population performs better in terms of fitness. However, it barely shows any signs of improvement after a local optimum has been reached, until the final generation of the simulation. This is unlike the narrow-perspective population, which shows a slight upward trend around the 300th generation, and some new best-ever artifacts of the population. Table 2 presents the highest-rated artifacts of both experiments along with some key statistics. Almost every artifact shows a clear trajectory on the canvas that is telling of the strategy that was used to produce it. Figure 6 below shows the highest-rated artifacts of the first 64 generations of both populations. We see that the sort of artifacts produced by both populations can easily be distinguished from approximately the 40th generation. From there on, we see that nearly all artifacts of the wide-vision population indicate a circular movement strategy, with little diversity among paintings.

Table 2. The highest-rated artifacts of all generations of wide-perspective and narrow-perspective populations and their key statistics.

Pers.	Fitness	Cov.	IC	PC	Gen.
Wide	401.05	36.05%	2.8339	0.0094	194
Narrow	251.82	21.33%	1.7714	0.0116	335

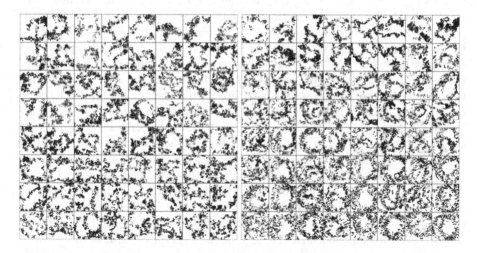

Wide   Narrow

The fitness results and artifacts of this population show that this strategy is further exploited in subsequent generations, likely because of its effective contribution to maximizing fitness. In contrast, the narrow-perspective population struggles to escape a local optimum early on but demonstrates far more diversity among its artifacts in all generations. This suggests that potentially fit strategies are being explored rather than being exploited.

Fig. 6. The best artifacts of the first 64 generations (top-left to bottom-right) of the narrow- (left) and the wide-perspective population (right).

The discrepancy between the fitness results and the type of artifacts produced by both populations led us to believe that coverage and fitness may be strongly positively correlated. To investigate, we plotted coverage against fitness (Fig. 7) and observed that coverage is an accurate predictor of fitness in the wide-perspective population, but not necessarily for the narrow-perspective population.

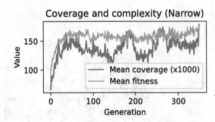 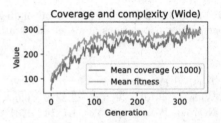

Fig. 7. Mean coverage and fitness in narrow- (left) and wide-perspective populations (right).

6   Discussion

Our results of the current experiment demonstrate a notable distinction between the narrow- and wide-perspective setup. In our experiment, we observe that virtual organisms with narrow-perspective vision trigger explorative search of the fitness landscape by the evolutionary algorithm and demonstrate more complex and distinct behavior. We also see that this is not necessarily in the interest of maximizing fitness. One explanation for this could be that relatively small adaptations to a narrow-perspective controller's weights lead to greater variations in the emerging painting strategy. In the agent's cognitive model, perception and action are closely coupled together. Therefore, distinct actions may be more likely to be triggered when visual observations are more volatile, as is the case with the narrow-perspective agents. This is in line with Brinck's [5] argument that art creation is a situated activity, noting that what the artist perceives is directly transformed into action. We further observe that narrow-perspective agents generally appear more sensitive to the environment in their painting strategies than wide-perspective agents. Narrow-perspective agents show more effective corrective behavior such as turning near the edge of the canvas. This is not as apparent in wide-perspective agents who barely appear to discernibly change their behavior near edges. Little response to edges is likely induced by the exploitation of circular movement patterns–evidently an effective strategy for painting highly fit artifacts. We further think that the widespread coverage of paint in the environment reinforces an agent's behavioral pattern. This may be due to the relatively poor compression quality of global features in visual observations of developed circular patterns, leading to similar encodings of z. Incidentally, this fact may have greatly contributed to finding the circular movement strategy.

From our observations, we theorize that volatile visual information, as demonstrated by the narrow-perspective experiment, considerably complicates the shape of the fitness landscape. For instance, a consistent circular movement strategy would be much more difficult to sustain over the length of a rollout, and over multiple generations, with narrow-perspective vision than with wide-perspective vision. Even more so, this automatically concerns any potential strategy. Although volatile visual information may impede the evolution of consistent action and perception, it does have creative merit in the sense that it elicits greater behavioral complexity in agents. Hence, the narrow-perspective population has explored the greatest *artifact space*. This is demonstrated in Fig. 8 which presents two random selections of artifacts created in both populations.

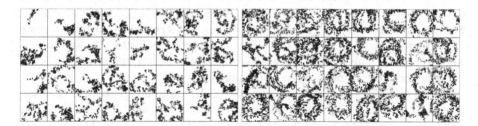

Fig. 8. Two random selections of artifacts drawn from all of the narrow-perspective population (left) and the wide-perspective population (right).

Considering our evaluation procedure; if we, hypothetically, consider Pollock's work as an aesthetic benchmark for this system (Table 1e), we consider the current fitness function helpful at guiding agents' technique towards this aesthetic up to a certain point. Figure 7 however suggests a possible perverse instantiation problem; at least one strategy exists in which coverage can be exploited to maximize fitness. However, we believe an adjustment to the fitness function would be premature. This is because, as the fitness function is based on complexity, coverage cannot be positively correlated with fitness as it approaches 50%. The highest recorded coverage of all artifacts in both populations is 36%, whereas the coverage of our Pollock example (Table 1e) is measured at 46%. We are confident that under the current time pressure of 240 s, it is physically not possible for agents to cover a significantly greater part of the canvas. Therefore, we believe that agents should be assigned sufficient time so that 50% coverage could be achieved. After this is explored, we believe that a worthwhile addition to the fitness function would be a novelty reward term to overcome local optima by encouraging exploration [27].

In our experiment, we see that a proxy for selection pressures based in aesthetic properties of an external artifact can evolve a virtual organism with some success. Our agents' artificially emergent and autonomous behaviors resemble those of simple biological organisms in some ways on a superficial level and are rather interesting to observe. Whether some of the resulting artifacts are aesthetically pleasing is up to the beholder. Their chaotic patterns and compositions certainly parallel abstract expressionist action paintings to some degree. The agents' paintings share an interesting connection to this art movement as all brushstrokes represent nothing but the actions themselves. With that, one could argue for their artistic value.

6.1 Future Work

We briefly propose future directions for the current research. Foremost, the system would highly benefit from a more robust visual model, as emphasized by the poor reconstruction quality of wide-perspective visual observations. This can be achieved by using a larger dataset of intermediate visual observations. Future work could assess whether granting a virtual organism continuous agency over its visual perspective, approximating the cognitive process of *attention*, is a worthwhile approach. This feature is trainable and could explore the nuance between the benefits of the demonstrated visual perspectives.

The morphology and environmental setup we chose for the task of painting is by no means the most suitable. We recommend that future work in embodied agent art should keep exploring the evolution of morphologies. This prevents authors from making predisposed choices about the most suitable body for a given task. A significant downside to this is that it requires a flexible network structure for the action controller model that is significantly more difficult to train. A search algorithm for appropriate morphology choice is another separate topic that could be further explored in the context of art-producing artificial organisms [27]. Furthermore, agents in the current work are limited to a single type of brush, paint color, and environment to explore. Therefore, future extensions could try implementing physically based painting systems, color palettes, and varying environments, each of which could bring about interesting new artifacts and behaviors. Ultimately, painting is only one method of artistic practice, and by no means the most suitable for embodied agents to practice. Computational organisms and environments allow for other artistic modes of expression to be explored such as sculpture, dance, music, poetry, etc. The possibilities are far-reaching and may one day perhaps exceed our imagination.

7 Conclusion

We have demonstrated that virtual organisms can be evolved to make aesthetically pleasing paintings using selection pressures based on aesthetic properties of the painting. The results from our experiments show notable behavioral differences between agents employed with wide-perspective and narrow-perspective vision. The wide-perspective population achieved the best results in terms of fitness by evolving a circular movement strategy effective at maximizing fitness early on, but later showing barely any signs of improvement. The narrow-perspective population performed worse and did not evolve an exploitable strategy. Instead, it brought about a diverse set of artifacts across all generations. From this we conclude that the wide-perspective setup may be more suited for maximizing aesthetic fitness while the narrow-vision setup induces more behavioral complexity and artifact diversity. Although, the scope of this research is limited, our results provided some interesting insights and discussions which provide directions for future applications of computational art systems employing virtual organisms.

References

1. Beer, R.D., Chiel, H.J., Sterling, L.S.: A biological perspective on autonomous agent design. Robot. Auton. Syst. **6**(1–2), 169–186 (1990)
2. Bentley, P.J.: Is evolution creative. In: Proceedings of the AISB, vol. 99, pp. 28–34 (1999)
3. Birkhoff, G.D.: Aesthetic Measure. Harvard University Press, Cambridge (1933)
4. Boden, M.A.: The Creative Mind: Myths and Mechanisms. Psychology Press, Hove (1990)
5. Brinck, I.: Situated cognition, dynamic systems, and art: on artistic creativity and aesthetic experience. Janus Head **9**(2), 407–431 (2007)
6. Clancey, W.J.: Situated Cognition: On Human Knowledge and Computer Representations. Cambridge University Press, Cambridge (1997)
7. Clark, A., Chalmers, D.: The extended mind. Analysis **58**(1), 7–19 (1998)
8. Colton, S., Wiggins, G.A., et al.: Computational creativity: the final frontier? In: ECAI, Montpelier, vol. 12, pp. 21–26 (2012)
9. Coumans, E.: Bullet Physics Library (2013). https://github.com/bulletphysics/bullet3
10. Dennett, D.C., Dennett, D.C.: Darwin's Dangerous Idea: Evolution and the Meanings of Life. Simon and Schuster, New York (1996)
11. Deussen, O., Lindemeier, T., Pirk, S., Tautzenberger, M.: Feedback-guided stroke placement for a painting machine. CAe **8** (2012)
12. Diamond, J.: Animal art: variation in bower decorating style among male bowerbirds Amblyornis inornatus. Proc. Natl. Acad. Sci. **83**(9), 3042–3046 (1986)
13. Dohm, K., Stahlhut, H., Hoffmann, J.: Kunstmaschinen Maschinenkunst. Kehrer Verlag (2007)
14. Dorigo, M., Bonabeau, E., Theraulaz, G.: Ant algorithms and stigmergy. Future Gener. Comput. Syst. **16**(8), 851–871 (2000)
15. Futuyma, D.J.: Natural selection and adaptation. Evolution, pp. 279–301 (2009)
16. Galanter, P.: Computational aesthetic evaluation: past and future. In: McCormack, J., d'Inverno, M. (eds.) Computers and Creativity, pp. 255–293. Springer, Heidelberg (2012). https://doi.org/10.1007/978-3-642-31727-9_10
17. Galanter, P.: Generative art theory. In: A Companion to Digital Art (2016)
18. Goldberg, D.E.: The race, the hurdle, and the sweet spot. In: Evolutionary Design by Computers (1999)
19. Ha, D., Schmidhuber, J.: World models (2018). arXiv:1803.10122
20. Hansen, N.: The CMA evolution strategy: a tutorial (2016). arXiv:1604.00772
21. Hansen, N., Akimoto, Y., Baudis, P.: CMA-ES/pycma on Github
22. Hansen, N., Auger, A., Ros, R., Finck, S., Pošík, P.: Comparing results of 31 algorithms from the black-box optimization benchmarking BBOB-2009. In: GECCO, pp. 1689–1696 (2010)
23. Hoenig, F.: Defining computational aesthetics. The Eurographics Association (2005)
24. Hülse, M., Wischmann, S., Manoonpong, P., von Twickel, A., Pasemann, F.: Dynamical systems in the sensorimotor loop: on the interrelation between internal and external mechanisms of evolved robot behavior. In: Lungarella, M., Iida, F., Bongard, J., Pfeifer, R. (eds.) 50 Years of Artificial Intelligence. LNCS (LNAI), vol. 4850, pp. 186–195. Springer, Heidelberg (2007). https://doi.org/10.1007/978-3-540-77296-5_18

25. Krčah, P.: Evolution and learning of virtual robots. Ph.D. thesis, Univerzita Karlova (2016)
26. Langton, C.G.: Artificial Life: An Overview. MIT Press, Cambridge (1997)
27. Lehman, J., Stanley, K.O.: Abandoning objectives: evolution through the search for novelty alone. Evol. Comput. **19**(2), 189–223 (2011)
28. Lehman, J., et al.: The surprising creativity of digital evolution: a collection of anecdotes from the evolutionary computation and artificial life research communities. Artif. Life **26**(2), 274–306 (2020)
29. Machado, P., Cardoso, A.: All the truth about NEvAr. Appl. Intell. **16**(2), 101–118 (2002). https://doi.org/10.1023/A:1013662402341
30. Machado, P., Romero, J., Nadal, M., Santos, A., Correia, J., Carballal, A.: Computerized measures of visual complexity. Acta Physiol. **160**, 43–57 (2015)
31. Matsuura, K.: A new pufferfish of the genus Torquigener that builds "mystery circles" on sandy bottoms in the Ryukyu Islands, Japan (Actinopterygii: Tetraodontiformes: Tetraodontidae). Ichthyol. Res. **62**(2), 207–212 (2015). https://doi.org/10.1007/s10228-014-0428-5
32. McCormack, J.: Niche constructing drawing robots. In: Correia, J., Ciesielski, V., Liapis, A. (eds.) EvoMUSART 2017. LNCS, vol. 10198, pp. 201–216. Springer, Cham (2017). https://doi.org/10.1007/978-3-319-55750-2_14
33. McCormack, J., Lomas, A.: Understanding aesthetic evaluation using deep learning. In: Romero, J., Ekárt, A., Martins, T., Correia, J. (eds.) EvoMUSART 2020. LNCS, vol. 12103, pp. 118–133. Springer, Cham (2020). https://doi.org/10.1007/978-3-030-43859-3_9
34. Moura, L.: A new kind of art: the robotic action painter. In: X Generative Art Conference. Politecnico di Milano University (2007)
35. Nake, F.: Information aesthetics: an heroic experiment. J. Math. Arts **6**(2–3), 65–75 (2012)
36. Redies, C.: Combining universal beauty and cultural context in a unifying model of visual aesthetic experience. Front. Hum. Neurosci. **9**, 218 (2015)
37. Scha, R., Bod, R.: Computationele Esthetica. Informatie en Informatiebeleid **11**(1), 54–63 (1993)
38. Schwefel, H.P.: Numerical Optimization of Computer Models. Wiley, Hoboken (1981)
39. Secretan, J., et al.: Picbreeder: a case study in collaborative evolutionary exploration of design space. Evol. Comput. **19**(3), 373–403 (2011)
40. Shimamura, A.P., Palmer, S.E.E.: Aesthetic Science: Connecting Minds, Brains, and Experience. OUP, New York (2012)
41. Sims, K.: Artificial evolution for computer graphics. In: PACMCGIT, vol. 18, pp. 319–328 (1991)
42. Sobel, I.: An isotropic 3×3 image gradient operator. In: Machine Vision for Three-Dimensional Scenes (1990)
43. Such, F.P., Madhavan, V., Conti, E., Lehman, J., Stanley, K.O., Clune, J.: Deep neuroevolution: genetic algorithms are a competitive alternative for training deep neural networks for reinforcement learning (2017). arXiv:1712.06567
44. Takagi, H.: Interactive evolutionary computation: fusion of the capabilities of EC optimization and human evaluation. Proc. IEEE **89**(9), 1275–1296 (2001)
45. Taylor, R.P., Micolich, A.P., Jonas, D.: Fractal analysis of Pollock's drip paintings. Nature **399**(6735), 422–422 (1999)
46. Todd, P.M., Werner, G.M.: Frankensteinian methods for evolutionary music. In: Musical Networks: Parallel Distributed Perception and Performance, pp. 313–340 (1999)

47. Todd, S., Latham, W.: Evolutionary Art & Computers. Academic Press Inc., Cambridge (1994)
48. Tresset, P., Deussen, O.: Artistically skilled embodied agents. In: AISB (2014)
49. Wilson, D.J.: An experimental investigation of Birkhoff's aesthetic measure. J. Abnorm. Soc. Psychol. **34**(3), 390 (1939)

Continuous Surrogate-Based Optimization Algorithms Are Well-Suited for Expensive Discrete Problems

Rickard Karlsson, Laurens Bliek⬤, Sicco Verwer, and Mathijs de Weerdt⁽⌧⁾⬤

Delft University of Technology, Delft, The Netherlands
m.m.deweerdt@tudelft.nl

Abstract. One method to solve expensive black-box optimization problems is to use a surrogate model that approximates the objective based on previous observed evaluations. The surrogate, which is cheaper to evaluate, is optimized instead to find an approximate solution to the original problem. In the case of discrete problems, recent research has revolved around discrete surrogate models that are specifically constructed to deal with these problems. A main motivation is that literature considers continuous methods, such as Bayesian optimization with Gaussian processes as the surrogate, to be sub-optimal (especially in higher dimensions) because they ignore the discrete structure by, e.g., rounding off real-valued solutions to integers. However, we claim that this is not true. In fact, we present empirical evidence showing that the use of continuous surrogate models displays competitive performance on a set of high-dimensional discrete benchmark problems, including a real-life application, against state-of-the-art discrete surrogate-based methods. Our experiments with different kinds of discrete decision variables and time constraints also give more insight into which algorithms work well on which type of problem.

Keywords: Surrogate models · Bayesian optimization · Expensive combinatorial optimization · Black-box optimization

1 Introduction

A principal challenge in optimization is to deal with black-box objective functions. The objective function is assumed to be unknown in this case, in contrast to traditional optimization that often utilizes an explicit formulation to compute the gradient or lower bounds. Instead, we assume to have an objective $y = f(\mathbf{x}) + \epsilon$ with some unknown function $f(\mathbf{x})$ together with additive noise ϵ. Furthermore, $f(\mathbf{x})$ can be expensive to evaluate in terms of time or another resource which restricts the number of evaluations allowed.

One type of method to solve these black-box optimization problems is the use of surrogate models. Surrogate-based algorithms approximate the objective function in search of the optimal solution, with the benefit that the surrogate model is cheaper to evaluate. Bayesian optimization [5] is an example of such a surrogate-based algorithm.

An active field of research is how to deal with discrete black-box optimization problems with an expensive objective function. There are many real-world examples

© Springer Nature Switzerland AG 2021
M. Baratchi et al. (Eds.): BNAIC/Benelearn 2020, CCIS 1398, pp. 48–63, 2021.
https://doi.org/10.1007/978-3-030-76640-5_4

of this, such as deciding on the architecture of a deep neural network [8] or designing molecules with desirable properties [17]. Furthermore, optimization over structured domains was highlighted as an important problem to address from the NIPS 2017 workshop on Bayesian optimization [11].

Discrete optimization problems can be solved with a continuous surrogate model, e.g., Bayesian optimization with Gaussian processes [5], by ignoring the discrete structure and rounding off the real-valued input to discrete values. However, literature in this field generally considers this to be a sub-optimal approach [1,9]. Therefore, research has revolved around inherently discrete models such as density estimators or decision trees, e.g., HyperOpt [2] or SMAC [13]. Another approach is to use continuous models that guarantee discrete optimal solutions, such as the piece-wise linear model IDONE [4].

In contrast to common belief, we present an empirical study that displays that continuous surrogate models, in this case Gaussian processes and linear combinations of rectified linear units, show competitive performance on expensive discrete optimization benchmarks by outperforming discrete state-of-the-art algorithms. Firstly, we will introduce the problem, the related work, and the considered benchmark problems. Then, in the remainder of the paper we 1) perform a benchmark comparison between continuous and discrete surrogate-based algorithms on different discrete optimization problems (including one real-life application), 2) investigate why continuous surrogate models perform well by testing different representations of the discrete input to the problems and visualizing the continuous surrogate models, and 3) perform a more realistic analysis that takes the time budget and evaluation time into account when comparing the algorithms. We conclude that continuous surrogates applied to discrete problems should get more attention, and leave some questions for interesting directions of future research in the domain of discrete expensive black-box optimization.

In this paper, we first present the problem description and surrogate-based optimization in Sect. 2. Then, Sect. 3 gives an overview of the related work and surrogate-based algorithms for discrete optimization problems. In Sect. 4 we explain the experimental setup and the combinatorial problems that we use in our benchmark comparison, and Sect. 5 presents the results from our experiments. Lastly, in Sect. 6 we give the conclusion from this work and propose future work.

2   Problem Description

Consider the following class of d-dimensional discrete optimization problems:

$$
\begin{aligned}
\underset{\mathbf{x}}{\text{minimize}} \quad & f(\mathbf{x}) \\
\text{subject to} \quad & \mathbf{x} \in \mathbb{Z}^d \\
& l_i \leq x_i \leq u_i, \ i = 1, \ldots, d
\end{aligned}
\tag{1}
$$

where l_i and u_i are the lower and upper bound for each integer-valued decision variable x_i. For black-box optimization problems, we assume to have no closed form expression for $f : \mathbb{Z}^d \to \mathbb{R}$. The only information which can be gathered about f comes from observing the output when evaluating $f(\mathbf{x})$ given some input $\mathbf{x}$. However, in many real-world applications we also have to deal with some noise $\epsilon \in \mathbb{R}$ such that we are given the output $y = f(\mathbf{x}) + \epsilon$ [5]. Performing an evaluation of $f(x)$ is also assumed to be expensive: it could require large computational power, human interaction with the system or time consuming simulations. Therefore it is of interest to obtain a good, but not necessarily optimal, solution to (1) with a limited number of evaluations B, also known as the budget. I.e., the problem is to search the space of candidate solutions to the objective function $f(x)$ so that the returned objective value is as small as possible using only B number of functions evaluations.

One way of approaching this class of problems is to make use of a so called surrogate model. A surrogate model is an auxiliary function M that approximates the objective function based on the points evaluated so far. This model is cheaper to evaluate in comparison to the original black-box objective function. Given a number m of already evaluated points, the surrogate model is constructed using the evaluation history $H = \{(\mathbf{x}^{(1)}, y^{(1)}), (\mathbf{x}^{(2)}, y^{(2)}), \ldots, (\mathbf{x}^{(m)}, y^{(m)})\}$. The surrogate can be utilized to predict promising points to evaluate next on. The next feasible solution $\mathbf{x}^{(m+1)}$ to evaluate on can be chosen based on this prediction. These steps, which are also described in Algorithm 1, are repeated until the budget B is reached.

Typically, an acquisition function $A(M, \mathbf{x})$ is used to propose the next point $\mathbf{x}^{(m+1)}$ to evaluate with the objective function. It predicts how promising a new point $\mathbf{x}$ is, based on a trade-off of exploitation (searching at or near already evaluated points that had a low objective) and exploration (searching in regions where the surrogate has high uncertainty). In general, the next point is chosen by finding the global optimum $\mathbf{x}^{(m+1)} = \operatorname*{argmax}_{\mathbf{x}} A(M, \mathbf{x})$.

Algorithm 1. Surrogate-based optimization

Require: budget B, surrogate model M, acquisition function A
 1: Initialize $\mathbf{x}^{(1)}$ randomly and an empty set H
 2: **for** $m = 1 : B$ **do**
 3:     $y^{(m)} \leftarrow f(\mathbf{x}^{(m)}) + \epsilon$
 4:     $H \leftarrow H \cup \{(\mathbf{x}^{(m)}, y^{(m)}))\}$
 5:     $M \leftarrow$ fit surrogate model using H
 6:     $\mathbf{x}^{(m+1)} \leftarrow \operatorname*{argmax}_{\mathbf{x}} A(M, \mathbf{x})$
 7: **end for**
 8: **return** optimal $(\mathbf{x}^*, y^*) \in H$

---

3   Related Work

Although discrete problem structures are difficult to handle in black-box optimization, multiple approaches have been proposed. A survey by M. Zaefferer [27] presents different strategies for dealing with discrete structures in surrogate-based algorithms. In our case, a discrete problem structure refers to a combinatorial problem that has either categorical, ordinal or binary decision variables. The first strategy is the naive way by simply ignoring the discrete structure. Another strategy is to use inherently discrete models such as tree-based models [2, 13]. These models can however fail if the problem structure is too complex or if there are both discrete and continuous variables involved [27]. Lastly, discrete structures can be dealt with by using a certain mapping. Although this strategy does not apply directly to a surrogate model, a suitable mapping can make the problem easier. For example, encoding integer solutions with a binary representation can be easier for some regression models to handle.

There are also other strategies such as using problem-specific feature extraction or customizing the model. However, these violate the black-box assumption which is why we will not discuss them.

We now discuss several surrogate-based optimization algorithms that can solve the expensive discrete optimization problem in Eq. (1) and that also have their code available online.

Bayesian optimization has a long history of success in expensive optimization problems [14], and has been applied in many domains such as chemical design and hyperparameter optimization for deep learning [10, 16]. It typically uses a Gaussian process as a surrogate to approximate the expensive objective. Several acquisition functions exist to guide the search, such as Expected Improvement, Upper Confidence Bound, or Thompson sampling [25], information-theoretic approaches such as Predictive Entropy Search [12], or simply the surrogate itself [6, 21]. Though Gaussian processes are typically used on continuous problems, they can be adapted for problems with discrete variables as well. The authors of [9] suggest three possible approaches, namely rounding to the nearest integer 1) when choosing where to evaluate the objective function, 2) when evaluating the objective function, or 3) inside the covariance function of the Gaussian process. The latter provides the best results but gives an acquisition function that is hard to optimize. The first option leads to the algorithm getting stuck by repeatedly evaluating the same points, although this can be circumvented by carefully balancing exploration and exploitation [19]. In this work, we will consider only the simpler second option, for which we do not need to modify any existing implementations.[1]

BOCS[2] [1] transforms the combinatorial problem into one that can be solved with semi-definite programming. It uses Thompson sampling as the acquisition function. However, it suffers from a large time complexity, which was only recently alleviated by using a submodular relaxation called the PSR method[3] [7].

COMBO[4] [26] uses an efficient approximation of a Gaussian process with random features, together with Thompson sampling as the acquisition function. Though this gives increased efficiency, COMBO deals with discrete search spaces by iterating over all possible candidate solutions, which is only possible for small-dimensional problems. Later, a different group proposed another algorithm with the same name[5], based on the graph Fourier transform [20]. However, this method uses approximately the same computational resources as BOCS.

---

[1] We consider the implementation from https://github.com/fmfn/BayesianOptimization in this work, which uses the Upper Confidence Bound acquisition function.

[2] https://github.com/baptistar/BOCS.

[3] https://github.com/aryandeshwal/Submodular_Relaxation_BOCS.

[4] https://github.com/tsudalab/combo.

[5] https://github.com/QUVA-Lab/COMBO.

HyperOpt[6] [2] makes use of a tree of Parzen estimators as the surrogate model. It can naturally deal with categorical or integer variables, and even with conditional variables that only exist if other variables take on certain values. The algorithm is known to perform especially well on hyperparameter tuning problems with hundreds of dimensions [3]. This is in sharp contrast with Bayesian optimization algorithms using Gaussian processes, which are commonly used on problems with less than 10 dimensions. A possible drawback for HyperOpt is that each dimension is modeled separately, i.e., no interaction between different variables is modeled. HyperOpt uses the Expected Improvement acquisition function.

SMAC[7] [13] is another surrogate-based algorithm that can naturally deal with integer variables. The main reason for this is that the surrogate model used in this algorithm is a random forest, which is an inherently discrete model. A point of critique for SMAC is that the random forests have worse predictive capabilities than Gaussian processes. Nevertheless, like HyperOpt, SMAC has been applied to problems with hundreds of dimensions [18]. SMAC uses the Expected Improvement acquisition function.

IDONE[8] [4] uses a linear combination of rectified linear units as its surrogate model. This is a continuous function, yet it has the special property that any local minimum of the model is located in a point where all variables take on integer values. This makes the method suitable for expensive discrete optimization problems, with the advantage that the acquisition function can be optimized efficiently with continuous solvers. IDONE uses the surrogate model itself as the acquisition function, but adds a random perturbation that lies in the range $\{-1, 0, 1\}^d$ to the optimum of the acquisition function to improve its exploration capabilities. Though the method is not as mature as SMAC or HyperOpt, it also has been applied to problems with more than 100 variables [4].

4   Benchmark Problems

We present the four different benchmark problems that are used to compare the surrogate-based algorithms. The purpose of the benchmarks is to compare the discrete surrogate-based algorithms presented in the previous section and investigate which algorithms are most suited for which type of problem.

The benchmarks have been selected to include binary, categorical and ordinal decision variables. Since we assume that the evaluation of the objective functions is expensive, we perform the benchmark with a relatively strict budget of at most 500 evaluations. The objective function is evaluated once per iteration in Algorithm 1. Furthermore, we are testing on relatively large problem sizes, ranging from 44 up to 150 decision variables with search spaces of around $\sim 10^{50}$ possibilities. This range is interesting considering that Bayesian optimization using Gaussian processes is typically applied on problems with less than 10 variables.

On top of that, it has been shown that a large dimensionality reduces the difference between using complicated acquisitions functions and more simple ones [21], which helps us doing a fair comparison between surrogates.

---

[6] https://github.com/hyperopt/hyperopt.

[7] https://github.com/automl/SMAC3.

[8] https://bitbucket.org/lbliek2/idone.

Moreover, we do an analysis of the performance of each algorithm where we limit the allowed time budget instead of the number of evaluations and simulate different evaluation times of the objective functions. The time budget includes both the total time to evaluate the objective function and the computation time of the optimization algorithm. Thus, it puts emphasis on the computation time of the algorithm in addition to their respective sample efficiency.

We present the four benchmark problems in detail below. Note that we present these problems in detail but that they are treated as black boxes by the optimization algorithms.

The Discrete Rosenbrock problem is a d-dimensional, non-convex function defined by the following function:

$$f(\mathbf{x}) = \sum_{i=1}^{d-1} [100(\mathbf{x}_{i+1} - \mathbf{x}_i^2)^2 + (1 - \mathbf{x}_i)^2] \tag{2}$$

where $\mathbf{x} \in \mathbb{Z}^d$. In the Rosenbrock problem, it is relatively easy to find candidate solutions with small objective values, but finding the global optimum $[1, 1, \dots, 1]$ is not. Introduced in 1960, this problem is often used for testing optimization algorithms [24]. As we are exploring discrete optimization problems, we consider a discrete variant of the problem such that only integer solutions are considered. We have $d = 49$ decision variables and each decision variable x_i is bounded by the range $[-5, 10]$. Thus, the problem's search space is in the order of 10^{59} candidate solutions. Lastly, the additive noise ϵ is normally distributed according to $N(\mu = 0, \sigma = 10^{-6})$.

The Weighted Max-Cut problem [15] is an NP-hard graph cutting problem, defined as follows: For an undirected weighted graph $G = (V, E)$, a *cut* in G creates the subset $S \subseteq V$ and its complement $\overline{S} = V \backslash S$. Then $E(S, \overline{S})$, is defined as the set of edges that have one vertex in S and the other in $\overline{S}$. The Max-Cut problem is to find the cut that maximizes the weight of the edges in $E(S, \overline{S})$. The problem is encoded with a binary string $x \in \{0, 1\}^d$ where either $x_i = 0$ or $x_i = 1$ indicates if node i lies in S or $\overline{S}$ respectively.

For the following experiments, the MaxCut problem instances are randomly generated as weighted graphs, with d nodes, edge probability $p = 0.5$ and a uniformly distributed edge weight in the range $[0, 10]$. The graph generator is initialized with the same random seed for every run, ensuring that all experiments of a given problem size are performed on the same graph. On top of that, the additive noise ϵ added to each evaluation is following a standard normal distribution $N(\mu = 0, \sigma = 1)$. Lastly, we are using a graph with $d = 150$ nodes which means that the size of the problem's search space is $2^{150} \approx 10^{57}$.

The Perturbed Traveling Salesman is a variant of the well-known sequential graph problem where, given a number of cities and the distances between these cities, a shortest path needs to be found that visits all cities and returns to the starting city. We consider the asymmetric case with k cities where the distance between cities is not the same in both directions. Moreover, noise $\epsilon \sim U(0, 1)$ is added to each distance during evaluation. While the perturbation can cause issues for problem-specific solvers, it creates a good benchmark for black-box optimization algorithms. To ensure a robust solution, each proposed route is also evaluated 100 times and the worst-case objective value is returned. Furthermore, we will consider problem instance *ftv44*. This is an instance with 44 cities taken from TSPLIB [23], a library of problem instances for the traveling salesman problem. An instance with 44 cities is chosen to closely match the number of decision variables in the ESP problem which has a fixed number of 49 decision variables.

The problem is encoded as in [4]: after choosing a fixed origin city, there are $d = k - 2$ ordered decision variables x_i for $i = 1, \ldots, d$ such that $x_1 \in \{1, 2, \ldots, k - 1\}$ where each integer represents a city other than the origin city. Then, the next decision variable $x_2 \in \{1, \ldots, k - 2\}$ selects between the cities that were not yet visited. This is repeated until all cities have been chosen in some order. Since the last decision variable $x_d \in \{1, 2\}$ selects between the two remaining cities, we can deduce afterward the two remaining edges which closes the route since there is one last city to visit before returning to the origin city. Thus, the total number of possible sequences is given by $(d - 1)! \approx 6 \cdot 10^{52}$ for this instance.

The Electrostatic Precipitator problem is a real-world industrial optimization problem first published by Rehbach et al. [22]. The Electrostatic Precipitator (ESP) is a crucial component for gas cleaning systems. It is a large device that is used when solid particles need to be filtered from exhaust gases, such as reducing pollution in fossil fueled power plants. Before gas enters the ESP, it passes through a gas distribution system that controls the gas flow into the ESP. The gas flow is guided by configurable metal plates which blocks the airflow to a varying degree. The configuration of these plates inside the gas distribution system is vital for the efficiency of the ESP. However, it is non-trivial to configure this system optimally.

The objective function is computed with a computationally intensive fluid dynamics simulation, taking about half a minute of computation time every time a configuration is tested. There are 49 slots where different types of plates can be placed or be left empty. In total, there are 8 different options available per slot. This is formalized such that each integer-valued solution $\mathbf{x}$ is subject to the inequality constraint $0 \leq \mathbf{x}_i \leq 7$ for $i = 1, \ldots, 49$. This gives a large solution space in the order of 10^{44} possibilities.

Lastly, the decision variables in this problem indicate the hole sizes of the metal plates, and are ordinal. However, as an indication of the complex problem structure we have noted that changing only a single variable does not affect the objective function.

5   Experiments

The goal of this section is to show a benchmark comparison between discrete and continuous surrogate-based algorithms on the discrete optimization problems of the previous section. The compared algorithms are HyperOpt and SMAC as two popular surrogate-based algorithms that make use of a discrete surrogate model if the search space is discrete, and Bayesian optimization as a popular surrogate-based algorithm for continuous problems. Though there exist several other algorithms that can deal with the discrete setting, these three are often used in practice because they are well established, can be used for a wide variety of problems, and have code available online. The most recent method we found online, namely the PSR variant of BOCS, requires too much memory and computation time for problems of the size we consider in this work and is therefore not included in the comparison. Other methods that are also especially designed for expensive discrete problems require even more resources. We do also include IDONE in the comparisons as a surrogate-based algorithm that uses a continuous surrogate model but is designed for discrete problems, and random search is included as a baseline.

All experiments were run on the same Unix-based laptop with a Dual-Core Intel Core i5 2.7 GHz CPU and 8 GB RAM. Each algorithm attempted to solve the benchmarks 5 times. The allowed evaluation budget was 500 evaluations for all problems except the ESP problem where 100 evaluations were allowed instead due to it being more computationally expensive.

We are using the default hyperparameters for all algorithms, which are decided by their respective code libraries, with two exceptions. We change the SMAC algorithm to deterministic mode, since it otherwise evaluates the same point several times, which deteriorates its performance significantly. Besides that, the first five iterations of IDONE are random evaluations, which is similar to what happens in the other algorithms. The other algorithms start with their default number of random evaluations (which is 5 for Bayesian optimization and 3 for SMAC and HyperOpt), however for a fair comparison we make sure that all of these initial random evaluations come from a uniform distribution over the search space. Unfortunately, more extensive hyperparameter tuning than stated above is too time-consuming for expensive optimization problems such as ESP.

In the following section we present the results from the benchmark comparison of the four surrogate-based optimization algorithms. The benchmark consists of the four problems which have varying discrete structures.

5.1 Results

In this section we describe the main results from comparing the algorithms on the discrete Rosenbrock, weighted Max-Cut, the travelling salesman and the ESP problems. Figure 2 shows the best average objective value found until a given iteration on each problem as well as their respective computation time. The computation time is the cumulative time up until iteration i which is required to perform the steps on line 5 and 6 in Algorithm 1. Furthermore, we also investigate how the algorithms perform if we introduce a time budget during optimization instead of constraining the number of evaluations.

Ordinal Decision Variables. We start by comparing the results from the 49-dimensional discrete Rosenbrock problem, see Eq. (2). In Fig. 2a, we see that Bayesian optimization (BO) is the only algorithm that comes close to the optimal objective value of zero. The other algorithms are not performing as well, where HyperOpt (HO) gets the closest to BO. Given that the problem is in fact a discrete version of an inherently continuous problem with ordinal variables, this can be considered to be well suited for continuous model regression. On the other hand, IDONE also uses a continuous surrogate, but it does not perform as well as BO. A possible explanation is that IDONE is less flexible since it is a piece-wise linear model.

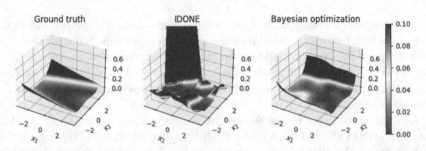

Fig. 1. Visualization of continuous surrogates that approximate the two-dimensional Rosenbrock, namely the linear combination of ReLUs from IDONE and Gaussian processes from BO. These models were picked based on the best performance from 15 different runs with 50 evaluations each. HyperOpt and SMAC are not visualized since this is not supported by their respective code libraries.

To investigate the quality of the surrogates from both BO and IDONE, we visualize their surfaces in Fig. 1 for the 2-dimensional case of the Rosenbrock problem. The Gaussian process from BO (which uses a Matérn 5/2 kernel in this case) predicts a smoother surface than IDONE which appears more rugged and uneven. Overall, BO looks more similar to the objective ground truth. This is likely the main reason why BO performs well while IDONE does not. BO seems suitable for the discrete Rosenbrock problem since the problem is originally a continuous one. Meanwhile, this problem's structure is apparently too complex for the piece-wise linear surrogate in IDONE, as seen in Fig. 1.

We also look at the real-life ESP problem, where the decision variables are ordinal. The results from this problem are found in Fig. 2c. It shows a more even performance among the algorithms compared to the discrete Rosenbrock problem, although BO still returns the best objective on average. This is closely followed by both SMAC and HO, while IDONE is doing worse than random search.

Based on the results from these two problems, it appears that BO works well with ordinal decision variables. However, this does not seem to hold true for all continuous surrogates considering the performance of IDONE. Still, the naive approach with BO outperforms the other state-of-the-art discrete algorithms on the problems that we have discussed so far. This is actually in line with experimental results from [9] on small problems (up to 6 dimensions) with both discrete and continuous parameters, though it was not the main conclusion of the authors. The difference with our work is that we consider purely discrete problems of higher dimensions, from a real-life application, and we include IDONE in the comparison.

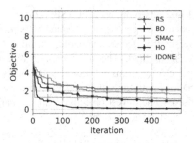

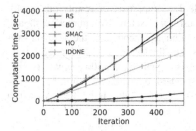

(a) Best average objective value versus iteration on the 49-dimensional discrete Rosenbrock.

(b) Average computation time versus iteration on the 49-dimensional discrete Rosenbrock.

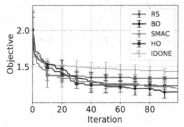

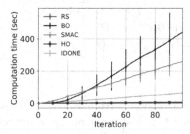

(c) Best average objective value versus iteration on the ESP problem.

(d) Average computation time versus iteration on the ESP problem.

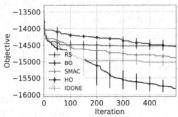

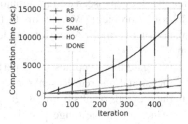

(e) Best average objective value versus iteration on the 150-dimensional weighted Max-Cut.

(f) Average computation time versus iteration on the 150-dimensional weighted Max-Cut.

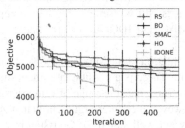

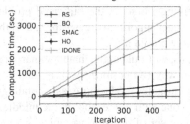

(g) Best average objective value versus iteration on the TSP with 44 cities.

(h) Average computation time versus iteration on the TSP with 44 cities.

Fig. 2. Comparison of objective value and computation time of Bayesian optimization (BO), SMAC, IDONE, HyperOpt (HO) and random search (RS) on four different benchmark problems. An average is computed from 5 runs and the standard deviation is plotted as the error. The objective value has been negated for Max-Cut since the maximization problem has been turned into a minimization problem. The evaluation budget was 500 evaluations for all problems except the ESP problem which was limited to 100 evaluations due to it being more computationally expensive.

Table 1. Comparison of results on the 49-dimensional discrete Rosenbrock with and without binary encoding of the decision variables. The final average objective value from 5 runs is presented after 500 evaluations with the standard deviation in parenthesis. The lowest objective value is marked as bold in each column.

Table 2. Comparison of TSP with 44 cities when the input has a sequential structure versus that decision variables' position have been shuffled. The final average objective value from 5 runs is presented after 500 evaluations with the standard deviation in parenthesis. The lowest objective value is marked as bold in each column.

Algorithm	Non-binary	Binary
BO	**0.067 (0.021)**	**0.37 (0.038)**
SMAC	1.61 (0.18)	1.28 (0.29)
HyperOpt	0.91 (0.13)	0.94 (0.14)
IDONE	1.13 (0.20)	0.61 (0.038)

Algorithm	Non-shuffled	Shuffled
BO	4713.2 (789.2)	4898.0 (292.4)
SMAC	4841.8 (184.7)	4784.9 (302.7)
HyperOpt	4971.9 (256.5)	4871.8 (221.9)
IDONE	**4122.8 (279.8)**	**4556.4 (175.7)**

Binary Decision Variables. We will now consider a graph problem, that is the weighted Max-Cut problem. From the results in Fig. 2e, we notice that BO clearly outperforms all other algorithms. Meanwhile, IDONE is the second best, followed by SMAC and then HO which performs worse than random search. Compared to the other problems that we have seen so far, a major difference is the binary decision variables in the Max-Cut problem. We use this to frame our hypothesis, namely that the good performance of BO on the Max-Cut problem is due to the binary representation of the problem.

To investigate this hypothesis, we perform an additional experiment by encoding the 49-dimensional discrete Rosenbrock problem with binary variables and compare this with the previous results from Fig. 2a. The original problem has 49 integer decision variables which lie in the range $[-5, 10]$, this is converted into a total of 196 binary decision variables for the binary-encoded version. Table 1 shows the performance of the algorithms on the binary-encoded, discrete Rosenbrock problem. Although BO is performing worse on the binarized problem, it is still performing the best compared to the other algorithms, even though both SMAC and IDONE perform better on the binarized problem.

Thus, we could argue that the binary representation of the Max-Cut problem can not explain why BO performs well on this problem. There is a possible argument that the binary variables might cause less rounding-off errors since the range of values is simply zero to one with a threshold in the middle. However, a counter-argument is that such a large number of decision variables is typically not well-suited for Gaussian processes regression. This is also indicated by the large computation time of BO on the Max-Cut, see Fig. 2f.

Ordering of Decision Variables. Even though TSP is a graph problem like the Max-Cut problem, there is an important difference. The encoding of the problem, as described in Sect. 4, causes strong interactions between adjacent decision variables, i.e., variables x_i and x_{i+1} for any i.

We continue by looking at the results from TSP in Fig. 2g. BO is now outperformed by IDONE even though it still performs better than SMAC and HO on average, although BO has a large variance on this problem. We suspect that this problem structure is well-suited for IDONE, as it explicitly fits some of its basis functions with adjacent variables in the input vector $(x_1, x_2, \ldots, x_d)$ [4].

To investigate whether this is the case, we test what happens when the order of the decision variables are re-shuffled in TSP such that the interactions with adjacent decision variables are removed. This is done by adding to the objective function a mapping that changes the order of the variables in the input vector $(x_1, x_2, \ldots, x_d)$ to a fixed arbitrarily chosen order. From Table 2 we see that IDONE performs worse without the original ordering. At the same time, the other algorithms show no large significant difference. However, IDONE returns the best objective on average both with and without re-shuffling the order of variables. The large variance on BO makes it more difficult to draw any strong conclusions, but since IDONE also uses a continuous surrogate model, we can still conclude that continuous surrogates perform better than the discrete counterparts on this problem.

Taking Computation Time into Consideration. Although BO performs well on the benchmark comparisons, we notice that it is more expensive with respect to computation time compared to the other surrogate-based methods. Figures 2b, 2d, 2f and 2h show the cumulative time on the problems.

In general, BO requires a vast amount of time compared to the other algorithms, especially on Max-Cut where the computations took one to two minutes per iteration. This is not surprising considering that regression with Gaussian processes is computationally intensive: its complexity grows as $O(n^3)$ where n are the number of observations [25]. This can be a big drawback if the evaluation time of the objective function is relatively small.

Meanwhile, the other algorithms share similar computation times which are often less than one second. The only exception is for IDONE which requires more computation time on TSP, see Fig. 2h.

So far, we have only considered experiments that restrict the number of evaluations. But in real-life applications, the computation time of an algorithm can be important to take into consideration when limited with some given time budget as well. In particular, the large computation time of BO motivates the question whether it would still perform well under a constrained time budget instead. By keeping track of both the evaluation times of the objective functions, as well as the computation time spent by the algorithms at every iteration, we can investigate the performance of the algorithms in different situations. We artificially adjust the evaluation time in the experiments from Fig. 2 to simulate the cost of the objective function. The evaluation time ranges from 10^1 to $1.5 \cdot 10^3$ s. Similarly, the time budget varies between 10^2 and 10^4 s.

Figure 3 displays which algorithm performs best on average for each problem, depending on the evaluation time and time budget. It also shows the objective value that was achieved by the best performing algorithm. Results only occur below the line $y = x$ because the time budget must be larger than the evaluation time. To ensure a fair comparison, we only present the algorithm with the best final average objective value

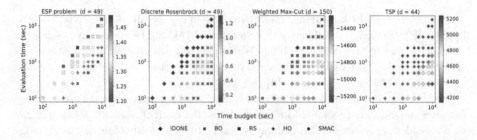

Fig. 3. The best algorithm on average for a given time budget and an evaluation time of the objective function is indicated with different shapes for each algorithm. The colors represent the objective value. The time budget includes both the evaluation time and the computation time of the algorithms. These results are obtained by adding an artificial evaluation time after running the experiments.

if the maximum number of evaluations from the previous benchmark experiments was not exceeded within the allocated time budget for all algorithms. As expected, on all problems, for a given evaluation time (value on the vertical axis), the objective values become lower (better) with an increase in the time budget.

For the ESP problem, the results are mixed. The best algorithm varies between BO, HO, SMAC and even random search, depending mostly on the ratio between the time budget and the evaluation time. For example, random search performs best when the evaluation time is around the order of 10^1 smaller than the time budget which gives relatively few evaluations. Meanwhile, BO performs best with a much larger ratio. On the discrete Rosenbrock benchmark, BO is clearly the best in almost all cases. The only exception is when the ratio between evaluation time and time budget is very small (so only 10–50 iterations can be performed), in which case IDONE performs better. For the weighted Max-Cut, on the other hand, we notice the opposite of what we see with the Rosenbrock benchmark. Thus, it seems like the growth in computation time of BO, see Fig. 2f, sometimes outweighs the good performance that we noted earlier when only taking an evaluation budget into consideration. Lastly, we see that IDONE and HyperOpt outperform other algorithms on TSP when constrained by a time budget.

This experiment gives a better picture of the performance of each algorithm, especially if we may consider it to be more realistic by taking time constraints into consideration. Thus, the experiment from Fig. 3 is a good complement to our benchmark comparison. In the following and last section, we summarize the conclusions that can be drawn from all of the above experiments.

6 Conclusion and Future Work

Based on the results from the benchmark comparison, we can show that the use of continuous surrogate models is a valid approach for expensive, discrete black-box optimization. Moreover, we give insight into what discrete problem structures are well-suited for the different methods.

We have shown that Bayesian optimization (BO) performs better than discrete state-of-the-art algorithms on the four tested, high-dimensional benchmarks problem with either ordinal or binary decision variables, as well problems with strong interaction between subsequent variables. IDONE, another continuous surrogate-based algorithm designed for discrete problems, outperforms BO on the TSP problem, but not on the three other benchmark problems.

In addition, we have investigated how the different algorithms deal with the different problem structures. Firstly, ordinal decision variables appear suitable for BO based on our experiments, especially if the objective function has an underlying continuous structure such as the discrete Rosenbrock problem. For binary decision variables, we noticed that BO is negatively affected by a binary representation, while IDONE and SMAC benefited from this transformation. However, BO still returned the best solution on the binary Max-Cut problem, even though a big drawback was its computation time. Lastly, we have seen that IDONE outperforms the other algorithms on a problem with a strong interaction between subsequent variables, even after negatively affecting it by changing the ordering.

We also investigated the algorithms under different time constraints by artificially changing the function evaluation times of the different benchmark problems. For lower time budgets, BO is held back by its large computation time in some cases. Even though BO is a time-intensive method, it mostly showed competitive performance when the evaluation time was relatively low and the time budget high, except for the binary Max-Cut problem. IDONE, HyperOpt, SMAC, and even random search all had specific problems and time budgets where they outperformed other algorithms. Lastly, based on our results, discrete surrogate-based methods could be more relevant in the setting with a limited time budget, in contrast to only limiting the number of evaluations.

Finally, we state some open questions which remain to be answered about continuous surrogates in the topic of expensive, discrete black-box optimization. Considering that we looked at a naive approach of BO, it is still an open question how the more advanced discrete BO variations would fare in the framework where time budgets and function evaluations times are taken into account like in this paper. This same framework would also lead to interesting comparisons between surrogate-based algorithms and other black-box algorithms such as local search or evolutionary algorithms, which are better suited for cheap function evaluations. It also remains unclear why BO performs best on the binary Max-Cut benchmark even though it is negatively affected by a binary representation on the discrete Rosenbrock function. Which other expensive discrete problems can be solved efficiently with continuous surrogate-based algorithms also remains for future work. Finally, it would be of great practical value if one could decide on the best surrogate-based algorithm in advance, given the time budget and evaluation time of a real-life optimization problem. This research is a first step in that direction.

Acknowledgment. This work is part of the research programme Real-time data-driven maintenance logistics with project number 628.009.012, which is financed by the Dutch Research Council (NWO). The authors would also like to thank Arthur Guijt for helping with the python code.

References

1. Baptista, R., Poloczek, M.: Bayesian optimization of combinatorial structures. In: International Conference on Machine Learning, pp. 471–480 (2018)
2. Bergstra, J., Yamins, D., Cox, D.D.: Hyperopt: a Python library for optimizing the hyperparameters of machine learning algorithms. In: Proceedings of the 12th Python in Science Conference, pp. 13–20 (2013)
3. Bergstra, J., Yamins, D., Cox, D.D.: Making a science of model search: hyperparameter optimization in hundreds of dimensions for vision architectures. In: Proceedings of the 30th International Conference on Machine Learning (2013). jmlr
4. Bliek, L., Verwer, S., de Weerdt, M.: Black-box combinatorial optimization using models with integer-valued minima. Ann. Math. Artif. Intell. 1–15 (2020). https://doi.org/10.1007/s10472-020-09712-4
5. Brochu, E., Cora, V.M., Freitas, N.D.: A tutorial on Bayesian optimization of expensive cost functions, with application to active user modeling and hierarchical reinforcement learning. ArXiv abs/1012.2599 (2010)
6. De Ath, G., Everson, R.M., Rahat, A.A., Fieldsend, J.E.: Greed is good: exploration and exploitation trade-offs in Bayesian optimisation. arXiv preprint arXiv:1911.12809 (2019)
7. Deshwal, A., Belakaria, S., Doppa, J.R.: Scalable combinatorial Bayesian optimization with tractable statistical models. arXiv preprint arXiv:2008.08177 (2020)
8. Elsken, T., Metzen, J.H., Hutter, F.: Neural architecture search: a survey. arXiv preprint arXiv:1808.05377 (2018)
9. Garrido-Merchán, E.C., Hernández-Lobato, D.: Dealing with categorical and integer-valued variables in Bayesian optimization with Gaussian processes. Neurocomputing **380**, 20–35 (2020)
10. Griffiths, R.R., Hernández-Lobato, J.M.: Constrained Bayesian optimization for automatic chemical design. arXiv preprint arXiv:1709.05501 (2017)
11. Hernández-Lobato, J.M., Gonzalez, J., Martinez-Cantin, R.: NIPS workshop on Bayesian optimization. https://bayesopt.github.io/. Accessed 22 Aug 2020
12. Hernández-Lobato, J.M., Hoffman, M.W., Ghahramani, Z.: Predictive entropy search for efficient global optimization of black-box functions. In: Advances in Neural Information Processing Systems, pp. 918–926 (2014)
13. Hutter, F., Hoos, H.H., Leyton-Brown, K.: Sequential model-based optimization for general algorithm configuration. In: Coello, C.A.C. (ed.) LION 2011. LNCS, vol. 6683, pp. 507–523. Springer, Heidelberg (2011). https://doi.org/10.1007/978-3-642-25566-3_40
14. Jones, D.R., Schonlau, M., Welch, W.J.: Efficient global optimization of expensive black-box functions. J. Glob. Optim. **13**(4), 455–492 (1998)
15. Karp, R.M.: Reducibility among combinatorial problems. In: Miller, R.E., Thatcher J.W., Bohlinger, J.D. (eds.) Complexity of Computer Computations. The IBM Research Symposia Series. Springer, Boston (1972). https://doi.org/10.1007/978-1-4684-2001-2_9
16. Klein, A., Falkner, S., Bartels, S., Hennig, P., Hutter, F.: Fast Bayesian optimization of machine learning hyperparameters on large datasets. In: Artificial Intelligence and Statistics, pp. 528–536 (2017)
17. Korovina, K., et al.: ChemBo: Bayesian optimization of small organic molecules with synthesizable recommendations. In: International Conference on Artificial Intelligence and Statistics, pp. 3393–3403. PMLR (2020)
18. Lindauer, M., Hutter, F.: Warmstarting of model-based algorithm configuration. arXiv preprint arXiv:1709.04636 (2017)
19. Luong, P., Gupta, S., Nguyen, D., Rana, S., Venkatesh, S.: Bayesian optimization with discrete variables. In: Liu, J., Bailey, J. (eds.) AI 2019. LNCS (LNAI), vol. 11919, pp. 473–484. Springer, Cham (2019). https://doi.org/10.1007/978-3-030-35288-2_38

20. Oh, C., Tomczak, J., Gavves, E., Welling, M.: Combinatorial Bayesian optimization using the graph cartesian product. In: Advances in Neural Information Processing Systems, pp. 2914–2924 (2019)
21. Rehbach, F., Zaefferer, M., Naujoks, B., Bartz-Beielstein, T.: Expected improvement versus predicted value in surrogate-based optimization. arXiv preprint arXiv:2001.02957 (2020)
22. Rehbach, F., Zaefferer, M., Stork, J., Bartz-Beielstein, T.: Comparison of parallel surrogate-assisted optimization approaches. In: Proceedings of the Genetic and Evolutionary Computation Conference, GECCO 2018, pp. 1348–1355. Association for Computing Machinery (2018)
23. Reinelt, G.: TSPlib. http://elib.zib.de/pub/mp-testdata/tsp/tsplib/tsplib.html. Accessed 31 July 2020
24. Rosenbrock, H.H.: An automatic method for finding the greatest or least value of a function. Comput. J. **3**(3), 175–184 (1960). https://doi.org/10.1093/comjnl/3.3.175
25. Shahriari, B., Swersky, K., Wang, Z., Adams, R.P., de Freitas, N.: Taking the human out of the loop: a review of Bayesian optimization. Proc. IEEE **104**(1), 148–175 (2016)
26. Ueno, T., Rhone, T.D., Hou, Z., Mizoguchi, T., Tsuda, K.: COMBO: an efficient Bayesian optimization library for materials science. Mater. Disc. **4**, 18–21 (2016)
27. Zaefferer, M.: Surrogate models for discrete optimization problems. Ph.D. thesis, Technische Universität Dortmund (2018)

Comparing Correction Methods
to Reduce Misclassification Bias

Kevin Kloos[1,5(✉)] (ID), Quinten Meertens[3,4,5(✉)] (ID), Sander Scholtus[5] (ID),
and Julian Karch[2] (ID)

[1] Mathematical Institute, Leiden University, Leiden, The Netherlands
kevinkloos29@gmail.com
[2] Institute of Psychology, Leiden University, Leiden, The Netherlands
[3] Leiden Centre of Data Science, Leiden University, Leiden, The Netherlands
[4] Center for Nonlinear Dynamics in Economics and Finance,
University of Amsterdam, Amsterdam, The Netherlands
q.a.meertens@uva.nl
[5] Statistics Netherlands, The Hague, The Netherlands

Abstract. When applying supervised machine learning algorithms to
classification, the classical goal is to reconstruct the true labels as accurately as possible. However, if the predictions of an accurate algorithm
are aggregated, for example by counting the predictions of a single
class label, the result is often still statistically biased. Implementing
machine learning algorithms in the context of official statistics is therefore impeded. The statistical bias that occurs when aggregating the predictions of a machine learning algorithm is referred to as misclassification bias. In this paper, we focus on reducing the misclassification bias
of binary classification algorithms by employing five existing estimation
techniques, or estimators. As reducing bias might increase variance, the
estimators are evaluated by their mean squared error (MSE). For three
of the estimators, we are the first to derive an expression for the MSE in
finite samples, complementing the existing asymptotic results in the literature. The expressions are then used to compute decision boundaries
numerically, indicating under which conditions each of the estimators
is optimal, i.e., has the lowest MSE. Our main conclusion is that the
calibration estimator performs best in most applications. Moreover, the
calibration estimator is unbiased and it significantly reduces the MSE
compared to that of the uncorrected aggregated predictions, supporting
the use of machine learning in the context of official statistics.

Keywords: Bias correction · Misclassification bias · Supervised
machine learning · Classification · Official statistics

The views expressed in this paper are those of the authors and do not necessarily reflect
the policy of Statistics Netherlands. The authors would like to thank Arnout van Delden
and three anonymous referees for their useful comments on previous versions of this
paper.

M. Baratchi et al. (Eds.): BNAIC/Benelearn 2020, CCIS 1398, pp. 64–90, 2021.
https://doi.org/10.1007/978-3-030-76640-5_5

1 Introduction

Currently, many researchers in the field of official statistics are examining the potential of machine learning algorithms. A typical example is estimating the proportion of houses in the Netherlands having solar panels, by employing a machine learning algorithm trained to classify satellite images [3]. However, as long as the algorithm's predictions are not error-free, the estimate of the relative occurrence of a class, also known as the *base rate*, can be biased [17,18]. This fact is also intuitively clear: if the number of false positives does not equal the number of false negatives, then the estimate of the base rate is biased, even if the false positive rate and false negative rate are both small. The statistical bias that occurs when aggregating the predictions of a machine learning algorithm is referred to as *misclassification bias* [5].

Misclassification bias occurs in a broad range of applications, including official statistics [13], land cover mapping [12], political science [9,21], and epidemiology [8]. The objective in each of these applications is to minimize a loss function at the level of aggregated predictions, in contrast to minimizing a loss function at the level of individual predictions. Within the field of machine learning, learning with that objective is referred to as quantification learning; see [6] for a recent overview. In quantification learning, the idea is not to train a classifier at all, but to directly estimate the base rate from the feature distribution. A drawback of that approach is that relatively large training and test datasets are needed to optimize hyperparameters and to obtain accurate estimates of the accuracy of the prediction, respectively. In the applications referred to before, labelled data are often expensive to obtain and therefore scarce. Hence, in this paper, we focus on what is referred to as quantifiers based on corrected classifiers [6]. In short, it entails that we first aggregate predictions of classification algorithms and then correct the aggregates in order to reduce misclassification bias.

In the literature on measurement error, several methods have been proposed to reduce misclassification bias when aggregating categorical data that is prone to measurement error; see [11] for a technical discussion and [1] for a more recent overview. Based on that literature, we propose a total of five estimators for the base rate that can be derived from the confusion matrix of a classification algorithm. As reducing bias might increase variance, the estimators are evaluated by their mean squared error (MSE). To the best of our knowledge, for three of the five estimators, only asymptotic expressions for the MSE are ever presented in the literature. In this paper, we derive the expressions for the MSE for finite datasets. As a first step, we restrict ourselves to binary classification problems. Nonetheless, we believe that the same proof strategies may be used for multi-class classification problems. The expressions for the MSE enable a theoretical comparison of the five estimators for finite datasets. It allows us, for the first time, to make solid recommendations on how to employ classification algorithms in official statistics and other disciplines interested in aggregate statistics.

The remainder of the paper is organized as follows. First, in Sect. 2, the five estimators are formally introduced and the mathematical expressions for their MSEs are presented. The derivations are included in the Appendix A. Then, in

Sect. 3, the decision boundaries are numerically derived. We can indicate under which condition, like the sensitivity and specificity of the learning algorithm and the size of the test set, each of the estimators has the lowest MSE. Finally, in Sect. 4, we draw our main conclusion and discuss directions for future research.

2   Methods

Consider a *target population* of N objects and assume that the objects can be separated into two classes. One of the two classes is the *class of interest*. We refer to the relative occurrence of the class of interest in the target population as the *base rate* and we denote that parameter by α. In the example mentioned in Sect. 1, the objects are houses in the Netherlands and the two classes are whether or not the house has solar panels on the roof [3]. The class of interest is having solar panels and hence α indicates the relative frequency of houses in the country having solar panels.

We assume that the true classifications are only known for objects in a small simple random sample of the target population. In the applications that we consider, these classifications are obtained by manual inspection of the objects in that sample. Objects that belong to the class of interest receive class label 1, the other objects receive class label 0. Then, the sample is split randomly into a training set and a test set. As usual, the training set is used for model selection through cross-validation and is then used to train the selected model. We will consider the result of that part of the process as given. The test set is used to estimate the classification performance of the trained algorithm, which we will discuss in more detail below. Finally, the classification algorithm is applied on the entire target population (minus the small random sample, but we will neglect that small difference) resulting in a predicted label for each object.

As we will encounter in Subsect. 2.2, simply computing the relative occurrence of objects predicted to belong to the class of interest will result in a biased estimate of α. That bias is referred to as *misclassification bias* [4]. In this section, five estimators for the base rate parameter α are formally introduced, many of which have been proposed decades ago; see [11] for an extensive discussion. We summarize the formulas for bias and variance that can be found in the literature and complement them with our own derivations.

In order to correct for misclassification bias, we need estimates of the algorithm's (mis)classification probabilities. Following [20], we assume that misclassifications are independent across objects and that the (mis)classification probabilities are the same for each object, conditional on their true class label. With this classification-error model in mind, we denote the probability that the algorithm predicts an object of class 0 correctly by p_{00} and we define p_{11} analogously. Observe that p_{11} and p_{00} correspond to the algorithm's sensitivity and specificity, respectively. The *confusion matrix* $\mathbf{P}$ is then defined as follows:

$$\mathbf{P} = \begin{pmatrix} p_{00} & 1 - p_{00} \\ 1 - p_{11} & p_{11} \end{pmatrix}. \tag{1}$$

Table 1. Contingency tables for test set (left) and target population (right)

(a)

		Estimated class		
		0	1	Tot
True class	0	n_{00}	n_{01}	n_{0+}
	1	n_{10}	n_{11}	n_{1+}
	Tot	n_{+0}	n_{+1}	n

(b)

		Estimated class		
		0	1	Tot
True class	0	N_{00}	N_{01}	N_{0+}
	1	N_{10}	N_{11}	N_{1+}
	Tot	N_{+0}	N_{+1}	N

The classification probabilities p_{00} and p_{11} are not known, but will be estimated using the test set. We write n for the size of the test set and introduce the notation n_{ij} and N_{ij} as depicted in Table 1. The classification probabilities are then estimated without bias by $\hat{p}_{00} = n_{00}/n_{0+}$ and $\hat{p}_{11} = n_{11}/n_{1+}$. (Here, the assumption is needed that the test set is a simple random sample from the target population.) Furthermore, the base rate α for the target population is defined formally as $\alpha = N_{1+}/N$.

Finally, we make the following technical assumptions. We assume that the algorithm is not perfect in predicting either of the classes, but that it is better than guessing for both of the classes, i.e., we assume that $0.5 < p_{ii} < 1$. Because the test set is a small (i.e., $n \ll N$) simple random sample from the population, n_{0+} may be assumed to follow a $Bin(n, \alpha)$-distribution, since α is considered fixed. Moreover, the classification-error model that we assume implies that the elements in the rows in Table 1, conditional on the corresponding row total, follow a binomial distribution as well, with the corresponding classification probability as success probability. For example, to name just two out of the eight entries, $n_{00} \mid n_{0+} \sim Bin(n_{0+}, p_{00})$ and $N_{10} \mid N_{1+} \sim Bin(N_{1+}, 1 - p_{11})$. Last, the assumption $n \ll N$ justifies our ultimate technical assumption, which is that the estimators for the entries in **P** based on the test set on the one hand and estimators for α based only on the predicted class labels for the target population on the other hand, are independent random variables.

2.1 Baseline Estimator - Random Sample

The baseline estimator for α is the proportion of data points in the test dataset for which the observed class label is equal to 1. The baseline estimator will be denoted by $\hat{\alpha}_a$. Under the assumptions discussed above, it is immediate that $\hat{\alpha}_a$ is an unbiased estimator for α, i.e.:

$$B\left[\hat{\alpha}_a\right] = 0. \tag{2}$$

Since we have assumed that the size n of the test dataset is much smaller than the size N of the population data, we may approximate the distribution of $n\hat{\alpha}_a$ by a binomial distribution with success probability α. The variance, and hence the MSE, of $\hat{\alpha}_a$ is then given by

$$MSE\left[\hat{\alpha}_a\right] = V\left[\hat{\alpha}_a\right] = \frac{\alpha(1-\alpha)}{n}. \tag{3}$$

This MSE will serve as the baseline value for the other estimators we discuss.

2.2 Classify and Count

When applying a trained machine learning algorithm on new data, we may simply count the number of data points for which the predicted class equals 1. The resulting estimator for α, which we will denote by $\hat{\alpha}^*$, is referred to as the 'classify-and-count' estimator, see [6]. In general, the classify-and-count estimator is (strongly) biased, and has almost zero variance. More specifically,

$$E\left[\hat{\alpha}^*\right] = \alpha p_{11} + (1-\alpha)(1-p_{00}), \tag{4}$$

and hence

$$B\left[\hat{\alpha}^*\right] = \alpha(p_{11}-1) + (1-\alpha)(1-p_{00}), \tag{5}$$

which is zero only if the point (p_{00}, p_{11}) lies on the line through $(1-\alpha, \alpha)$ and $(1,1)$ in $\mathbb{R}^2$, as shown in [17]. The variance of the classify-and-count estimator is derived in [2] and equals

$$V\left[\hat{\alpha}^*\right] = \frac{\alpha p_{11}(1-p_{11}) + (1-\alpha)p_{00}(1-p_{00})}{N}. \tag{6}$$

If the population size N is large, the variance of $\hat{\alpha}^*$ is low. In some literature, this low variance is misinterpreted as high accuracy, by claiming intuitively that the large size of the dataset implies that the noise cancels out (cf. [16]). However, the nonzero bias is neglected in such arguments. Therefore, we are interested in the MSE because it considers both bias and variance. It equals

$$MSE\left[\hat{\alpha}^*\right] = \left[\alpha(p_{11}-1) + (1-\alpha)(1-p_{00})\right]^2 + O\left(\frac{1}{N}\right). \tag{7}$$

Here and below, the notation $O(1/x)$ indicates a remainder term that, for sufficiently large values of $x > 0$, is always contained inside an interval $(-C/x, C/x)$ for some constant $C > 0$; see, e.g., [19, p. 147]. Observe how, in general, the MSE does not converge to 0 as N tends to ∞.

2.3 Subtracting Estimated Bias

Knowing that the classify-and-count estimator $\hat{\alpha}^*$ is biased see Eq. (5), we may attempt to estimate that bias and subtract it from $\hat{\alpha}^*$. As briefly mentioned in [17], we may estimate that bias by the plug-in estimator, that is, we substitute the unknown quantities in Eq. (5) by their estimates. More precisely, the bias is estimated as

$$\widehat{B}\left[\hat{\alpha}^*\right] = \hat{\alpha}^*(\hat{p}_{00} + \hat{p}_{11} - 2) + (1-\hat{p}_{00}), \tag{8}$$

in which the estimators $\hat{p}_{00}$ and $\hat{p}_{11}$ are based on the test dataset. The resulting estimator $\hat{\alpha}_b$ for α equals

$$\hat{\alpha}_b = \hat{\alpha}^* - \hat{B}[\hat{\alpha}^*] = \hat{\alpha}^*(3 - \hat{p}_{00} - \hat{p}_{11}) - (1 - \hat{p}_{00}). \tag{9}$$

To the best of our knowledge, the bias and variance of the estimator $\hat{\alpha}_b$ have not been published in the scientific literature. Therefore, we have derived both, up to terms of order $1/n^2$, yielding the following result.

Theorem 1. *The bias of $\hat{\alpha}_b$ as estimator for α is given by*

$$B[\hat{\alpha}_b] = (1 - p_{00})(2 - p_{00} - p_{11}) - \alpha(p_{00} + p_{11} - 2)^2. \tag{10}$$

The variance of $\hat{\alpha}_b$ equals

$$V[\hat{\alpha}_b] = \frac{[\alpha(p_{00} + p_{11} - 1) - p_{00}]^2 \, p_{00}(1 - p_{00})}{n(1 - \alpha)} \left(1 + \frac{\alpha}{n(1 - \alpha)}\right)$$

$$+ \frac{[\alpha(p_{00} + p_{11} - 1) + (1 - p_{00})]^2 \, p_{11}(1 - p_{11})}{n\alpha} \left(1 + \frac{1 - \alpha}{n\alpha}\right)$$

$$+ O\left(\max\left[\frac{1}{n^3}, \frac{1}{N}\right]\right). \tag{11}$$

Proof. See Appendix A.

In particular, Theorem 1 implies that $B[\hat{\alpha}_b] = (2 - p_{00} - p_{11})B[\hat{\alpha}^*]$, compare Eqs. (10) and (5). Hence, $|B[\hat{\alpha}_b]| \leq |B[\hat{\alpha}^*]|$, because $1 < p_{00} + p_{11} < 2$.

2.4 Misclassification Probabilities

Let $\mathbf{P}$ be the row-normalized confusion matrix of the machine learning algorithm that we have trained, as defined in Eq. (1). That is, entry p_{ij} is the probability that the algorithm predicts class j for a data point that belongs to class i. The probabilities p_{ij} are referred to as misclassification probabilities. In the binary setting, we write $\boldsymbol{\alpha}$ for the column vector $(1 - \alpha, \alpha)^T$ (similarly for $\hat{\boldsymbol{\alpha}}^*$). Under the assumption that the probabilities p_{ij} are identical for each data point, we obtain the expression $E[\hat{\boldsymbol{\alpha}}^*] = \mathbf{P}^T\boldsymbol{\alpha}$. If the true values of all entries p_{ij} of $\mathbf{P}$ were known and if $p_{00} + p_{11} \neq 1$, then $\hat{\boldsymbol{\alpha}}_p = (\mathbf{P}^T)^{-1}\hat{\boldsymbol{\alpha}}^*$ would be an unbiased estimator for α. Using the plug-in estimator $\hat{\mathbf{P}}$ for $\mathbf{P}$, estimated on the test set, the following estimator for α is obtained:

$$\hat{\alpha}_p = \frac{\hat{\alpha}^* + \hat{p}_{00} - 1}{\hat{p}_{00} + \hat{p}_{11} - 1}. \tag{12}$$

It is known that the estimator $\hat{\alpha}_p$ is consistent (asymptotically unbiased) for α, see [1]. In [7], the variance of this estimator is analysed for an arbitrary number of classes. For the binary case, a simple analytic expression for the bias and variance of $\hat{\alpha}_p$ for finite datasets has not been given, as far as we know. Therefore, we have derived the bias and variance for finite datasets, yielding the following result.

Theorem 2. *The bias of $\hat{\alpha}_p$ as estimator for α is given by*

$$B\left[\hat{\alpha}_p\right] = \frac{p_{00} - p_{11}}{n(p_{00} + p_{11} - 1)} + O\left(\frac{1}{n^2}\right). \tag{13}$$

The variance of $\hat{\alpha}_p$ is given by

$$V[\hat{\alpha}_p] = \frac{(1 - \alpha)p_{00}(1 - p_{00})\left[1 + \frac{\alpha}{n(1-\alpha)}\right] + \alpha p_{11}(1 - p_{11})\left[1 + \frac{1-\alpha}{n\alpha}\right]}{n(p_{00} + p_{11} - 1)^2}$$

$$+ O\left(\max\left[\frac{1}{n^2}, \frac{1}{N}\right]\right). \tag{14}$$

Proof. See Appendix A.

2.5 Calibration Probabilities

Let $\mathbf{C}$ be the column-normalized confusion matrix of the machine learning algorithm that we have trained. That is, entry c_{ij} is the probability that the true class of a data point is j given that the algorithm has predicted class i. The probabilities c_{ij} are referred to as calibration probabilities [11]. The vector $\mathbf{C}\hat{\alpha}^*$ is an unbiased estimator for α, if $\mathbf{C}$ is known.

Using the plug-in estimator $\hat{\mathbf{C}}$ for $\mathbf{C}$, which is estimated on the test dataset analogously to $\hat{\mathbf{P}}$, the following estimator $\hat{\alpha}_c$ for α is obtained:

$$\hat{\alpha}_c = \hat{\alpha}^* \frac{n_{11}}{n_{+1}} + (1 - \hat{\alpha}^*)\frac{n_{10}}{n_{+0}}, \tag{15}$$

in which each n_{ij} and n_{+j} should be considered as random variables. It has been shown that $\hat{\alpha}_c$ is a consistent estimator for α [1]. Under the assumptions we have made in this paper, it can be shown that $\hat{\alpha}_c$ is in fact an unbiased estimator for α. To the best of our knowledge, we are also the first to give an approximation (up to terms of order $1/n^2$) of the variance of $\hat{\alpha}_c$. Both results are summarized in the following theorem.

Theorem 3. *The calibration estimator $\hat{\alpha}_c$ is an unbiased estimator for α:*

$$B\left[\hat{\alpha}_c\right] = 0. \tag{16}$$

The variance of $\hat{\alpha}_c$ is equal to the following expression:

$$V(\hat{\alpha}_c) = \left[\frac{(1 - \alpha)(1 - p_{00}) + \alpha p_{11}}{n} + \frac{(1 - \alpha)p_{00} + \alpha(1 - p_{11})}{n^2}\right]$$

$$\times \left[\frac{\alpha p_{11}}{(1 - \alpha)(1 - p_{00}) + \alpha p_{11}}\left(1 - \frac{\alpha p_{11}}{(1 - \alpha)(1 - p_{00}) + \alpha p_{11}}\right)\right]$$

$$+ \left[\frac{(1 - \alpha)p_{00} + \alpha(1 - p_{11})}{n} + \frac{(1 - \alpha)(1 - p_{00}) + \alpha p_{11}}{n^2}\right]$$

$$\times \left[\frac{(1 - \alpha)p_{00}}{(1 - \alpha)p_{00} + \alpha(1 - p_{11})}\left(1 - \frac{(1 - \alpha)p_{00}}{(1 - \alpha)p_{00} + \alpha(1 - p_{11})}\right)\right]$$

$$+ O\left(\max\left[\frac{1}{n^3}, \frac{1}{Nn}\right]\right). \tag{17}$$

Proof. See Appendix A.

Hereby, the overview of the five estimators for α is complete. The expressions that we have derived for the bias and variance of these five estimators will now be used to compare the (root) mean squared error of the five estimators, both theoretically as well as by means of simulation studies.

3 Results

The aim of this section is to derive empirically which of the five estimators of α that we presented in Sect. 2 has the lowest MSE, and under which conditions. For a given population size N, the MSE of each estimator depends on four parameters (i.e., $\alpha, p_{00}, p_{11}, n$), so visualizations would have to be 5-dimensional. To reduce dimensions, we will first present a simulation study in which all four parameters are fixed. For the fixed parameter setting, the sampling distributions of the estimators are compared using boxplots. Second, we will fix several values of α and n and use plots to compare the MSE of the estimators for varying p_{00} and p_{11}. The latter analysis will already be sufficient in order to reach a final conclusion on which estimator has the lowest MSE.[1]

3.1 Sampling Distributions of the Estimators

Here, we present two simple simulation studies to gain some intuition for the difference in the sampling distributions of the five estimators. In the first simulation study, we consider a class-balanced dataset, that is, $\alpha = 0.5$, with a small test dataset of size $n = 1000$, a large population dataset $N = 3 \times 10^5$ and a rather poor classifier having classification probabilities $p_{00} = 0.6$ and $p_{11} = 0.7$. We deliberately choose $p_{00} \neq p_{11}$, as otherwise the classify-and-count estimator $\hat{\alpha}^*$ would be unbiased: (p_{00}, p_{11}) would be on the line between $(1 - \alpha, \alpha)$ and $(1, 1)$, see also Eq. (5).

Table 2 summarizes the bias, variance and root mean squared error (RMSE), computed using the analytic approximations presented in Sect. 2. The classify-and-count estimator is highly biased and therefore it has a high RMSE, despite having the lowest variance of all estimators. The RMSE of the classify-and-count estimator can indeed be improved by subtracting an estimate of the bias ($\hat{\alpha}_b$). The subtraction reduces the absolute bias and only slightly increases the variance. A further bias reduction is obtained by the misclassification estimator $\hat{\alpha}_p$. However, inverting the row-normalized confusion matrix $\mathbf{P}$ (that is, the misclassification probabilities) for values of p_{00} and p_{11} close to $p_{00} + p_{11} = 1$ significantly increases the variance of the estimator, leading to the highest RMSE

---

[1] The results in this section have been obtained using the statistical software R. All visualizations have been implemented in a Shiny dashboard, which in addition includes interactive 3D-plots of the RMSE surface for each of the estimators. The code, together with the Appendix A, can be retrieved from https://github.com/kevinkloos/Misclassification-Bias.

of all estimators considered. Finally, the calibration estimator $\hat{\alpha}_c$ is unbiased and has the lowest variance among the estimators that make use of the test dataset. In particular, note that the variance is also lower than that of the baseline esti-mator. In this example, the estimator based on the calibration probabilities has the lowest RMSE, and it is the only estimator with a lower RMSE than the baseline estimator $\hat{\alpha}_a$.

Table 2. A comparison of the bias, variance and RMSE of each of the five estimators for α, where $\alpha = 0.5$, $p_{00} = 0.6$, $p_{11} = 0.7$, $n = 1000$ and $N = 3 \times 10^5$.

Estimator	Symbol	Bias $\times 10^{-2}$	Variance $\times 10^{-4}$	RMSE $\times 10^{-2}$
Baseline	$\hat{\alpha}_a$	0.000	2.500	1.581
Classify-and-count	$\hat{\alpha}^*$	5.000	0.000	5.000
Subtracted-bias	$\hat{\alpha}_b$	3.500	2.244	3.807
Misclassification	$\hat{\alpha}_p$	−0.033	25.025	5.003
Calibration	$\hat{\alpha}_c$	0.000	2.275	1.508

To gain insight in the sampling distribution of the estimators, in addition to the metrics presented in Table 2, we simulated a large number $R = 10000$ of confusion matrices for datasets of size $n = 1000$ and $N = 3 \times 10^5$. Each confusion matrix was created as follows. First, take a random draw from a $Bin(N, \alpha)$-distribution, resulting in a number N_{1+}. Then, take a random draw from a $Bin(N_{1+}, p_{11})$-distribution to obtain N_{11} and a random draw from a $Bin(N - N_{+1}, p_{00})$-distribution to obtain N_{00}. This computes the theoretical confusion matrix for the target population. Use this confusion matrix to draw a sample from a multivariate hypergeometric distribution, with its parameters from the drawn theoretical confusion matrix. These draws precisely give the number of true and false positives and negatives needed to fill a confusion matrix. Each confusion matrix can be used to compute the five estimators. Repeating this procedure $R = 10000$ times gave rise to the sampling distributions of the five estimators as presented in Fig. 1. It nicely visualizes the bias and variance of the five estimators, supporting the results in Table 2. In addition, it shows that, due to the bias, the variances of the classify-and-count estimator $\hat{\alpha}^*$ and the subtracted-bias estimator $\hat{\alpha}_b$ cannot be used to obtain reliable confidence intervals for α.

In the second simulation study, we consider a highly imbalanced dataset, namely $\alpha = 0.98$. We again assume that the available test dataset has size $n = 1000$, but we assume a classifier having classification probabilities $p_{00} = 0.94$ and $p_{11} = 0.97$. Table 3 summarizes the bias, variance and RMSE of each of the estimators and Fig. 2 shows the sampling distributions of each of the estimators. It can be noticed that subtracted-bias estimator and the misclassification esti-mator both have estimates of α that exceed 1. It is obvious that such values

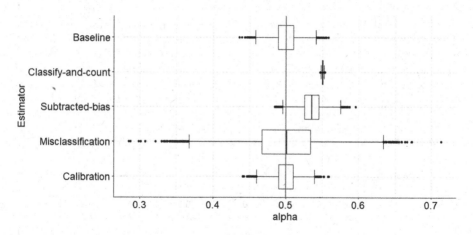

Fig. 1. The boxplots show the sampling distribution of the estimators for α, where $\alpha = 0.5$, $p_{00} = 0.6$, $p_{11} = 0.7$, $n = 1000$ and $N = 3 \times 10^5$. The true value of α is highlighted by a vertical line.

cannot occur in the population. For the method with the misclassification probabilities, this effect gets stronger when $p_{00} + p_{11}$ gets closer to 1. Furthermore, the baseline estimator performs well compared to the other estimators when the dataset is highly imbalanced: its RMSE is slightly higher than the RMSE of the method with calibration probabilities and much lower than the method with the misclassification probabilities. Finally, it is shown that the classify-and-count estimator is highly biased, even though p_{00} and p_{11} are both fairly close to 1.

Table 3. A comparison of the bias, variance and RMSE of each of the five estimators for α, where $\alpha = 0.98$, $p_{00} = 0.94$, $p_{11} = 0.97$, $n = 1000$ and $N = 3 \times 10^5$.

Method	Symbol	Bias $\times 10^{-2}$	Variance $\times 10^{-5}$	RMSE $\times 10^{-3}$
Baseline	$\hat{\alpha}_a$	0.000	1.960	4.427
Classify-and-count	$\hat{\alpha}^*$	−2.820	0.000	28.200
Subtracted-bias	$\hat{\alpha}_b$	−0.254	3.377	6.342
Misclassification	$\hat{\alpha}_p$	−0.003	3.587	5.989
Calibration	$\hat{\alpha}_c$	0.000	1.289	3.591

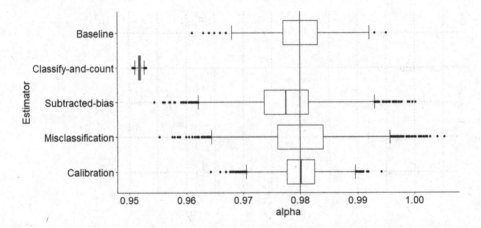

Fig. 2. The boxplots show the sampling distribution of the estimators for α, where $\alpha = 0.98$, $p_{00} = 0.94$, $p_{11} = 0.97$, $n = 1000$ and $N = 3 \times 10^5$. The true value of α is highlighted by a vertical line.

3.2   Finding the Optimal Estimator

The aim of this subsection is to find the optimal estimator, i.e., the estimator with the lowest RMSE, for every combination of values of the parameters α, p_{00}, p_{11} and n. First, suppose that (p_{00}, p_{11}) is close to the line in the plane through the points $(1 - \alpha, \alpha)$ and $(1, 1)$. As noted before, it implies that the classify-and-count estimator $\hat{\alpha}^*$ has low bias. Consequently, the subtracted-bias estimator $\hat{\alpha}_b$ has low bias as well. Thus, these two estimators will have the lowest RMSE in the described region, whose size decreases as n increases. Figure 3 visualizes the described region for $\alpha = 0.2$ and two different values of n. We remark that the biased estimators $\hat{\alpha}^*$ and $\hat{\alpha}_b$ perform worse (relative to the other estimators) when the sample size n of the test dataset increases. The biased methods, like Classify-and-count and Subtracted-bias, perform well when the classification probabilities are high for the largest group.

As we have seen in both Table 2 and Table 3, the calibration estimator $\hat{\alpha}_c$ competes with the baseline estimator in having the lowest RMSE. In general, the calibration estimator will have lower RMSE if the classification probabilities p_{00} and p_{11} are higher, while the baseline estimator does not depend on these classification probabilities. In a neighbourhood of $p_{00} = p_{11} = 0.5$, the baseline estimator will always have lower RMSE than the calibration estimator. However, for every α and n, there must exist a curve in the (p_{00}, p_{11})-plane beyond which the calibration estimator will have lower RMSE than the baseline estimator. The left-hand panels in Fig. 4 show this curve for $\alpha = 0.2$ and two different values of n. For larger values of n, the curve where the calibration estimator performs better than the baseline estimator gets closer to $p_{00} = p_{11} = 0.5$ and therefore covers a larger area in the (p_{00}, p_{11})-plane.

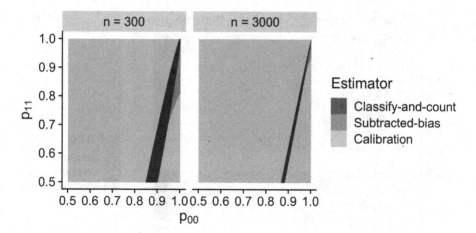

Fig. 3. For each coordinate (p_{00}, p_{11}), the depicted color indicates which estimator has the lowest RMSE, considering only the classify-and-count estimator (green), the subtracted-bias estimator (orange) and the calibration estimator (purple). In the left panel, we have set $\alpha = 0.2$ and $n = 300$, whereas $\alpha = 0.2$ and $n = 3000$ in the right panel. The red and green regions are smaller in the right panel, as the variance of the calibration estimator is decreasing in n, while the bias of the classify-and-count estimator and of the subtracted-bias estimator do not depend on n. (Color figure online)

Table 2 and Table 3 have shown that the misclassification estimator only performs well if p_{00} and p_{11} are high, which is confirmed by the expression of the bias and variance: both have a singularity at $p_{00} + p_{11} = 1$, see Eqs. (13) and (14). The right-hand panels in Fig. 4 show, for $\alpha = 0.2$ and two different values of n, the curve in the (p_{00}, p_{11})-plane beyond which the misclassification estimator has lower RMSE than the baseline estimator. Observe that an increase in the size n of the test dataset does not have much impact on the position of the curve. The reason is that the misclassification estimator has a singularity at $p_{00} = p_{11} = 0.5$. The shape of the curve also depends on the value of α. If $\alpha = 0.8$ instead of 0.2, the curves are line-symmetric in the line $p_{00} = p_{11}$. The curve is also line symmetric in $p_{00} = p_{11}$ for $\alpha = 0.5$. The area where the misclassification estimator performs better than the baseline estimator decreases when α gets closer towards 0 or 1. The main reason why this happens is that the variance of the baseline estimator decreases fast when α gets closer towards 0 or 1. Thus, the baseline estimator performs better than the misclassification estimator either if the classifier performs badly in general or performs badly in classifying the largest group.

The final analysis of this paper is to compare the calibration estimator and the misclassification estimator for high values of p_{00} and p_{11}. In Theorem 4 it is proven that, for all possible combinations of α and sufficiently large n, the MSE of the calibration estimator is consistently lower than that of the misclassification estimator.

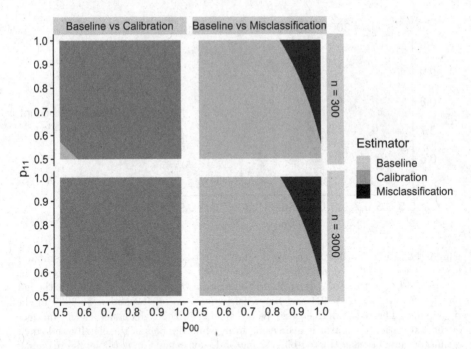

Fig. 4. For each coordinate (p_{00}, p_{11}), the depicted color indicates which estimate has the lowest RMSE, considering only the baseline estimator (green), the calibration estimator (orange) and the misclassification estimator (purple). The top-row panels consider $\alpha = 0.2$ and $n = 300$, while the bottom-row panels consider $\alpha = 0.2$ and $n = 3000$. (Color figure online)

Theorem 4. *Let $\widetilde{MSE}[\hat{\alpha}_p]$ and $\widetilde{MSE}[\hat{\alpha}_c]$ denote the approximate mean squared errors, up to terms of order $1/n$, of the misclassification estimator and the calibration estimator, respectively. It holds that:*

$$\widetilde{MSE}[\hat{\alpha}_p] - \widetilde{MSE}[\hat{\alpha}_c] = \frac{\left[(1-\alpha)p_{00}(1-p_{00}) + \alpha p_{11}(1-p_{11})\right]^2}{n(p_{00} + p_{11} - 1)^2 \beta(1-\beta)}, \tag{18}$$

in which $\beta := (1-\alpha)(1-p_{00}) + \alpha p_{11}$.

Proof. See Appendix A.

Thus, neglecting terms of order $1/n^2$ and higher, the result implies that the calibration estimator has a lower mean squared error than the misclassification estimator, except that both are equal if and only if $p_{00} = p_{11} = 1$. (Note that $0 < \beta < 1$.)

We do remark that the difference in MSE is large in particular for values of p_{00} and p_{11} close to $\frac{1}{2}$. More specifically, it diverges when $p_{00} + p_{11} \to 1$. It is the result of the misclassification estimator having a singularity at $p_{00} + p_{11} = 1$ (see Eq. (14)), while the variance of the calibration estimator is bounded. An unpleasant consequence of the singularity at $p_{00} + p_{11} = 1$ is that, for fixed n and α, the probability that $\hat{\alpha}_p$ takes values outside the interval $[0, 1]$ increases as $p_{00} + p_{11} \to 1$; see [14] for a discussion and a possible solution.

4   Conclusion and Discussion

In this paper, we have studied the effect of classification errors on five estimators of the base rate parameter α that are obtained from machine learning algorithms. In general, a straightforward classify-and-count estimator will lead to biased estimates and some form of bias correction should be considered. As reducing bias might increase variance, we evaluated the (root) mean squared error (MSE) of the five estimators, both theoretically as well as numerically.

From our results we may draw the following main (three-part) conclusion regarding which estimator for α has lowest mean squared error. First, when dealing with small test datasets and rather poor algorithms, that is p_{00} and p_{11} both close to 0.5, the baseline estimator $\hat{\alpha}_a$ has the lowest MSE. Second, when dealing with algorithms for which the classification probabilities p_{00} and p_{11} are in a small neighbourhood around the line $(p_{11} - 1)\alpha + (1 - p_{00})(1 - \alpha) = 0$ in the (p_{00}, p_{11})-plane, the classify-and-count estimator and the subtracted-bias estimator will have the lowest MSE. As the size of the test dataset increases, the size of that neighbourhood decreases. Third, in any other situation, the calibration estimator will have the lowest MSE. In practice, the test dataset will have to be used to determine which of the three scenarios applies to the data and the algorithm at hand. It is an additional estimation problem that we have not discussed in this paper.

We would like to close the paper by pointing out three interesting directions for future research. First, the results could be generalized to multi-class classification problems. The theoretical derivations of the bias and variance are more complicated and involve matrix-vector notation, but the proof strategy is similar. However, it is more challenging to compare the MSE of the five estimators visually in the multi-class case.

Second, the assumptions that we have made could be relaxed. In particular, a trained and implemented machine learning model is, in practice, often used over a longer period of time. A shift in the base rate parameter α, also known as prior probability shift [15], is then inevitable. Consequently, we may no longer assume that the conditional distribution of the class label given the features in the test dataset is similar to that in the population. It implies that the calibration estimator is no longer unbiased, which might have a significant effect on our main conclusion.

Third and finally, a combination of estimators might have a substantially lower MSE than that of the individual estimators separately. Therefore, it might be interesting to study different methods of model averaging applied to the problem of misclassification bias. It could be fruitful especially when the assumptions that we have made are relaxed.

A Appendix

This appendix contains the proofs of the theorems presented in the paper entitled "Comparing Correction Methods to Reduce Misclassification Bias". Recall that we have assumed a population of size N in which a fraction $\alpha := N_{1+}/N$ belongs to the class of interest, referred to as the class labelled as 1. We assume that a binary classification algorithm has been trained that correctly classifies a data point that belongs to class $i \in \{0,1\}$ with probability $p_{ii} > 0.5$, independently across all data points. In addition, we assume that a test set of size $n \ll N$ is available and that it can be considered a simple random sample from the population. The classification probabilities p_{00} and p_{11} are estimated on that test set as described in Sect. 2. Finally, we assume that the classify-and-count estimator $\hat{\alpha}^*$ is distributed independently of $\hat{p}_{00}$ and $\hat{p}_{11}$, which is reasonable (at least as an approximation) when $n \ll N$.

It may be noted that the estimated probabilities $\hat{p}_{11}$ and $\hat{p}_{00}$ defined in Sect. 2 cannot be computed if $n_{1+} = 0$ or $n_{0+} = 0$. Similarly, the calibration probabilities c_{11} and c_{00} cannot be estimated if $n_{+1} = 0$ or $n_{+0} = 0$. We assume here that these events occur with negligible probability. This will be true when n is sufficiently large so that $n\alpha \gg 1$ and $n(1 - \alpha) \gg 1$.

Preliminaries

Many of the proofs presented in this appendix rely on the following two mathematical results. First, we will use univariate and bivariate Taylor series to approximate the expectation of non-linear functions of random variables. That is, to estimate $E[f(X)]$ and $E[g(X,Y)]$ for sufficiently differentiable functions f and g, we will insert the Taylor series for f and g at $x_0 = E[X]$ and $y_0 = E[Y]$ up to terms of order 2 and utilize the linearity of the expectation. Second, we will use the following conditional variance decomposition for the variance of a random variable X:

$$V(X) = E[V(X \mid Y)] + V(E[X \mid Y]). \tag{19}$$

The conditional variance decomposition follows from the tower property of conditional expectations [10]. Before we prove the theorems presented in the paper, we begin by proving the following lemma.

Lemma 1. *The variance of the estimator $\hat{p}_{11}$ for p_{11} estimated on the test set is given by*

$$V(\hat{p}_{11}) = \frac{p_{11}(1 - p_{11})}{n\alpha}\left[1 + \frac{1 - \alpha}{n\alpha}\right] + O\left(\frac{1}{n^3}\right). \tag{20}$$

Similarly, the variance of $\hat{p}_{00}$ is given by

$$V(\hat{p}_{00}) = \frac{p_{00}(1 - p_{00})}{n(1 - \alpha)}\left[1 + \frac{\alpha}{n(1 - \alpha)}\right] + O\left(\frac{1}{n^3}\right). \tag{21}$$

Moreover, $\hat{p}_{11}$ and $\hat{p}_{00}$ are uncorrelated: $C(\hat{p}_{11}, \hat{p}_{00}) = 0$.

Proof (of Lemma 1). We approximate the variance of $\hat{p}_{00}$ using the conditional variance decomposition and a second-order Taylor series, as follows:

$$V(\hat{p}_{00}) = V\left(\frac{n_{00}}{n_{0+}}\right)$$

$$= E_{n_{0+}}\left[V\left(\frac{n_{00}}{n_{0+}} \mid n_{0+}\right)\right] + V_{n_{0+}}\left[E\left(\frac{n_{00}}{n_{0+}} \mid n_{0+}\right)\right]$$

$$= E_{n_{0+}}\left[\frac{1}{n_{0+}^2}V(n_{00} \mid n_{0+})\right] + V_{n_{0+}}\left[\frac{1}{n_{0+}}E(n_{00} \mid n_{0+})\right]$$

$$= E_{n_{0+}}\left[\frac{n_{0+}p_{00}(1-p_{00})}{n_{0+}^2}\right] + V_{n_{0+}}\left[\frac{n_{0+}p_{00}}{n_{0+}}\right]$$

$$= E_{n_{0+}}\left[\frac{1}{n_{0+}}\right]p_{00}(1-p_{00})$$

$$= \left[\frac{1}{E[n_{0+}]} + \frac{1}{2}\frac{2}{E[n_{0+}]^3} \times V[n_{0+}]\right]p_{00}(1-p_{00}) + O\left(\frac{1}{n^3}\right)$$

$$= \frac{p_{00}(1-p_{00})}{E[n_{0+}]}\left[1 + \frac{V[n_{0+}]}{E[n_{0+}]^2}\right] + O\left(\frac{1}{n^3}\right)$$

$$= \frac{p_{00}(1-p_{00})}{n(1-\alpha)}\left[1 + \frac{\alpha}{n(1-\alpha)}\right] + O\left(\frac{1}{n^3}\right).$$

The variance of $\hat{p}_{11}$ is approximated in the exact same way.

Finally, to evaluate $C(\hat{p}_{11}, \hat{p}_{00})$ we use the analogue of Eq. (19) for covariances:

$$C(\hat{p}_{11}, \hat{p}_{00}) = C\left(\frac{n_{11}}{n_{1+}}, \frac{n_{00}}{n_{0+}}\right)$$

$$= E_{n_{1+},n_{0+}}\left[C\left(\frac{n_{11}}{n_{1+}}, \frac{n_{00}}{n_{0+}} \mid n_{1+}, n_{0+}\right)\right]$$

$$\quad + C_{n_{1+},n_{0+}}\left[E\left(\frac{n_{11}}{n_{1+}} \mid n_{1+}, n_{0+}\right), E\left(\frac{n_{00}}{n_{0+}} \mid n_{1+}, n_{0+}\right)\right]$$

$$= E_{n_{1+},n_{0+}}\left[\frac{1}{n_{1+}n_{0+}}C(n_{11}, n_{00} \mid n_{1+}, n_{0+})\right]$$

$$\quad + C_{n_{1+},n_{0+}}\left[\frac{1}{n_{1+}}E(n_{11} \mid n_{1+}), \frac{1}{n_{0+}}E(n_{00} \mid n_{0+})\right].$$

The second term is zero as before. The first term also vanishes because, conditional on the row totals n_{1+} and n_{0+}, the counts n_{11} and n_{00} follow independent binomial distributions, so $C(n_{11}, n_{00} \mid n_{1+}, n_{0+}) = 0$.

Note: in the remainder of this appendix, we will not add explicit subscripts to expectations and variances when their meaning is unambiguous.

Subtracted-Bias Estimator

We will now prove the bias and variance approximations for the subtracted-bias estimator $\hat{\alpha}_b$ that was defined in Eq. (9).

Proof (of Theorem 1). The bias of $\hat{\alpha}_b$ is given by

$$
\begin{aligned}
B(\hat{\alpha}_b) &= E\left[\hat{\alpha}^* - \hat{B}[\hat{\alpha}^*]\right] - \alpha \\
&= E[\hat{\alpha}^* - \alpha] - E\left[\hat{B}[\hat{\alpha}^*]\right] \\
&= B[\hat{\alpha}^*] - E\left[\hat{B}[\hat{\alpha}^*]\right] \\
&= [\alpha(p_{00} + p_{11} - 2) + (1 - p_{00})] - E\left[\hat{\alpha}^*(\hat{p}_{00} + \hat{p}_{11} - 2) + (1 - \hat{p}_{00})\right].
\end{aligned}
$$

Because $\hat{\alpha}^*$ and $(\hat{p}_{00} + \hat{p}_{11} - 2)$ are assumed to be independent, the expectation of their product equals the product of their expectations:

$$
\begin{aligned}
B(\hat{\alpha}_b) &= \alpha(p_{00} + p_{11} - 2) + (1 - p_{00}) - E[\hat{\alpha}^*](p_{00} + p_{11} - 2) - (1 - p_{00}) \\
&= (\alpha - E[\hat{\alpha}^*])(p_{00} + p_{11} - 2) \\
&= B[\hat{\alpha}^*](2 - p_{00} - p_{11}) \\
&= (1 - p_{00})(2 - p_{00} - p_{11}) - \alpha(p_{00} + p_{11} - 2)^2.
\end{aligned}
$$

This proves the formula for the bias of $\hat{\alpha}_b$ as estimator for α. To approximate the variance of $\hat{\alpha}_b$, we apply the conditional variance decomposition of Eq. (19) conditional on $\hat{\alpha}^*$ and look at the two resulting terms separately. First, consider the expectation of the conditional variance:

$$
\begin{aligned}
E\left[V(\hat{\alpha}_b \mid \hat{\alpha}^*)\right] &= E\left[V(\hat{\alpha}^*(3 - \hat{p}_{00} - \hat{p}_{11}) - (1 - \hat{p}_{00}) \mid \hat{\alpha}^*)\right] \\
&= E\big[V(\hat{\alpha}^*(3 - \hat{p}_{00} - \hat{p}_{11}) \mid \hat{\alpha}^*) + V(1 - \hat{p}_{00} \mid \hat{\alpha}^*) \\
&\quad - 2C(\hat{\alpha}^*(3 - \hat{p}_{00} - \hat{p}_{11}), 1 - \hat{p}_{00} \mid \hat{\alpha}^*)\big] \\
&= E\big[(\hat{\alpha}^*)^2\, V(3 - \hat{p}_{00} - \hat{p}_{11} \mid \hat{\alpha}^*) + V(1 - \hat{p}_{00} \mid \hat{\alpha}^*) \\
&\quad - 2\hat{\alpha}^* C(3 - \hat{p}_{00} - \hat{p}_{11}, 1 - \hat{p}_{00} \mid \hat{\alpha}^*)\big] \\
&= E\big[(\hat{\alpha}^*)^2\, [V(\hat{p}_{00}) + V(\hat{p}_{11})] + V(\hat{p}_{00}) - 2\hat{\alpha}^* V(\hat{p}_{00})\big] \\
&= E\left[(\hat{\alpha}^*)^2\right][V(\hat{p}_{00}) + V(\hat{p}_{11})] + V(\hat{p}_{00}) - 2E[\hat{\alpha}^*]\, V(\hat{p}_{00}).
\end{aligned}
$$

In the penultimate line, we used that $C(\hat{p}_{11}, \hat{p}_{00}) = 0$. The second moment $E\left[(\hat{\alpha}^*)^2\right]$ can be written as $E[\hat{\alpha}^*]^2 + V(\hat{\alpha}^*)$. Because $V(\hat{\alpha}^*)$ is of order $1/N$, it can be neglected compared to $E[\hat{\alpha}^*]^2$, which is of order 1. In particular, we find that the expectation of the conditional variance equals:

$$
\begin{aligned}
E\left[V(\hat{\alpha}_b \mid \hat{\alpha}^*)\right] &= E\left[(\hat{\alpha}^*)\right]^2[V(\hat{p}_{00}) + V(\hat{p}_{11})] + V(\hat{p}_{00}) - 2E[\hat{\alpha}^*]\, V(\hat{p}_{00}) + O\left(\frac{1}{N}\right) \\
&= V(\hat{p}_{00})\, [E[\hat{\alpha}^*] - 1]^2 + V(\hat{p}_{11})E[\hat{\alpha}^*]^2 + O\left(\frac{1}{N}\right).
\end{aligned}
$$

Next, the variance of the conditional expectation can be seen to be equal the following:

$$
\begin{aligned}
V\left[E(\hat{\alpha}_b \mid \hat{\alpha}^*)\right] &= V\left[E(\hat{\alpha}^*(3 - \hat{p}_{00} - \hat{p}_{11}) - (1 - \hat{p}_{00}) \mid \hat{\alpha}^*)\right] \\
&= V\left[\hat{\alpha}^* E(3 - \hat{p}_{00} - \hat{p}_{11} \mid \hat{\alpha}^*) - E(1 - \hat{p}_{00} \mid \hat{\alpha}^*)\right] \\
&= V(\hat{\alpha}^*)(3 - p_{00} - p_{11})^2.
\end{aligned}
$$

Because $V(\hat{\alpha}^*)$ is of order $1/N$, it can be neglected in the final formula. Furthermore, the variances of $\hat{p}_{00}$ and $\hat{p}_{11}$ can be written out using the result from Lemma 1:

$$V(\hat{\alpha}_b) = \frac{[\alpha(p_{00} + p_{11} - 1) - p_{00}]^2 \, p_{00}(1 - p_{00})}{n(1 - \alpha)} \left[1 + \frac{\alpha}{n(1-\alpha)}\right]$$
$$+ \frac{[\alpha(p_{00} + p_{11} - 1) + (1 - p_{00})]^2 \, p_{11}(1 - p_{11})}{n\alpha} \left[1 + \frac{1 - \alpha}{n\alpha}\right]$$
$$+ O\left(\max\left[\frac{1}{n^3}, \frac{1}{N}\right]\right).$$

This concludes the proof of Theorem 1.

Misclassification Estimator

We will now prove the bias and variance approximations for the misclassification estimator $\hat{\alpha}_p$ as defined in Eq. (12).

Proof (of Theorem 2). Under the assumption that $\hat{\alpha}^*$ is distributed independently of $(\hat{p}_{00}, \hat{p}_{11})$, it holds that

$$E(\hat{\alpha}_p) = E\left(\frac{\hat{p}_{00} - 1}{\hat{p}_{00} + \hat{p}_{11} - 1}\right) + E\left[E\left(\frac{\hat{\alpha}^*}{\hat{p}_{00} + \hat{p}_{11} - 1} \,\Big|\, \hat{\alpha}^*\right)\right]$$
$$= E\left(\frac{\hat{p}_{00} - 1}{\hat{p}_{00} + \hat{p}_{11} - 1}\right) + E(\hat{\alpha}^*)E\left(\frac{1}{\hat{p}_{00} + \hat{p}_{11} - 1}\right). \tag{22}$$

$E(\hat{\alpha}^*)$ is known from Eq. (4). To evaluate the other two expectations, we use a second-order Taylor series approximation. The first- and second-order partial derivatives of $f(x, y) = 1/(x + y - 1)$ and $g(x, y) = (x - 1)/(x + y - 1) = 1 - [y/(x + y - 1)]$ are given by:

$$\frac{\partial f}{\partial x} = \frac{\partial f}{\partial y} = \frac{-1}{(x + y - 1)^2}, \tag{23}$$
$$\frac{\partial^2 f}{\partial x^2} = \frac{\partial^2 f}{\partial y^2} = \frac{2}{(x + y - 1)^3},$$
$$\frac{\partial g}{\partial x} = \frac{y}{(x + y - 1)^2}, \tag{24}$$
$$\frac{\partial g}{\partial y} = \frac{-(x - 1)}{(x + y - 1)^2},$$
$$\frac{\partial^2 g}{\partial x^2} = \frac{-2y}{(x + y - 1)^3},$$
$$\frac{\partial^2 g}{\partial y^2} = \frac{2(x - 1)}{(x + y - 1)^3}. \tag{25}$$

Now also using that $C(\hat{p}_{11}, \hat{p}_{00}) = 0$, we obtain for the first expectation:

$$E\left(\frac{1}{\hat{p}_{00} + \hat{p}_{11} - 1}\right) = \frac{1}{p_{00} + p_{11} - 1} + \frac{V(\hat{p}_{00}) + V(\hat{p}_{11})}{(p_{00} + p_{11} - 1)^3} + O(n^{-2})$$

$$= \frac{1}{p_{00} + p_{11} - 1}\left[1 + \frac{\frac{p_{00}(1-p_{00})}{n(1-\alpha)} + \frac{p_{11}(1-p_{11})}{n\alpha}}{(p_{00} + p_{11} - 1)^2}\right] + O(n^{-2}).$$

(26)

Here, we have included only the first term of the approximations to $V(\hat{p}_{00})$ and $V(\hat{p}_{11})$ from Lemma 1, since this suffices to approximate the bias up to terms of order $O(1/n)$. Similarly, for the second expectation we obtain:

$$E\left(\frac{\hat{p}_{00} - 1}{\hat{p}_{00} + \hat{p}_{11} - 1}\right) = \frac{p_{00} - 1}{p_{00} + p_{11} - 1} + \frac{(p_{00} - 1)V(\hat{p}_{11}) - p_{11}V(\hat{p}_{00})}{(p_{00} + p_{11} - 1)^3} + O(n^{-2})$$

$$= \frac{p_{00} - 1}{p_{00} + p_{11} - 1}\left[1 + p_{11}\frac{\frac{1-p_{11}}{n\alpha} + \frac{p_{00}}{n(1-\alpha)}}{(p_{00} + p_{11} - 1)^2}\right] + O(n^{-2}). \quad (27)$$

Using Eqs. (22), (4), (26) and (27), we conclude that:

$$E(\hat{\alpha}_p) = \frac{\alpha(p_{00} + p_{11} - 1) - (p_{00} - 1)}{p_{00} + p_{11} - 1}\left[1 + \frac{\frac{p_{00}(1-p_{00})}{n(1-\alpha)} + \frac{p_{11}(1-p_{11})}{n\alpha}}{(p_{00} + p_{11} - 1)^2}\right]$$

$$+ \frac{p_{00} - 1}{p_{00} + p_{11} - 1}\left[1 + p_{11}\frac{\frac{1-p_{11}}{n\alpha} + \frac{p_{00}}{n(1-\alpha)}}{(p_{00} + p_{11} - 1)^2}\right] + O\left(\frac{1}{n^2}\right).$$

From this, it follows that an approximation to the bias of $\hat{\alpha}_p$ that is correct up to terms of order $O(1/n)$ is given by:

$$B(\hat{\alpha}_p) = \frac{\alpha(p_{00} + p_{11} - 1) - (p_{00} - 1)}{n(p_{00} + p_{11} - 1)^3}\left[\frac{p_{00}(1 - p_{00})}{1 - \alpha} + \frac{p_{11}(1 - p_{11})}{\alpha}\right]$$

$$+ \frac{(p_{00} - 1)p_{11}}{n(p_{00} + p_{11} - 1)^3}\left[\frac{1 - p_{11}}{\alpha} + \frac{p_{00}}{1 - \alpha}\right] + O\left(\frac{1}{n^2}\right).$$

By expanding the products in this expression and combining similar terms, the expression can be simplified to:

$$B(\hat{\alpha}_p) = \frac{p_{11}(1 - p_{11}) - p_{00}(1 - p_{00})}{n(p_{00} + p_{11} - 1)^2} + O\left(\frac{1}{n^2}\right).$$

Finally, using the identity $p_{11}(1 - p_{11}) - p_{00}(1 - p_{00}) = (p_{00} + p_{11} - 1)(p_{00} - p_{11})$, we obtain the required result for $B(\hat{\alpha}_p)$.

To approximate the variance of $\hat{\alpha}_p$, we apply the conditional variance decomposition conditional on $\hat{\alpha}^*$ and look at the two resulting terms separately. First, consider the variance of the conditional expectation:

$$V\left[E(\hat{\alpha}_p \mid \hat{\alpha}^*)\right] = V\left[E\left(\hat{\alpha}^* \frac{1}{\hat{p}_{00} + \hat{p}_{11} - 1} + \frac{\hat{p}_{00} - 1}{\hat{p}_{00} + \hat{p}_{11} - 1} \mid \hat{\alpha}^*\right)\right]$$

$$= V\left[\hat{\alpha}^* \frac{1}{p_{00} + p_{11} - 1}\right]$$

$$= \frac{1}{(p_{00} + p_{11} - 1)^2} V\left[\hat{\alpha}^*\right] = O\left(\frac{1}{N}\right), \tag{28}$$

where in the last line we used Eq. (6). Note: the factor $1/(p_{00} + p_{11} - 1)^2$ can become arbitrarily large in the limit $p_{00} + p_{11} \to 1$. It will be seen below that this same factor also occurs in the lower-order terms of $V(\hat{\alpha}_p)$; hence, the relative contribution of Eq. (28) remains negligible even in the limit $p_{00} + p_{11} \to 1$.

Next, we compute the expectation of the conditional variance.

$$E\left[V(\hat{\alpha}_p \mid \hat{\alpha}^*)\right] = E\left[V\left(\hat{\alpha}^* \frac{1}{\hat{p}_{00} + \hat{p}_{11} - 1} + \frac{\hat{p}_{00} - 1}{\hat{p}_{00} + \hat{p}_{11} - 1} \mid \hat{\alpha}^*\right)\right]$$

$$= E\left[V\left(\hat{\alpha}^* \frac{1}{\hat{p}_{00} + \hat{p}_{11} - 1} \mid \alpha^*\right) + V\left(\frac{\hat{p}_{00} - 1}{\hat{p}_{00} + \hat{p}_{11} - 1} \mid \hat{\alpha}^*\right)\right.$$

$$\left. + 2C\left(\hat{\alpha}^* \frac{1}{\hat{p}_{00} + \hat{p}_{11} - 1}, \frac{\hat{p}_{00} - 1}{\hat{p}_{00} + \hat{p}_{11} - 1} \mid \hat{\alpha}^*\right)\right]$$

$$= E\left[(\hat{\alpha}^*)^2\right] V\left[\frac{1}{\hat{p}_{00} + \hat{p}_{11} - 1}\right] + V\left[\frac{\hat{p}_{00} - 1}{\hat{p}_{00} + \hat{p}_{11} - 1}\right]$$

$$+ 2E\left[\hat{\alpha}^*\right] C\left[\frac{1}{\hat{p}_{00} + \hat{p}_{11} - 1}, \frac{\hat{p}_{00} - 1}{\hat{p}_{00} + \hat{p}_{11} - 1}\right]$$

$$= E\left[\hat{\alpha}^*\right]^2 \left[1 + O\left(\frac{1}{N}\right)\right] V\left[\frac{1}{\hat{p}_{00} + \hat{p}_{11} - 1}\right] + V\left[\frac{\hat{p}_{00} - 1}{\hat{p}_{00} + \hat{p}_{11} - 1}\right]$$

$$+ 2E\left[\hat{\alpha}^*\right] C\left[\frac{1}{\hat{p}_{00} + \hat{p}_{11} - 1}, \frac{\hat{p}_{00} - 1}{\hat{p}_{00} + \hat{p}_{11} - 1}\right]. \tag{29}$$

To approximate the variance and covariance terms, we use a first-order Taylor series. Using the partial derivatives in Eqs. (23), (24) and (25), we obtain:

$$V\left[\frac{1}{\hat{p}_{00} + \hat{p}_{11} - 1}\right] = \frac{V(\hat{p}_{00}) + V(\hat{p}_{11})}{(p_{00} + p_{11} - 1)^4} + O(n^{-2})$$

$$V\left[\frac{\hat{p}_{00} - 1}{\hat{p}_{00} + \hat{p}_{11} - 1}\right] = \frac{V(\hat{p}_{00})(p_{11})^2}{(p_{00} + p_{11} - 1)^4} + \frac{V(\hat{p}_{11})(1 - p_{00})^2}{(p_{00} + p_{11} - 1)^4} + O(n^{-2})$$

$$C\left[\frac{1}{\hat{p}_{00} + \hat{p}_{11} - 1}, \frac{\hat{p}_{00} - 1}{\hat{p}_{00} + \hat{p}_{11} - 1}\right] = \frac{V(\hat{p}_{00})(-p_{11})}{(p_{00} + p_{11} - 1)^4} + \frac{V(\hat{p}_{11})(p_{00} - 1)}{(p_{00} + p_{11} - 1)^4} + O(n^{-2}).$$

Substituting these terms into Eq. (29) and accounting for Eq. (28) yields:

$$V(\hat{\alpha}_p) = \frac{V(\hat{p}_{00})\left[E\left[\hat{\alpha}^*\right]^2 - 2p_{11}E\left[\hat{\alpha}^*\right] + p_{11}^2\right]}{(p_{00} + p_{11} - 1)^4}$$

$$+ \frac{V(\hat{p}_{11})\left[E\left[\hat{\alpha}^*\right]^2 - 2(1-p_{00})E\left[\hat{\alpha}^*\right] + (1-p_{00})^2\right]}{(p_{00} + p_{11} - 1)^4} + O\left(\max\left[\frac{1}{n^2}, \frac{1}{N}\right]\right)$$

$$= \frac{V(\hat{p}_{00})\left[E\left[\hat{\alpha}^*\right] - p_{11}\right]^2}{(p_{00} + p_{11} - 1)^4} + \frac{V(\hat{p}_{11})\left[E\left[\hat{\alpha}^*\right] - (1-p_{00})\right]^2}{(p_{00} + p_{11} - 1)^4} + O\left(\max\left[\frac{1}{n^2}, \frac{1}{N}\right]\right)$$

$$= \frac{V(\hat{p}_{00})(1-\alpha)^2}{(p_{00} + p_{11} - 1)^2} + \frac{V(\hat{p}_{11})\alpha^2}{(p_{00} + p_{11} - 1)^2} + O\left(\max\left[\frac{1}{n^2}, \frac{1}{N}\right]\right).$$

Finally, inserting the expressions for $V(\hat{p}_{00})$ and $V(\hat{p}_{11})$ from Lemma 1 yields:

$$V(\hat{\alpha}_p) = \frac{\frac{p_{00}(1-p_{00})}{n(1-\alpha)}\left[1 + \frac{\alpha}{n(1-\alpha)}\right](1-\alpha)^2}{(p_{00} + p_{11} - 1)^2} + \frac{\frac{p_{11}(1-p_{11})}{n\alpha}\left[1 + \frac{1-\alpha}{n\alpha}\right]\alpha^2}{(p_{00} + p_{11} - 1)^2}$$

$$+ O\left(\max\left[\frac{1}{n^2}, \frac{1}{N}\right]\right),$$

from which Eq. (14) follows. This concludes the proof of Theorem 2.

Calibration Estimator

We will now prove the bias and variance approximations for the calibration estimator $\hat{\alpha}_c$ that was defined in Eq. (15).

Proof (of Theorem 3). To compute the expected value of $\hat{\alpha}_c$, we first compute its expectation conditional on the 4-vector $\boldsymbol{N} = (N_{00}, N_{01}, N_{10}, N_{11})$:

$$E(\hat{\alpha}_c \mid \boldsymbol{N}) = E\left[\hat{\alpha}^* \frac{n_{11}}{n_{+1}} + (1 - \hat{\alpha}^*)\frac{n_{10}}{n_{+0}} \mid \boldsymbol{N}\right]$$

$$= \hat{\alpha}^* E\left[\frac{n_{11}}{n_{+1}} \mid \boldsymbol{N}\right] + (1 - \hat{\alpha}^*)E\left[\frac{n_{10}}{n_{+0}} \mid \boldsymbol{N}\right]$$

$$= \hat{\alpha}^* E\left[E\left(\frac{n_{11}}{n_{+1}} \mid \boldsymbol{N}, n_{+1}\right) \mid \boldsymbol{N}\right]$$

$$+ (1 - \hat{\alpha}^*)E\left[E\left(\frac{n_{10}}{n_{+0}} \mid \boldsymbol{N}, n_{+0}\right) \mid \boldsymbol{N}\right]$$

$$= \frac{N_{+1}}{N}E\left[\frac{1}{n_{+1}}n_{+1}\frac{N_{11}}{N_{+1}} \mid \boldsymbol{N}\right] + \frac{N_{+0}}{N}E\left[\frac{1}{n_{+0}}n_{+0}\frac{N_{10}}{N_{+0}} \mid \boldsymbol{N}\right]$$

$$= \frac{N_{11}}{N} + \frac{N_{10}}{N}$$

$$= \frac{N_{1+}}{N} = \alpha. \tag{30}$$

By the tower property of conditional expectations, it follows that $E[\hat{\alpha}_c] = E\left[E(\hat{\alpha}_c \mid \boldsymbol{N})\right] = \alpha$. This proves that $\hat{\alpha}_c$ is an unbiased estimator for α.

To compute the variance of $\hat{\alpha}_c$, we use the conditional variance decomposition, again conditioning on the 4-vector $\boldsymbol{N}$. We remark that N_{0+} and N_{1+} are deterministic values, but that N_{+0} and N_{+1} are random variables. As shown above in Eq. (30), the conditional expectation is deterministic, hence it has no variance: $V(E[\hat{\alpha}_c \mid \mathbf{N}]) = 0$. The conditional variance decomposition then simplifies to the following:

$$V(\hat{\alpha}_c) = E\left[V(\hat{\alpha}_c \mid \mathbf{N})\right]. \tag{31}$$

The conditional variance $V(\hat{\alpha}_c \mid \mathbf{N})$ can be written as follows:

$$
\begin{aligned}
V[\hat{\alpha}_c \mid \mathbf{N}] &= V\left[\hat{\alpha}^* \frac{n_{11}}{n_{+1}} + (1 - \hat{\alpha}^*)\frac{n_{10}}{n_{+0}} \mid \mathbf{N}\right] \\
&= (\hat{\alpha}^*)^2\, V\left[\frac{n_{11}}{n_{+1}} \mid \mathbf{N}\right] + (1 - \hat{\alpha}^*)^2\, V\left[\frac{n_{10}}{n_{+0}} \mid \mathbf{N}\right] \\
&\quad + 2\hat{\alpha}^*(1 - \hat{\alpha}^*)C\left[\frac{n_{11}}{n_{+1}}, \frac{n_{10}}{n_{+0}} \mid \mathbf{N}\right]. \tag{32}
\end{aligned}
$$

We will consider these terms separately. First, the variance of n_{11}/n_{+1} can be computed by applying an additional conditional variance decomposition:

$$V\left[\frac{n_{11}}{n_{+1}} \mid \mathbf{N}\right] = V\left[E\left(\frac{n_{11}}{n_{+1}} \mid \mathbf{N}, n_{+1}\right) \mid \mathbf{N}\right] + E\left[V\left(\frac{n_{11}}{n_{+1}} \mid \mathbf{N}, n_{+1}\right) \mid \mathbf{N}\right].$$

The first term is zero, which can be shown as follows:

$$
\begin{aligned}
V\left[E\left(\frac{n_{11}}{n_{+1}} \mid \mathbf{N}, n_{+1}\right)\right] &= V\left[\frac{1}{n_{+1}}E(n_{11} \mid \mathbf{N}, n_{+1}) \mid \mathbf{N}\right] \\
&= V\left[\frac{1}{n_{+1}}n_{+1}\frac{N_{11}}{N_{+1}} \mid \mathbf{N}\right] \\
&= V\left[\frac{N_{11}}{N_{+1}} \mid \mathbf{N}\right] = 0.
\end{aligned}
$$

For the second term, we find under the assumption that $n \ll N$:

$$
\begin{aligned}
E\left[V\left(\frac{n_{11}}{n_{+1}} \mid \mathbf{N}, n_{+1}\right) \mid \mathbf{N}\right] &= E\left[\frac{1}{n_{+1}^2}V(n_{11} \mid \mathbf{N}, n_{+1}) \mid \mathbf{N}\right] \\
&= E\left[\frac{1}{n_{+1}^2}n_{+1}\frac{N_{11}}{N_{+1}}(1 - \frac{N_{11}}{N_{+1}}) \mid \mathbf{N}\right] \\
&= E\left[\frac{1}{n_{+1}} \mid \mathbf{N}\right]\frac{N_{11}N_{01}}{N_{+1}^2}.
\end{aligned}
$$

The expectation of $\frac{1}{n_{+1}}$ can be approximated with a second-order Taylor series:

$$
\begin{aligned}
V\left[\frac{n_{11}}{n_{+1}} \mid \mathbf{N}\right] &= \left[\frac{1}{E[n_{+1} \mid \mathbf{N}]} + \frac{1}{2}\frac{2}{E[n_{+1} \mid \mathbf{N}]^3}V[n_{+1} \mid \mathbf{N}]\right]\frac{N_{11}N_{01}}{N_{+1}^2} + O(n^{-3}) \\
&= \frac{1}{E[n_{+1} \mid \mathbf{N}]}\left[1 + \frac{V[n_{+1} \mid \mathbf{N}]}{E[n_{+1} \mid \mathbf{N}]^2}\right]\frac{N_{11}N_{01}}{N_{+1}^2} + O(n^{-3}) \\
&= \frac{1}{n\hat{\alpha}^*}\left[1 + \frac{1 - \hat{\alpha}^*}{n\hat{\alpha}^*}\right]\frac{N_{11}N_{01}}{N_{+1}^2} + O(n^{-3}). \tag{33}
\end{aligned}
$$

The variance of n_{10}/n_{+0} can be approximated in the same way, which yields the following expression:

$$V\left[\frac{n_{10}}{n_{+0}} \mid \mathbf{N}\right] = \frac{1}{n(1-\hat{\alpha}^*)}\left[1 + \frac{\hat{\alpha}^*}{n(1-\hat{\alpha}^*)}\right]\frac{N_{00}N_{10}}{N_{+0}^2} + O(n^{-3}). \quad (34)$$

Finally, it can be shown that the covariance in the final term is equal to zero:

$$\begin{aligned}
C\left[\frac{n_{11}}{n_{+1}}, \frac{n_{10}}{n_{+0}} \mid \mathbf{N}\right] &= E\left[C\left(\frac{n_{11}}{n_{+1}}, \frac{n_{10}}{n_{+0}} \mid \mathbf{N}, n_{+0}, n_{+1}\right) \mid \mathbf{N}\right] \\
&\quad + C\left[E\left(\frac{n_{11}}{n_{+1}} \mid \mathbf{N}, n_{+0}, n_{+1}\right), E\left(\frac{n_{10}}{n_{+0}} \mid \mathbf{N}, n_{+0}, n_{+1}\right) \mid \mathbf{N}\right] \\
&= E\left[\frac{1}{n_{+0}n_{+1}}C\left(n_{11}, n_{10} \mid \mathbf{N}, n_{+0}, n_{+1}\right) \mid \mathbf{N}\right] \\
&\quad + C\left[\frac{1}{n_{+1}}E\left(n_{11} \mid \mathbf{N}, n_{+0}, n_{+1}\right), \frac{1}{n_{+0}}E\left(n_{10} \mid \mathbf{N}, n_{+0}, n_{+1}\right) \mid \mathbf{N}\right] \\
&= 0 + C\left[\frac{1}{n_{+1}}n_{+1}\frac{N_{11}}{N_{+1}}, \frac{1}{n_{+0}}n_{+0}\frac{N_{10}}{N_{+0}} \mid \mathbf{N}\right] = 0. \quad (35)
\end{aligned}$$

Combining Eqs. (33), (34), (35), with Eq. (32) gives:

$$\begin{aligned}
V[\hat{\alpha}_c \mid \mathbf{N}] &= \frac{N_{+1}^2}{N^2}\frac{1}{n\hat{\alpha}^*}\left[1 + \frac{1-\hat{\alpha}^*}{n\hat{\alpha}^*}\right]\frac{N_{11}N_{01}}{N_{+1}^2} \\
&\quad + \frac{N_{+0}^2}{N^2}\frac{1}{n(1-\hat{\alpha}^*)}\left[1 + \frac{\hat{\alpha}^*}{n(1-\hat{\alpha}^*)}\right]\frac{N_{00}N_{10}}{N_{+0}^2} + O(n^{-3}) \\
&= \frac{1}{n\hat{\alpha}^*}\left[1 + \frac{1-\hat{\alpha}^*}{n\hat{\alpha}^*}\right]\frac{N_{11}N_{01}}{N^2} \\
&\quad + \frac{1}{n(1-\hat{\alpha}^*)}\left[1 + \frac{\hat{\alpha}^*}{n(1-\hat{\alpha}^*)}\right]\frac{N_{00}N_{10}}{N^2} + O(n^{-3}).
\end{aligned}$$

Recall from Eq. (31) that $V[\hat{\alpha}_c] = E[V[\hat{\alpha}_c \mid \mathbf{N}]] = E[E[V[\hat{\alpha}_c \mid \mathbf{N}] \mid N_{+1}]]$. Hence,

$$\begin{aligned}
V[\hat{\alpha}_c] &= E\left[\frac{1}{n\hat{\alpha}^*}\left(1 + \frac{1-\hat{\alpha}^*}{n\hat{\alpha}^*}\right)E\left(\frac{N_{11}N_{01}}{N^2} \mid N_{+1}\right)\right. \quad (36) \\
&\quad \left. + \frac{1}{n(1-\hat{\alpha}^*)}\left(1 + \frac{\hat{\alpha}^*}{n(1-\hat{\alpha}^*)}\right)E\left(\frac{N_{00}N_{10}}{N^2} \mid N_{+1}\right)\right] + O(n^{-3}).
\end{aligned}$$

To evaluate the expectations in this expression, we observe that, conditional on the column total N_{+1}, N_{11} is distributed as $Bin(N_{+1}, c_{11})$, where c_{11} is a calibration probability as defined in Section 2.5. Hence,

$$E[N_{11} \mid N_{+1}] = N_{+1}c_{11} = \frac{N_{+1}\alpha p_{11}}{(1-\alpha)(1-p_{00}) + \alpha p_{11}} \quad (37)$$

$$V[N_{11} \mid N_{+1}] = N_{+1}c_{11}(1 - c_{11}).$$

Similarly, since $N = N_{+1} + N_{+0}$ is fixed,

$$E[N_{00} \mid N_{+1}] = N_{+0}c_{00} = \frac{N_{+0}(1-\alpha)p_{00}}{(1-\alpha)p_{00} + \alpha(1-p_{11})} \tag{38}$$

$$V[N_{00} \mid N_{+1}] = N_{+0}c_{00}(1-c_{00}).$$

Using these results, we obtain:

$$E\left[\frac{N_{11}N_{01}}{N^2} \mid N_{+1}\right] = \frac{1}{N^2}E[N_{11}N_{01} \mid N_{+1}]$$

$$= \frac{1}{N^2}E[N_{11}(N_{+1} - N_{11}) \mid N_{+1}]$$

$$= \frac{1}{N^2}\left[N_{+1}E[N_{11} \mid N_{+1}] - E[N_{11}^2 \mid N_{+1}]\right]$$

$$= \frac{1}{N^2}\left[N_{+1}E[N_{11} \mid N_{+1}] - V[N_{11} \mid N_{+1}] - E[N_{11} \mid N_{+1}]^2\right]$$

$$= \frac{1}{N^2}\left[N_{+1}^2 c_{11} - N_{+1}c_{11}(1-c_{11}) - N_{+1}^2 c_{11}^2\right]$$

$$= \frac{N_{+1}^2}{N^2}c_{11}(1-c_{11}) + O\left(\frac{1}{N}\right), \tag{39}$$

and similarly

$$E\left[\frac{N_{00}N_{10}}{N^2} \mid N_{+1}\right] = \frac{N_{+0}^2}{N^2}c_{00}(1-c_{00}) + O\left(\frac{1}{N}\right). \tag{40}$$

Substituting Eqs. (39) and (40) into Eq. (36) and noting that $N_{+1}^2/N^2 = (\hat{\alpha}^*)^2$ and $N_{+0}^2/N^2 = (1-\hat{\alpha}^*)^2$, we obtain:

$$V[\hat{\alpha}_c] = E\left[\frac{\hat{\alpha}^*}{n}\left(1 + \frac{1-\hat{\alpha}^*}{n\hat{\alpha}^*}\right)c_{11}(1-c_{11})\right.$$

$$\left. + \frac{1-\hat{\alpha}^*}{n}\left(1 + \frac{\hat{\alpha}^*}{n(1-\hat{\alpha}^*)}\right)c_{00}(1-c_{00})\right] + O\left(\max\left[\frac{1}{n^3}, \frac{1}{Nn}\right]\right)$$

$$= \left[\frac{E(\hat{\alpha}^*)}{n} + \frac{1-E(\hat{\alpha}^*)}{n^2}\right]c_{11}(1-c_{11})$$

$$+ \left[\frac{1-E(\hat{\alpha}^*)}{n} + \frac{E(\hat{\alpha}^*)}{n^2}\right]c_{00}(1-c_{00}) + O\left(\max\left[\frac{1}{n^3}, \frac{1}{Nn}\right]\right).$$

Finally, substituting the expressions for $E(\hat{\alpha}^*)$ from Eq. (4) and the expressions for c_{11} and c_{00} from Eqs. (37) and (38), the desired Eq. (17) is obtained. This concludes the proof of Theorem 3.

Comparing Mean Squared Errors

To conclude, we present the proof of Theorem 4, which essentially shows that the mean squared error (up to and including terms of order $1/n$) of the calibration estimator is lower than that of the misclassification estimator.

Proof (of Theorem 4). Recall that the bias of $\hat{\alpha}_p$ as an estimator for α is given by

$$B[\hat{\alpha}_p] = \frac{p_{00} - p_{11}}{n(p_{00} + p_{11} - 1)} + O\left(\frac{1}{n^2}\right).$$

Hence, $(B[\hat{\alpha}_p])^2 = O(1/n^2)$ is not relevant for $\widetilde{MSE}[\hat{\alpha}_p]$. It follows that $\widetilde{MSE}[\hat{\alpha}_p]$ is equal to the variance of $\hat{\alpha}_p$ up to order $1/n$. From Eq. (14) we obtain:

$$\widetilde{MSE}[\hat{\alpha}_p] = \frac{1}{n}\left[\frac{(1-\alpha)p_{00}(1-p_{00}) + \alpha p_{11}(1-p_{11})}{(p_{00} + p_{11} - 1)^2}\right]. \tag{41}$$

Recall that $\hat{\alpha}_c$ is an unbiased estimator for α, i.e., $B[\hat{\alpha}_c] = 0$. Also recall the notation $\beta = (1-\alpha)(1-p_{00}) + \alpha p_{11}$. It follows from Eq. (17) that the variance, and hence the MSE, of $\hat{\alpha}_c$ up to terms of order $1/n$ can be written as:

$$\begin{aligned}\widetilde{MSE}[\hat{\alpha}_c] &= \frac{1}{n}\left[\beta\frac{\alpha p_{11}}{\beta}\left(1 - \frac{\alpha p_{11}}{\beta}\right) + (1-\beta)\frac{(1-\alpha)p_{00}}{1-\beta}\left(1 - \frac{(1-\alpha)p_{00}}{1-\beta}\right)\right] \\ &= \frac{\alpha(1-\alpha)}{n}\left[\frac{(1-p_{00})p_{11}}{\beta} + \frac{p_{00}(1-p_{11})}{1-\beta}\right]. \end{aligned} \tag{42}$$

To prove Eq. (18), first note that

$$\frac{(1-p_{00})p_{11}}{\beta} + \frac{p_{00}(1-p_{11})}{1-\beta} = \frac{(1-p_{00})p_{11} + \beta(p_{00} - p_{11})}{\beta(1-\beta)}. \tag{43}$$

The numerator of this equation can be rewritten as follows:

$$\begin{aligned}&(1-p_{00})p_{11} + \beta(p_{00} - p_{11}) \\ &= (1-p_{00})p_{11} + (1-\alpha)p_{00}(1-p_{00}) + \alpha p_{00}p_{11} - (1-\alpha)(1-p_{00})p_{11} - \alpha p_{11}^2 \\ &= (1-\alpha)p_{00}(1-p_{00}) + \alpha p_{00}p_{11} + \alpha(1-p_{00})p_{11} - \alpha p_{11}^2 \\ &= (1-\alpha)p_{00}(1-p_{00}) + \alpha p_{11}(1-p_{11}).\end{aligned}$$

Note that the obtained expression is equal to the numerator of Eq. (41). Write $T = (1-\alpha)p_{00}(1-p_{00}) + \alpha p_{11}(1-p_{11})$ for that expression. It follows that

$$\begin{aligned}&\widetilde{MSE}[\hat{\alpha}_p] - \widetilde{MSE}[\hat{\alpha}_c] \\ &= \frac{T}{n(p_{00} + p_{11} - 1)^2} - \frac{T\alpha(1-\alpha)}{n\beta(1-\beta)} \\ &= \frac{T}{n(p_{00} + p_{11} - 1)^2\beta(1-\beta)}\left[\beta(1-\beta) - \alpha(1-\alpha)(p_{00} + p_{11} - 1)^2\right].\end{aligned}$$

Writing out the second factor in the last expression gives the following:

$$\beta(1 - \beta) - \alpha(1 - \alpha)(p_{00} + p_{11} - 1)^2$$
$$= (1 - \alpha)^2 p_{00}(1 - p_{00}) + \alpha(1 - \alpha)\Big((1 - p_{00})(1 - p_{11}) + p_{00}p_{11}\Big) + \alpha^2 p_{11}(1 - p_{11})$$
$$\quad - \alpha(1 - \alpha)(p_{00} + p_{11} - 1)^2$$
$$= (1 - \alpha)^2 p_{00}(1 - p_{00}) + \alpha(1 - \alpha)\Big(p_{00}(1 - p_{00}) + p_{11}(1 - p_{11})\Big) + \alpha^2 p_{11}(1 - p_{11})$$
$$= (1 - \alpha)p_{00}(1 - p_{00}) + \alpha p_{11}(1 - p_{11})$$
$$= T.$$

This concludes the proof of Theorem 4.

References

1. Buonaccorsi, J.P.: Measurement Error: Models, Methods, and Applications. Chapman & Hall/CRC, Boca Raton (2010)
2. Burger, J., Delden, A.v., Scholtus, S.: Sensitivity of mixed-source statistics to classification errors. J. Offic. Stat. **31**(3), 489–506 (2015). https://doi.org/10.1515/jos-2015-0029
3. Curier, R., et al.: Monitoring spatial sustainable development: semi-automated analysis of satellite and aerial images for energy transition and sustainability indicators. arXiv preprint arXiv:1810.04881 (2018)
4. Czaplewski, R.L.: Misclassification bias in areal estimates. Photogram. Eng. Remote Sens. **58**(2), 189–192 (1992)
5. Czaplewski, R.L., Catts, G.P.: Calibration of remotely sensed proportion or area estimates for misclassification error. Remote Sens. Environ. **39**(1), 29–43 (1992). https://doi.org/10.1016/0034-4257(92)90138-A
6. González, P., Castaño, A., Chawla, N.V., Coz, J.J.D.: A review on quantification learning. ACM Comput. Surv. **50**(5), 74:1–74:40 (2017). https://doi.org/10.1145/3117807
7. Grassia, A., Sundberg, R.: Statistical precision in the calibration and use of sorting machines and other classifiers. Technometrics **24**(2), 117–121 (1982). https://doi.org/10.1080/00401706.1982.10487732
8. Greenland, S.: Sensitivity analysis and bias analysis. In: Ahrens, W., Pigeot, I. (eds.) Handbook of Epidemiology, pp. 685–706. Springer, New York (2014). https://doi.org/10.1007/978-0-387-09834-0_60
9. Hopkins, D.J., King, G.: A method of automated nonparametric content analysis for social science. Am. J. Polit. Sci. **54**(1), 229–247 (2010). https://doi.org/10.1111/j.1540-5907.2009.00428.x
10. Knottnerus, P.: Sample Survey Theory: Some Pythagorean Perspectives. Springer, New York (2003). https://doi.org/10.1007/978-0-387-21764-2
11. Kuha, J., Skinner, C.J.: Categorical data analysis and misclassification. In: Lyberg, L., et al. (eds.) Survey Measurement and Process Quality, pp. 633–670. Wiley, New York (1997)
12. Löw, F., Knöfel, P., Conrad, C.: Analysis of uncertainty in multi-temporal object-based classification. ISPRS J. Photogramm. Remote Sens. **105**, 91–106 (2015). https://doi.org/10.1016/j.isprsjprs.2015.03.004

13. Meertens, Q.A., Diks, C.G.H., Herik, H.J.v.d., Takes, F.W.: A data-driven supply-side approach for estimating cross-border internet purchases within the European union. J. Royal Stat. Soc. Ser. A (Stat. Soc.) **183**(1), 61–90 (2020). https://doi.org/10.1111/rssa.12487

14. Meertens, Q.A., Diks, C.G.H., Herik, H.J.v.d., Takes, F.W.: A Bayesian approach for accurate classification-based aggregates. In: Berger-Wolf, T.Y., et al. (eds.), Proceedings of the 19th SIAM International Conference on Data Mining, pp. 306–314 (2019). https://doi.org/10.1137/1.9781611975673.35

15. Moreno-Torres, J.G., Raeder, T., Alaiz-Rodríguez, R., Chawla, N.V., Herrera, F.: A unifying view on dataset shift in classification. Pattern Recogn. **45**(1), 521–530 (2012). https://doi.org/10.1016/j.patcog.2011.06.019

16. O'Connor, B., Balasubramanyan, R., Routledge, B., Smith, N.: From Tweets to polls: linking text sentiment to public opinion time series. In: Proceedings of the International AAAI Conference on Weblogs and Social Media, Washington, DC (2010)

17. Scholtus, S., Delden, A.v.: On the accuracy of estimators based on a binary classifier, Discussion Paper No. 202007, Statistics Netherlands, The Hague (2020)

18. Schwartz, J.E.: The neglected problem of measurement error in categorical data. Soc. Methods Res. **13**(4), 435–466 (1985). https://doi.org/10.1177/0049124185013004001

19. Strichartz, R.S.: The Way of Analysis. Jones & Bartlett Learning, Sudbury (2000)

20. Delden, A.v., Scholtus, S., Burger, J.: Accuracy of mixed-source statistics as affected by classification errors. J. Official Stat. **32**(3), 619–642 (2016). https://doi.org/10.1515/jos-2016-0032

21. Wiedemann, G.: Proportional classification revisited: automatic content analysis of political manifestos using active learning. Soc. Sci. Comput. Rev. **37**(2), 135–159 (2019). https://doi.org/10.1177/0894439318758389

A Spiking Neuron Implementation of Genetic Algorithms for Optimization

Siegfried Ludwig[1]([✉]) [iD], Joeri Hartjes[1], Bram Pol[1], Gabriela Rivas[1],
and Johan Kwisthout[2] [iD]

[1] School for Artificial Intelligence, Radboud University, Montessorilaan 3,
6525 HR Nijmegen, Netherlands
siegfried.m.ludwig@protonmail.ch
[2] Donders Center for Cognition, Radboud University, Montessorilaan 3,
6525 HR Nijmegen, Netherlands
j.kwisthout@donders.ru.nl

Abstract. We designed freely scalable ensembles of spiking neurons to carry out the operations required to run a genetic algorithm, thereby opening up possibilities for making use of efficient neuromorphic hardware. Two types of implementation are explored that offer a complexity trade-off between computational space and time, with both designs having linear energy complexity. The designs were implemented in a simulator to successfully solve the one-max optimization problem, serving as a proof of concept for running genetic algorithms as spiking neural networks.

Keywords: Neuromorphic computing · Genetic algorithm · Spiking neural networks

1   Introduction

Neuromorphic computing ranges back to the term being coined in 1990 [9], in which the first implementation consisted of very large scale integration (VLSI) with analog components mimicking the biological neural systems. Much research has been done since this time, and in the last few years the energy efficiency of such architectures have become an increasingly dominant research subject. Spiking neural networks (SNN) are known as a type of neuromorphic implementation which have exceptional energy saving properties, compared to other systems [12]. SNNs augment artificial neural networks with the spiking dynamics found in biological neurons [4]. Based on leaky integrate-and-fire (LIF) neurons [2], SNNs transmit information by means of timing and energy spikes, released when the potential difference inside a neuron reaches a certain threshold. This is because such hardware is modeled after the brain in that its activation is event-driven and asynchronous. On top of that, SNN's property of local information storage effectively avoids the von Neumann bottleneck arising from an idling processor

M. Baratchi et al. (Eds.): BNAIC/Benelearn 2020, CCIS 1398, pp. 91–105, 2021.
https://doi.org/10.1007/978-3-030-76640-5_6

while retrieving data from memory [15]. Researching the possibility of implementing various existing algorithms in such SNNs leads the way to a future in which real life applications of such algorithms currently implemented on von Neumann architectures could be replaced.

Implementing algorithms as SNNs to run them on neuromorphic hardware has been done for sorting [1], constraint satisfaction [14], shortest path and neighborhood subgraph extraction problems [11]. The striking similarity between a genetic sequence and a neural spike train inspires the implementation of a genetic algorithm (GA) as a SNN, which could make use of recent hardware developments in neuromorphic computing.

The use of evolution-inspired algorithms has been proven a viable solution for tackling problems of optimization, bringing in advantages for optimization over traditional methods. For instance, GA systems [5,6] may provide the opportunity for difficult problem solving such as multi-objective optimization [3] and have found applications in various practical settings (see [7] for a review). As in natural evolution, GAs work by modifying the characteristics of individuals in a population across several iterations. This is done by means of reproduction (*crossover*) and random gene mutation. With each run, individuals with an arrangement of genes with a higher fitness value are allowed to preferentially reproduce and carry over their genetic information into the next *generation*. In this study, each individual solution (*chromosome*) is represented as a binary bit sequence, in which each bit represents the value of a gene.

Our main aim was to investigate the feasibility of implementing a GA using spiking neurons with the potential for future implementation on neuromorphic hardware, such as Intel's Loihi [8] or IBM's TrueNorth [10]. Our design consists of binary genetic sequences, which are represented as neuronal spikes and are processed by LIF neurons with context-dependent parameters. The chosen optimization problem is the *one-max problem* due to its simplicity and wide use in the literature on genetic algorithms; the objective of which is to produce a fully active genetic sequence, in this case a fully active spike train. The neural network was implemented and tested using a spiking neuron simulator[1].

We considered two candidate possibilities for encoding the binary genetic sequence in neural ensembles. Firstly, the genetic sequence can be represented sequentially as a spike train, with a spike indicating a 1 and no spike indicating a 0. An ensemble in this design processes one bit at a time. The second way of representing a binary genetic sequence is parallel, using a separate neuron for each position of the genetic sequence. These two encodings are expected to offer a complexity trade-off between computational space and time.

First, we present the high-level architecture of the SNN (Sect. 2), followed by details on the sequential and parallel implementations (Sects. 3). We then conduct a complexity analysis of both implementations with regard to space, time and energy, in order to assess the tractability of our design (Sect. 4).

---

[1] https://gitlab.socsci.ru.nl/j.kwisthout/neuromorphic-genetic-algorithm.

2   High-Level Architecture

The genetic algorithm consists of initializing and evaluating a starting population and then repeatedly performing selection, crossover, mutation, and evaluation on the population until termination. It is implemented as a single recurrent SNN, consisting of specialized neural ensembles for each operation (Fig. 1). The topology of the network gives a fitness hierarchy, with the fittest chromosomes being at the top and conversely the least fit chromosomes being at the bottom. The network architecture is static during run-time and no learning of the weights is required.

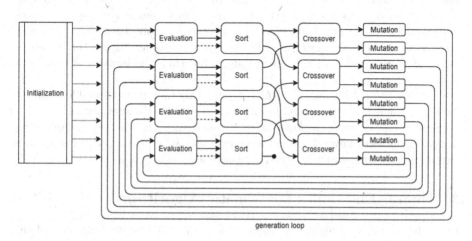

Fig. 1. High-level architecture of the genetic algorithm network, depicted with 8 chromosome lanes as solid arrows (each arrow can represent multiple neural connections in the parallel design). After *mutation*, all chromosomes are connected back to *evaluation* to close the generation loop, resulting in a single large neural network. The dashed arrows from *evaluation* to *sort* represent the evaluation result. To increase the number of chromosomes, the pattern of the second pair of the four lane pairs is repeated.

After initialization, the chromosomes enter the evaluation ensembles in pairs, where they are evaluated against each other and then potentially swapped to bring the chromosome with higher fitness to the top. This setup corresponds to a single pairwise bubble sort step and over time ranks chromosomes by their fitness, which is necessary for selection. The use of only a limited number of bubble sort steps in each generation will lead to incomplete sorting, but is more efficient and leads to some variety in the ranking of the chromosomes while still avoiding the removal of very promising individuals from the bottom. This design is related to the ranking selection mechanism [13].

Selection is implemented in the connections from the sorting ensembles to the crossover ensembles, by eliminating the bottom chromosome and connecting the top chromosome twice. This results in better solutions propagating more successfully over time. In addition to potentially moving up one lane in the sorting ensemble itself, the winner of the pairwise evaluations moves up by another lane after sorting to ensure upwards mobility, as otherwise the same pairs would be compared each iteration. Conversely, the inferior chromosome moves down by a number of lanes after sorting.

Crossover is then performed on each pair of chromosomes. This reproduction is implemented with a stochastic crossover method, which splits two sequences at a random point and swaps all subsequent genes between the individuals.

After crossover, each chromosome is processed individually in a mutation ensemble. Mutation is carried out by assigning a probability for flipping the activity of each bit in a given sequence. In our designs, we use a probability of $p = \frac{1}{n}$, where n is the length of the chromosome, but other mutation rates are possible. We do not apply mutation on the top two chromosomes of each generation in order to allow for stable one-max solutions. Again, this choice is more up to the design of the genetic algorithm than the implementation as a spiking neural network.

To close the generation loop, the outputs of the mutation ensembles connect back into the evaluation ensembles, forming a recurrent neural network.

Scaling the network up for a larger population size or longer chromosomes is straight-forward beyond a small minimum size, by repeating whole ensembles and repeated elements within certain ensembles.

3   Neural Ensembles for Genetic Algorithms

In the following, we present the sequential and parallel implementations of the neuromorphic genetic algorithm. While both designs process many chromosomes in parallel, the genes making up each individual chromosome are either processed sequentially or all at once, which leads to a trade-off in computational space and time. Both designs consist of specialized neural ensembles, which implement the necessary processing steps to complete a genetic algorithm.

3.1   Sequential Design

In our sequential design of the GA, the chromosome is processed one bit at a time, which more closely resembles genetic processing in nature. Sequential processing allows a small neural ensemble to process arbitrary lengths of chromosomes over time without itself growing in size. The implementation relies on a lead bit, which precedes every chromosome and is always active. This allows the signaling of the arrival of a new chromosome, ensuring correct processing. In the following, neurons will be ascribed different types based on their function in the ensemble. However, they are all based on the LIF neuron model.

Evaluation Ensemble. The sequential one-max evaluation ensemble (Fig. 2) makes use of 8 neurons and 11 internal connections. It takes as input two chromosomes and gives as output two chromosomes as well as a spike on a separate neuron serving as an indicator in case the bottom chromosome has a higher fitness than the top chromosome. The membrane potential of the accumulator neuron (ACC) is increased with each active bit in the bottom chromosome, and decreased with each active bit in the top chromosome. Note that the ACC neuron is like all other neuron types used here just a LIF neuron with specific parameters. The activation neuron (A), activated by the lead bit, then makes the ACC neuron fire or not based on the final membrane potential of the ACC neuron. Only in the case of a membrane potential higher than zero will the indicator neuron fire, and will the chromosomes' ranking switch. A reset neuron (R) is responsible for spiking but suppressing the ACC as to prevent interference of previous chromosome comparisons with current iterations. Clearing the potential of the ACC neuron could alternatively be done using membrane leakage over time, but that would result in a less predictable design.

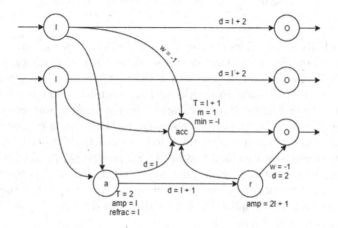

Fig. 2. Sequential one-max evaluation ensemble. (I) Input, (acc) Accumulator neuron, (a) Activation neuron, (r) Reset neuron, (o) Output.

Bubble Sort Ensemble. The bubble sort ensemble (Fig. 3) consists of 10 neurons and 15 internal connections. It takes two chromosomes plus a fitness indication as input and gives two chromosomes as output. It uses gate (G) neurons to open or close the identity and swap lanes connecting input and output and thereby controlling whether the incoming chromosomes are swapped or propagated as identity. This is achieved by giving the swap gate neurons a threshold of two, which means they can only fire if an input comes from the gate control (GC) neuron. The GC neuron is activated by the gate control activation (GCA) neuron, which takes the fitness indicator input coming from the evaluation ensemble. The GC neuron uses a recurrent connection to keep the swap gates open and the identity gates closed until the chromosomes passed through entirely, at which point it is deactivated by a delayed spike coming from the GCA neuron.

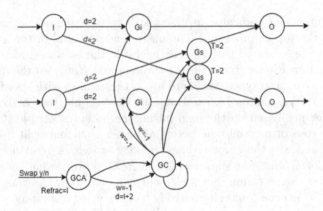

Fig. 3. Bubble sort ensemble in the sequential design. (I) input, (Gi) identity gate, (Gs) swap gate, (GC) gate control, (GCA) gate control activation, (O) output.

Crossover Ensemble. The crossover ensemble (Fig. 4) works similarly to the bubble sort ensemble, except that identity and swap gates are not open or closed for the whole chromosome, but switch activation at a random point. It uses 13 neurons and 27 internal connections. The ensemble could be simplified to only use one gate control (GC) neuron as in the bubble sort ensemble, but has been implemented with two in this project. The random crossover point is implemented via a stochastic (S) neuron and a stochasticity control (SC) neuron. The S neuron gets constant input from the SC neuron, while also generating a random membrane potential each time step. If this combined potential crosses the S neuron's threshold the identity GC neuron is deactivated and the swap GC neuron is activated. If S spikes, The S neuron also deactivates the SC neuron, since only one crossover point is desired.

Mutation Ensemble. Finally, the mutation ensemble (Fig. 5) stochastically turns a 0 into a 1 and conversely a 1 into a 0, independently for each bit excluding the lead bit. It uses 6 neurons and 12 internal connections. The first stochastic neuron (S1) gets a positive input from each spike in the input and adds a random membrane potential, which can cross the threshold and lead to a spike. A spike from S1 suppresses the ensemble output, thereby turning a 1 into a 0. The other stochastic neuron (S2) always gets input from the control (C) neuron and adds a random membrane potential, but it is suppressed by every spike in the input. If no spike comes from the input, it has a chance of firing and turning the ensemble output from a 0 to a 1. The control neuron is activated and finally deactivated by the control activation (CA) neuron.

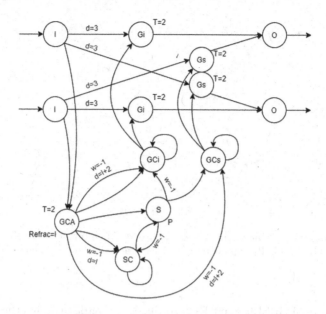

Fig. 4. Crossover ensemble in the sequential design. (I) input, (Gi) identity gate, (Gs) swap gate, (GCi) identity gate control, (GCs) swap gate control, (GCA) gate control activation, (S) stochastic, (SC) stochasticity control, (O) output.

Full Network Behavior. Each chromosome is passed through the ensembles in its lane, as described in the high-level architecture (see Fig. 1). In the sequential design, a chromosome can still be processed in one ensemble while already entering into the next (e.g. crossover to mutation), since here each bit can be handled independently. An exception to this is the evaluation ensemble, which needs to accumulate the full chromosome to make an evaluation. It therefore breaks the time-constant flow through the other ensembles and leads to a time dependency on the chromosome length. On the upside this prevents chromosomes from being longer than the execution cycle, which could otherwise lead to the beginning of the next generation interfering with the end of the last for long chromosomes.

3.2 Parallel Design

In the parallel implementation, every gene of the chromosome gets processed at the same time. Instead of using a single spike train to represent the chromosome, multiple neurons are used that each represent one gene of the chromosome. A set of neurons can then represent the binary code of the chromosome by either spiking or not. Its advantage is that the entire binary code of the chromosomes can be conveyed in a single time step, but requires more neurons as chromosomes get longer. A generation of the entire algorithm in parallel design takes exactly eleven simulation time steps. Again, all neuron types presented here are simple LIF neurons with specific parameters. The different ensembles used in the algorithm will be explained below.

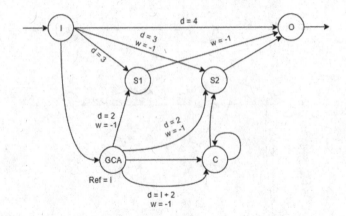

Fig. 5. Mutation ensemble in the sequential design. (I) input, (S1) stochastically flips 1 to 0, (S2) stochastically flips 0 to 1, (C) constant, (GCA) gate control activation, (O) output.

Evaluation and Bubble Sort Ensemble. In the parallel design the evaluation step is combined with the bubble sort step. The goal of the evaluation is to have the chromosome with the highest fitness be transferred to the first n output neurons where n is the length of the chromosome. One lead bit is present for each chromosome pair which enables functionality in the other ensembles of the GA, however for this segment it is of no use and therefore linked directly to its corresponding output neuron. Also for this reason the decision was made to omit the lead bit altogether in Fig. 6. By taking advantage of all information contained in the chromosome being available at once, the evaluation and sorting ensembles could be combined. This enables the comparison of the fitness through the use of one Accumulator neuron (ACC) to which all input genes are connected (excluding the lead bit). The sign of the connection weights leading to the ACC results in it becoming active only if the lower chromosome has a greater fitness than the top chromosome by at least one gene. Subsequently, the activation of the ACC will determine whether either the identity gates or the swap gates are activated. These are responsible for transferring the activity from the input to the output neuron of the same, or the 'adversarial chromosome', respectively.

Each of the input neurons are connected to both a dedicated identity gate and a dedicated swap gate, with these being connected to the identity neuron or the neuron on the other chromosome in the same position. The connection from the input to the gates is delayed by one time step, however, to allow for synchronous arrival of the spike and the spike coming from the ACC. The connections between the ACC and the gates are weighted such that by default the identity gates have a threshold low enough that a spike from the input neurons will be enough to spike the gate as well while the threshold of the swap gates is too high. As soon as the ACC is activated however this spike is no longer enough for the identity gates, while the extra activation coming from the ACC to the swap gates lowers their threshold enough to let the spike pass from the input neuron to the correct output neuron on the side of the 'adversarial chromosome'.

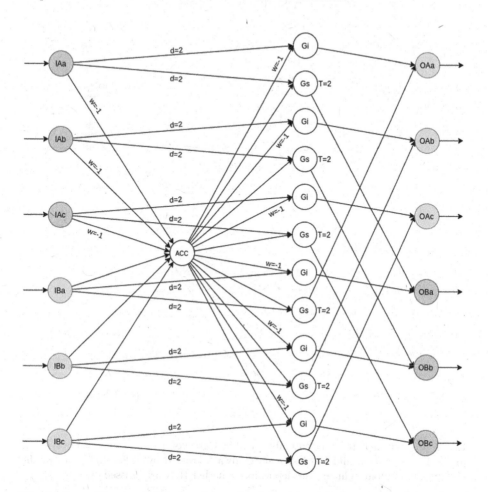

Fig. 6. Ensemble responsible for the evaluation and sorting in the parallel design, applied to a pair of chromosomes consisting of three genes each. Using an accumulator neuron (ACC), the ensemble determines which of the chromosomes has higher fitness and places the winner in the top lanes.

Crossover Ensemble. The parallel crossover ensemble can be seen in Fig. 7. The first gene of every chromosome always ends up in the same output chromosome. The last gene is always crossed over and ends up in the opposite chromosome. To decide where the genes in between go, a 'random point maker' has been designed (see Fig. 8), which is activated by the lead bit. The input to the second layer of the random point maker spikes with a probability of $p = \frac{1}{n-2}$, where n is the chromosome length. If activated, the node in this second layer transfers this spike to all nodes in the third layer on the same level or below, ensuring that once a gate opens the gates below also open.

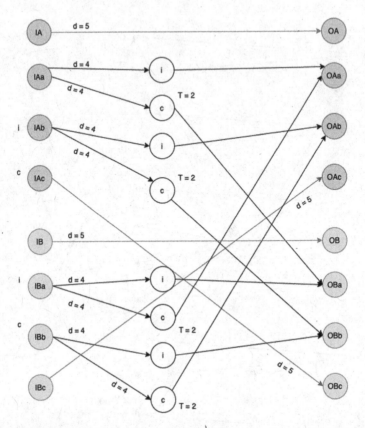

Fig. 7. The parallel crossover ensemble. The first gene of a chromosome is always sent to the same position and the last gene is always crossed over. For the genes in the middle, the random point maker determines whether they are crossed over or not.

The third layer of the random point maker (the gates) connect to the identity and crossover nodes in the crossover ensemble. When a gate neuron of the random point maker gets a spike, it closes the identity gate and opens the crossover gate of both chromosomes at that level. This way, initially the crossover ensemble will transfer genes to the same output chromosome, but at a random point will switch to crossing genes over to the other output chromosome. The crossover ensemble, together with the random point maker, takes five time steps to run for any chromosome length n. The number of neurons in the ensemble is $10n - 11$, meaning linear growth. The number of connections does not show linear growth, because the connections between the second and third layer of the random point maker grow with $\frac{n^2 + n}{2}$, which is quadratic growth. Because of this, the number of connections in the whole ensemble grows quadratically.

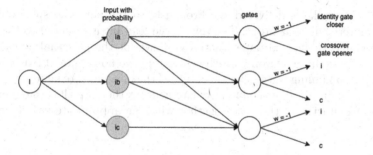

Fig. 8. The random point maker that connects to the gates of the crossover ensemble. This ensemble determines the point of the chromosomes where the identity ends and the swapping of genes with each other starts. It makes sure that there is an equal probability for every point in the chromosome to be the start of crossing over the remaining genes.

Mutation Ensemble. The final ensemble in the parallel design is responsible for the stochastic mutation of the genes in the chromosomes, meaning turning a 1 into a 0 or vice versa (Fig. 9). The way it is implemented is through assigning a probability P to each of the genes, and therefore neurons, to switch their activity. Except for the lead bit (Ia), every input-neuron (Ib, Ic) is connected to two neurons, and both of their thresholds are influenced by the switching-probability through $T = 2 - P$. A noise factor is present in both intermediate neurons, its function being to add randomness as to whether a neuron will mutate or not. In the diagram the first of the two intermediate neurons is responsible for potentially turning off the activation in case that the input neuron has spiked, and the other is responsible for the opposite. Each of the input neurons is connected directly to its corresponding output neuron, however this connection is delayed

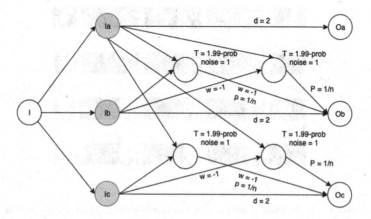

Fig. 9. The parallel mutation ensemble. This ensemble makes sure that every gene's bit has a chance to be swapped.

such that its spike is delivered synchronously to the potential spike of one of the two intermediate neurons. The role of the lead bit is essential to the mutation ensemble, as its guaranteed activity allows for the potential activation of the two intermediate neurons, which otherwise have no chance of reaching their threshold. Combining the stochastic nature of the intermediate neurons, together with the configuration of the intermediate neurons then has the desired effect of a random mutation of the gene together with the appropriate switching of its value.

4   Analysis

A raster plot of the output neurons of the sequential bubble sort ensemble is given in Fig. 10. It shows the improving solution quality over time, with the top chromosome reaching one-max, and also shows some resemblance of the fitness hierarchy, with better solutions being closer to the top (subject to imperfect sorting). Figure 11 confirms that the top chromosome in the hierarchy has a higher than average fitness, which specifically shows that even the single pairwise bubble sort step at each generation is enough to at least approximate a fitness ranking.

To assess the tractability of our two designs, a complexity analysis is performed. Computational complexity for neuromorphic computing is considered in terms of space, time, and energy, measured as the number of spikes. For this analysis, all three complexities have been considered with regard to the number of chromosomes and the chromosome length. Comparing the complexity of

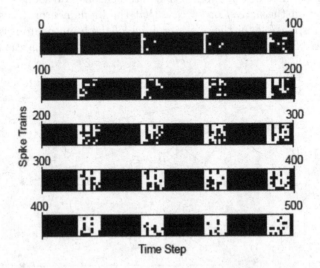

Fig. 10. Raster plot of bubble sort output neurons over time in the sequential design (8 chromosomes of length 8, for 500 steps). Each row of pixels depicts a neural spike train over 500 simulation steps. The solution quality is improving over time, with the top chromosome reaching one-max.

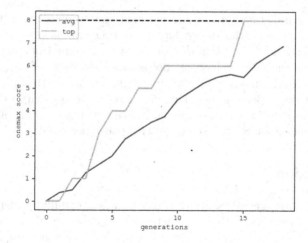

Fig. 11. Average and best solution quality over generations (8 chromosomes of length 8, for 500 steps). The fitness hierarchy results in the top chromosome having better fitness than the average. While this plot comes from the sequential design, the parallel design behaves similarly.

the sequential and parallel design shows a space-time trade-off between the two (Table 1), with the sequential design requiring less space but more time. Both designs have linear space complexity in the number of chromosomes, both in terms of the number of neurons and the number of connections. The sequential design has much lower space requirements however.

Table 1. Complexity analysis of space, time, and energy (number of spikes) for both the sequential and the parallel design. There is a trade-off between space and time comparing the two designs, with the sequential design requiring less space but more time.

		n_chromosomes		len_chromosomes	
		Sequential	Parallel	Sequential	Parallel
Space	Neurons	$O(n)$	$O(n)$	$O(1)$	$O(n)$
	Connections	$O(n)$	$O(n)$	$O(1)$	$O(n^2)$
Time		$O(1)$	$O(1)$	$O(n)$	$O(1)$
Energy		$O(n)$	$O(n)$	$O(n)$	$O(n)$

Regarding the chromosome length, the sequential design has constant space complexity, while the parallel design is linear in the number of neurons and quadratic in the number of connections. This is the least favorable of all measured behaviors. It is specifically caused by the current implementation of randomly determining a crossover point. Both designs have constant time complexity in the number of chromosomes, with time measured in simulation steps per generation.

While the parallel design also has constant time complexity in the chromosome length, the sequential design has linear time complexity. The sequential design inherently needs to have at least linear time complexity in the chromosome length, as the full chromosome needs to be accessed before an evaluation can be made. This is an advantage for the parallel design, as the full chromosome is available at once. Both designs have linear energy complexity in the number of chromosomes and in the chromosome length, when measuring energy as the average number of spikes required to process one generation.

5   Discussion

A fully functioning genetic algorithm has been successfully implemented as a spiking neural network with two different designs, representing chromosomes sequentially as a spike train over time or as parallel spikes at a single time step. Both implementations are freely scalable beyond a small minimum number of chromosomes, with arbitrary chromosome lengths. The complexity analysis of space, time and energy shows the tractability of this approach with the exception of the quadratically growing number of connections required for the parallel design when increasing chromosome length. The sequential design is at most linear in any of the analyzed complexities. There is a trade-off between the increased time complexity of the former and increased space complexity of the latter.

The design has not yet been implemented on neuromorphic hardware. Since fairly standard leaky integrate-and-fire neurons were used, however, and no learning is required, translating the design to an implementation in neuromorphic hardware should be relatively straight-forward.

For future work, the design of the crossover ensembles could be adapted to support gene lengths of more than one bit (a chromosome consists of a number of genes, which itself could consist of a number of bases/bits). Practically this just means that the random crossover point should only be allowed at transition points between genes, so at fixed intervals. This would allow for more complex behavior of the genetic algorithm.

More work needs to be done on the evaluation strategy, which under the current design requires a unique neural ensemble purpose-built for the optimization task at hand and thereby presents a hurdle for practical application. One possibility for a more general approach would be to train a spiking neural network to perform approximate evaluations for the given task, instead of hand-engineering the neural ensemble for exact solutions as is performed in this paper.

References

1. Bagchi, S., Bhat, S.S., Kumar, A.: O(1) time sorting algorithms using spiking neurons. In: 2016 International Joint Conference on Neural Networks (IJCNN), pp. 1037–1043. IEEE (2016). https://doi.org/10.1109/ijcnn.2016.7727312

2. Burkitt, A.N.: A review of the integrate-and-fire neuron model: I. Homogeneous synaptic input. Biol. Cybernet. **95**(1), 1–19 (2006). https://doi.org/10.1007/s00422-006-0068-6
3. Deb, K.: Multi-objective Optimization Using Evolutionary Algorithms, vol. 16. Wiley, New York (2001)
4. Ghosh-Dastidar, S., Adeli, H.: Spiking neural networks. Int. J. Neural Syst. **19**(04), 295–308 (2009). https://doi.org/10.1142/s0129065709002002
5. Holland, J.H.: Genetic algorithms. Sci. Am. **267**(1), 66–73 (1992)
6. Koza, J.R.: Genetic Programming: On the Programming of Computers by Means of Natural Selection, vol. 1. MIT Press, Cambridge (1992)
7. Kumar, M., Husain, M., Upreti, N., Gupta, D.: Genetic algorithm: review and application. Available at SSRN **3529843** (2010). https://doi.org/10.2139/ssrn.3529843
8. Lin, C.K., et al.: Programming spiking neural networks on intel's Loihi. Computer **51**(3), 52–61 (2018). https://doi.org/10.1109/mc.2018.157113521
9. Mead, C.: Neuromorphic electronic systems. Proc. IEEE **78**(10), 1629–1636 (1990). https://doi.org/10.1109/5.58356
10. Merolla, P.A., et al.: A million spiking-neuron integrated circuit with a scalable communication network and interface. Science **345**(6197), 668–673 (2014). https://doi.org/10.1126/science.1254642
11. Schuman, C.D., et al.: Shortest path and neighborhood subgraph extraction on a spiking memristive neuromorphic implementation. In: Proceedings of the 7th Annual Neuro-inspired Computational Elements Workshop, pp. 1–6 (2019). https://doi.org/10.1145/3320288.3320290
12. Schuman, C.D., et al.: A survey of neuromorphic computing and neural networks in hardware. arXiv preprint arXiv:1705.06963 (2017)
13. Whitley, L.D., et al.: The genitor algorithm and selection pressure: why rank-based allocation of reproductive trials is best. In: ICGA. vol. 89, pp. 116–123. Fairfax, VA (1989)
14. Yakopcic, C., Rahman, N., Atahary, T., Taha, T.M., Douglass, S.: Solving constraint satisfaction problems using the Loihi spiking neuromorphic processor. In: 2020 Design, Automation & Test in Europe Conference & Exhibition (DATE), pp. 1079–1084. IEEE (2020). https://doi.org/10.23919/date48585.2020.9116227
15. Young, A.R., Dean, M.E., Plank, J.S., Rose, G.S.: A review of spiking neuromorphic hardware communication systems. IEEE Access **7**, 135606–135620 (2019). https://doi.org/10.1109/access.2019.2941772

Solving Hofstadter's Analogies Using Structural Information Theory

Geerten Rijsdijk$^{(\boxtimes)}$ and Giovanni Sileno$^{(\boxtimes)}$

Informatics Institute, University of Amsterdam, Amsterdam, The Netherlands
geerten.rijsdijk@student.uva.nl, g.sileno@uva.nl

Abstract. Analogies are common part of human life; our ability to handle them is critical in problem solving, humor, metaphors and argumentation. This paper introduces a method to solve string-based (symbolic) analogies based on hybrid inferential process integrating Structural Information Theory—a framework used to predict phenomena of perceptual organization—with some metric-based processing. Results are discussed against two empirical experiments, one of which conducted along this work, together with the development of a Python version of the SIT encoding algorithm PISA.

Keywords: Analogical reasoning · Symbolic analogies · Compression · Structural information theory · Complexity

1 Introduction

Analogies are common part of human life; our ability to handle them is critical in problem solving, humor, metaphors and argumentation [8]. In psychology, analogy is seen as the process of understanding new information by means of structural similarities with previously acquired information [10], and analogical reasoning is one of the predominantly measured abilities on IQ tests. Because of their importance to cognition, analogies have interested researchers in the field of artificial intelligence. Systems for the computation of analogies have been created since the '60s for many different purposes such as solving puzzles based on objects in images [3], obtaining information by inference [9], understanding the development in analogical reasoning in children [16], or even as support in suggesting specialized care for patients with dementia [21]. Recent contributions in natural language processing [14] have suggested that analogical inference can be directly performed as vector operations on word vectors (e.g., `Paris` $\approx$ `France` + `Berlin` − `Germany`). However, even if some machine learning methods have proven to be unexpectedly good at reproducing some of these inferences, the overall results are not yet conclusive [18]. The centrality of analogies in human reasoning motivates to continue the effort to find a better understanding of their underlying mechanisms.

The aim of this paper is to offer an alternative solution to string-based (or symbolic) analogies as those proposed by Hofstadter [8]. The contribution is a hybrid inferential process integrating *Structural Information Theory* (SIT),

© Springer Nature Switzerland AG 2021
M. Baratchi et al. (Eds.): BNAIC/Benelearn 2020, CCIS 1398, pp. 106–121, 2021.
https://doi.org/10.1007/978-3-030-76640-5_7

introduced to predict phenomena of perceptual organization, with some metric-based processing depending on the atomic components of the input. Thanks to an anonymous reviewer we discovered that such an application of SIT has been explored before [1], with a investigation on the algebraic properties of SIT extended with domain-dependent operators (e.g., *succ* to produce consecutive symbols). However, that work was presented before the creation of the minimal encoding algorithm PISA used in the present research to conduct our experiments. Even if preliminary, the results of the method we propose go beyond the state of art both in terms of the types of analogy it can deal with and its speed. Additionally, we report on the development of a Python version of the SIT encoding algorithm PISA, modified to consider various methods to compute (descriptive) complexity. The code used for this work is publicly available.[1]

The paper proceeds as follows: in the remainder of this section, Hofstadter's analogies and Structural Information Theory are briefly introduced. Section 2 outlines the analogy solving algorithm, and presents in detail the different components. Section 3 briefly discusses the Python implementation of PISA. In Sect. 4, the algorithm is evaluated on two datasets, and its performance is compared to that of *Metacat*. The paper ends with a discussion and a conclusion.

1.1 Hofstadter's Analogies

Schematically, an analogy can often be expressed as "A is to B what C is to D" (also known as *proportional analogy*). In order to model and perform simple but relevant experiments on analogical reasoning, Douglas Hofstadter proposed a micro-world for analogy-making at the end of the '80s [15]. In this microworld, the objects used for the analogies are strings of letters. An example of such an analogy is:

ABC:*ABD*::*BCD*:?

which should be read as: "*ABC* is to *ABD* like *BCD* is to?". The answer commonly given by respondents to this test is *BCE*.

In order to predict human answers, Hofstadter created a computer program called Copycat [15]. To complete a given analogy, the program works with "agents", which gradually build up structures representing the understanding of the problem, eventually reaching a solution. Later the Copycat program was improved to Metacat [13], which adds a memory, allowing the program to prevent itself from performing actions it has previously tried. *Metacat*, which was last updated in 2016[2], represents plausibly the state of the art of algorithms available for this problem.

1.2 Structural Information Theory

Structural Information Theory, or SIT, is a theory about perception with roots in *Gestalt* psychology. Central to SIT is the *simplicity principle*, in practice a

---

[1] http://github.com/GeertenRijsdijk/SIT_analogies.
[2] http://science.slc.edu/~jmarshall/metacat/.

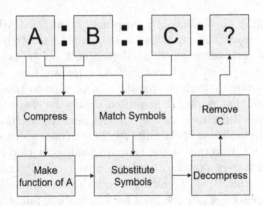

Fig. 1. Outline of the process used to answer an analogy of the form $A{:}B{::}C{:}?$.

formalization of Occam's razor: the simplest explanation for data is likely to be the correct one [11]. SIT has been empirically validated in several cognitive experiments with human participants [6,11].

SIT proposes to map the application of the simplicity principle to the Minimal Encoding Problem using the SIT language: given a string, use regularities to find an encoding with as little *complexity* as possible [11]. Such encoding can also be seen as a *compression*, since it may greatly decrease the amount of memory needed to store strings. There are three regularities/operators considered in the SIT coding language: *iteration* (I-form), *symmetry* (S-form) and *alternation* (A-form). They are defined in the following way:

I-form: $n * (y)$ $\Rightarrow yyy...y$ (n times, $n \geq 2$)
S-form: $S[(x_0)(x_1)...(x_n),(p)]$ $\Rightarrow x_0x_1...x_npx_n...x_1x_0$
S-form: $S[(x_0)(x_1)...(x_n)]$ $\Rightarrow x_0x_1...x_nx_n...x_1x_0$
A-form: $<(y)>/<(x_0)(x_1)...(x_n)> \Rightarrow yx_0yx_1...yx_n$
A-form: $<(x_0)(x_1)...(x_n)>/<(y)> \Rightarrow x_0yx_1...yx_ny$

(The p in a S-form is an optional element, called *pivot*.) These regularities have been proven to be the only ones which are *holographic* and *transparent* [5]. Holographic means invariant under growth, e.g., a repetition of n symbols can have that same symbol added to it forever, and will remain a repetition. Transparent means that the arguments of a regularity occur linearly in the original string it encodes. With alternations, while the arguments can occur non-consecutively, they still occur in the same linear order.

2   Analogy Solving

Analogies rely on a perceived underlying structures (see e.g., Structural Mapping Theory [4]). Both Copycat [15] and Metacat [13] are based on the idea that there are structures on one side of the analogy that need to be replicated on the other side. Their "agents" are functionally meant to identify the structures to be mapped. At functional level, however, what these agents do is nothing else than *compressing* the symbolic input, and this means that other compressors may work as well.

Figure 1 outlines the higher-level process that was followed to produce an analogical inference. In an analogy of form A:B::C:?, it is expected that there exists a certain structure in the left-hand side A:B, which can be extracted by means of some compression method. By applying this same structure to the partially available right-hand side C, decompressing the resulting code and taking away the part C, a possible answer to the analogy can be found.

2.1 Structural Compression

The SIT encoding defines a way—empirically validated on perceptual experiments—to compress strings and is therefore a plausible candidate for describing regularities emerging from the input. Indeed, handling strings—here seen as ordered lists of characters, not as words from some language—seems to be based primarily on perceptual mechanisms rather than on semantics.

Applying SIT on analogical inference, we decided to extract the structure of A:B focusing on the concatenated string A+B. The idea of compressing A and B together, rather than separately, is inspired by the technique used in the famous paper by Li and Vitanji on the *Similarity Metric* [12], in which concatenations a.o. of DNA-sequences of two species were compressed to find a measure of their similarity. In our case, we used for compression the PISA algorithm (Parameter load plus ISA-rules) [7], a minimal coding algorithm proposed specifically for SIT [7]. For example, in the problem $ABC{:}ABD{::}IJK{:}?$, the minimal code (or compression) of the concatenated left-hand side $ABC{:}ABD$ would be $S[(AB),(C)]D$ or $<(AB)><(C)(D)>$. PISA is currently the most optimized algorithm for performing this task, being only weakly exponential. Along with this work, a Python implementation of this algorithm is presented.

2.2 Generating Symbols from Symbols

To apply the structure extracted from the left-hand side of the analogy (namely from A+B) to the right-hand side (C+?), this structure needs to be defined only as a function of symbols in A, as only the first part of the right hand is known. The symbols in B need to be generated from the symbols in A, and for this some invertible function capturing an adequate relationship between the atomic symbols is needed. The SIT coding language cannot do this; the only relationship this language considers is the *identity* relationship: denoting an atomic component of perception with a or z is completely arbitrary; the only assumption is that all a or z map to the same type of atomic component.

In contrast, Hofstadter's analogies seem to rely on some metrical information. For instance, d is the most natural answer to the analogy $a{:}b{::}c{:}?$, obtained by *contrasting* the b and a (as objects in an alphabet) and applying the output of this operation on c. The role of contrast in concept construction, similarity and description generation is indeed central [2, 20]. For alphabetic characters as in Hofstadter's analogies, contrast between symbols can be simply defined as a directional distance between the positions of those symbols in the alphabet. So, for example, the distance between b and a is 1, and the distance between a and e is -4. This allow us to rewrite symbols in B as one of the symbol in A and a directional distance. A challenge that arises with this approach is *which symbol the distance should be calculated from*. We attempted multiple approaches to this problem, some of which were more useful in different situations than others.

Previous Symbol Strategy. The simplest way of deciding which symbol to calculate distance from is to choose the *previous symbol*. For example, in the analogy $a{:}bcd{::}i{:}?$, the left part $abcd$ can be described as $a(\$+1)(\$+1)(\$+1)$, where $\$$ refers here to the last symbol used in the code. This same structure can be applied to obtain the plausible (see Sect. 4) right-hand side $i{:}jkl$.

Last New Symbol Strategy. There are however analogies where this approach fails. Take the analogy $aba{:}aca{::}ada{:}?$, in which $abaaca$ gets encoded as $S[(a),(b)]$ $S[(a),(c)]$. When distances are applied, the code becomes $S[(a),(b)]$ $S[(a),((\$+2))]$. Now, when the symbol b is substituted by the symbol d, the decompressed code becomes $adaaca$, resulting in solution aca, whereas aea is a much more plausible answer. An approach solving this issue is choosing the *last new symbol* in the organization extracted using SIT. In the previous example, the last new symbol is b, the mapping would then result in $S[(a),(b)]$ $S[(a),((\$\$+1))]$, where $\$\$$ is the last new symbol used in the organization. Substituting b with d would result in $S[(a),(d)]$ $S[(a),((\$\$+1))]$, decompressing into the expected $adaaea$.

Same Position Strategy. These approaches do not use the actual position of symbols in the input string, but this does seem to play a role at times. Consider for instance $ae{:}bd{::}cc{:}?$. Here, a plausible answer would be db, where the change applied to the string is an increase by 1 for the first element, and a decrease by 1 for the second. In a case like this, a position-based approach would be useful, resulting in code $ae(a+1)(e-1)$ or $ae(\$\$\$+1)(\$\$\$-1)$, where $\$\$\$$ is the object in A in the same position of the object in B. However, this approach cannot be used when parts A, B and C of the analogy have different lengths.

2.3   Symbol Substitution

Once the compression of A+B has been defined using only symbols present in A, a substitution (or replacement) of the symbols in A with the symbols in C can be performed. In order to do so, A and C need to be represented in ways that allow the mapping of their components. Here too, different strategies have been tried, selecting the best depending on the case.

Representation as Strings. The simplest way to represent A and C is in their input form: strings, i.e., ordered lists of characters, in which each symbol counts as one element. However, there are cases in which this method is not applicable, as for instance when A and C do not share the same length.

Representation by Compression. The number of elements in the representation can be reduced by compressing the string and seeing it as a list of symbols and *highest level operators*. For example, $ijjkkk$ can be compressed into $i2*(j)3*(k)$, which is then split into i, $2*(j)$ and $3*(k)$. When a highest level operator has been used to replace a symbol, this operator itself will count as one symbol for the purposes of calculating new symbols from distances. If a distance was calculated from a symbol that has since been replaced by an operator, the entire operator will be carried over as the new element, and each individual symbol in this operator is increased by the distance. Consider the analogy abc:abd::$ijjkkk$:?:

- structure of A+B: $<(ab)>/<(c)(($ +1))>$
- structure of C: $i\ 2*(j)\ 3*(k)$
- substitution: $(a \rightarrow i), (b \rightarrow 2*(j)), (c \rightarrow 3*(k))$
- structure of C+D: $<(i2*(j))>/<(3*(k))(($ +1))>$
- distances removed: $<(i2*(j))>/<(3*(k))(3*(l))>$
- decompression: $ijjkkkijjlll$
- result D: $ijjlll$

Representation by Chunking. Alternatively, A and C can be represented in terms of *chunkings*, meaning divisions of the concatenated input symbol strings into chunks. These chunks can then be replaced as if they concerned one element. For example, $abcd$ could be chunked into $[ab, cd], [a, bc, d], [a, b, c, d]$, and so on. For A, the chunkings are derived from the compression of A+B, e.g.,:

- $[a, b, c]$ is a chunking of abc in the compression $S[(a)(b), (c)]c$.
- $[ab, c]$ is a chunking of abc in the compression $ab2*(c)(\$ +1)(\$ +1)$.
- $[ab, c]$ is a chunking of abc in the compression $<(ab)>/<(c)(($ +1))>$.
- $[abc]$ is a chunking of abc in the compression $2*(abc)$.

For C, there is no pre-existing structure present that determines how it should be chunked. However, we considered sound to chunk C in such a way that it best corresponds to the chunking of A.

We call the process of creating a chunking of C as similar as possible to a chunking of A *chunking-element matching*, and works as follows: a list is created for the number of symbols in each element in the chunking of A. (e.g., $[a, bc, def]$ results in $[1, 2, 3]$). Next, if the sum of the numbers does not equal the number of symbols in C, as a simple heuristic, the largest number in this list is increased/decreased. Now, this list of numbers can be used to split C into chunks, which can be used to substitute the original elements of the chunking of A. The following example shows how this chunking matching is used to solve an analogy abc:abd::$ijklm$:?

- structure of A+B: $<(ab)>/<(c)(($ +1))>$
- chunking of A in A+B: $[ab, c]$
- lengths of chunking elements of A: $[2, 1]$
- matching chunking lengths of C: $[4, 1]$
- chunking of C: $[ijkl, m]$

- substitution: $(ab \rightarrow ijkl), (c \rightarrow m)$
- structure of C+D: $<(ijkl)>/<(m)(($ $+1))>$
- distances removed: $<(ijkl)>/<(m)(n)>$
- decompression: $ijklmijkln$
- result D: $ijkln$

Representation by Consecutive Chunking. A special type of chunking is a *consecutive chunking*. A chunking is consecutive if all elements of the chunking contain exactly one symbol; the elements of the chunking together form all arguments of a single operator. For instance, $[a, b, c]$ is a consecutive chunking of abc in the code $<(a)(b)(c)>/<(d)>$, and $[a, b, c]$ is a consecutive chunking of abc in the code $S[(a)(b), (c)]$. Consecutive chunkings can be substituted in a special way: instead of replacing individual symbols or elements, the entire chunking can be replaced by a new chunking. The new chunking has one element for every symbol in C. When this consecutive chunking is applied, the entire argument string forming A is replaced with this new chunking (with the corresponding number of parentheses per element). For instance in $abc:cba::ijklm:?$:

- structure of A+B: $S[(a)(b)(c)]$
- consecutive chunking of A in A+B: $[a, b, c]$
- consecutive chunking of C: $[i, j, k, l, m]$
- substitution: $([(a), (b), (c)] \rightarrow [(i), (j), (k), (l), (m)])$
- structure of C+D: $S[(i)(j)(k)(l)(m)]$
- decompression: $ijklmmlkji$
- result D: $mlkji$

2.4   Structure in Parameters

Consider the analogy $aaabb:aabbb::eeeeef:?$. One way to look at it is that the analogy simply swaps the number of times the first symbol occurs with the number of times the second symbol occurs. However, PISA assigns to A+B the structure $3 * (a)S[2 * ((b))(a)]b$, which does not seem to capture this intuition, as there is no symbol substitution that results in the expected answer *efffff*. The core of this analogy problem does not lie in the structure of the symbols, but in the structure of the structure. By looking at the structure as a series of iterations, this becomes clear; in $3 * (a)2 * (b)2 * (a)3 * (b)$, the parameters of the iterations form a symmetry, namely $S[(3)(2)]$. It is this symmetry that forms a plausible basis for solving this analogy. The function written to apply this strategy is separated from the rest of the algorithm. It encodes A+B as a sequence of iterations. Next, the parameters of these iterations are compressed, distances are added and symbol substitution is performed in essentially the same way as described before. This results in new parameters which, combined with symbol substitution on the actual symbols, can produce an answer to the analogy.

However, problems of this type can easily become more complex. When the parameters of a structure can have a structure, the parameters of *that* structure could also have a structure, which could again have parameters with some structure. With larger codes, this 'parameter depth' could become very high.

Algorithm 1: PISA-based compressor

```
 1  Function compress_pisa(graph)
 2  │   new_hyperstrings = []
 3  │   for hyperstring h in graph do
 4  │   │   Q = QUIS(h)
 5  │   │   Create and encode S-graphs of h using Q
 6  │   │   for w in h.nodes[1 ... N] do
 7  │   │   │   Create and encode A-graphs of h using Q, up to node w
 8  │   │   │   for v in h.nodes[w ... 0] do
 9  │   │   │   │   find best possible code for v → w
10  │   │   │   │   add best code to h as edge v → w
11  │   │   │   │   for u in h.nodes[0 ... v] do
12  │   │   │   │   │   if c(u, w) > c(u,v) + c(v,w) then
13  │   │   │   │   │   │   new_code = u → v + v → w
14  │   │   │   │   │   │   add new_code to h as edge u → w
15  │   │   add h to new_hyperstrings;
16  │   return combine(new_hyperstrings);
```

Furthermore, relationships between parameters at different 'depths' are also possible. Take for instance the analogy $abc\!:\!aaabbbccc\!:\!:\!abcd\!:$. The structure of the parameters could be written as $3*(1)3*(3)$ (neglecting the internal relationships between symbols). To get to a plausible answer $aaaabbbbccccdddd$, there would need to be a relationship between the two 3s out of brackets, and the 3 inside the brackets, which are at different parameter depths. In short, structure in parameters can be very complex. In this work, it has only been explored at a surface level. Other configurations are left to future work.

2.5   Inversion Trick

When A:B::C:? does not have a structure that is easily worked with, it is also possible to rearrange the analogy to hopefully obtain better answers. This rearrangement is analogous to this numeric equivalence: $\frac{a}{b} = \frac{c}{d} \Leftrightarrow \frac{a}{c} = \frac{b}{d}$. In our case, while the two forms of analogies might often result in the same answers, one of the two forms might be more solvable using the approach proposed here. An example of this is the analogy $abac\!:\!adae\!:\!:\!baca\!:\!?$. A+B has a structure of form $<(a)>/<(.)>$, while the left side has a structure of form $<(.)>/<(a)>$. This change in structure is a problem for our algorithm, since it tries to apply the same structure to C+D. Changing the analogy to $abac\!:\!baca\!:\!:\!adae\!:\!?$ results in the structure $S[(a)(bac)]$, which is a structure the solver can deal with more easily.

3   Python Implementation of PISA

A string of length N can be represented by up to a superexponential $O(2^{N log(N)})$ number of codes [7]. To find the one with the lowest complexity, one could generate each possible code and compare all of these. For long strings this can be very time consuming. The PISA (Parameter load plus ISA-rules) algorithm was designed to efficiently find the minimal coding of a string in the SIT coding language [7]. PISA is significantly faster than a method which generates all possible encodings, being only weakly exponential. A dissection of the PISA algorithm can be found in Chapter 5 of *Simplicity in Vision* [6]. Here, we will briefly discuss our re-implementation in Python.

The PISA-based compressor created for this research is written in an object-oriented fashion (the original version[3], being in C, does not support classes), with a central *hyperstring* class. The general outline of the algorithm written for this research can be seen in Algorithm 1. The algorithm processes each hyperstring in the input graph separately (line 3). In line 4, the QUIS algorithm [6] is called for each hyperstring to create an intermediate structure to more efficient representations. The output matrix is indeed used in line 5 and 7 to create S- and A-graphs, representing symmetries and alternations present in the hyperstring. These graphs are themselves also encoded using this function. Lines 6 and 8 loop over every combination of two nodes (v, w) in the hyperstring. For each pair, lines 9 looks for the best possible code for the substring between these two nodes. Using the complexity metric, this best code is chosen from: the current code; the best possible iteration, if any; the best possible symmetry, if any, calculated using the S-graph that has a pivot halfway in between the two nodes; the best possible alternation, if any, calculated for every A-graph. Once the best code has been selected, line 10 adds an edge representing the code to the hyperstring. Next, line 11 iterates over every node that comes before node v. Line 12 looks at the complexities of the codes between u, v and w. If the complexity of the edge $u \to w$ can be reduced by creating a combination of the codes in edges $u \to v$ and $v \to w$, this is done. At the end of the algorithm, all encoded hyperstrings are recombined into a new graph. This graph is then returned.

Given a hyperstring that represents a mere string, the same hyperstring is returned with added edges that represent the best code for each substring, and the code of the edge connecting the first and last node of the hyperstring will be the best encoding of the entire string.

3.1   Configurable Complexity Metric

Besides reproducibility, a major reason why we reimplemented PISA was to gain control over its components, in particular the way in which complexity is measured. The original PISA relies only on one metric, the I_{new} load [7]. We considered instead as basis the more general principles of Kolmogorov complexity [19]. At a more fundamental level, SIT has been conceived for structural information, but analogies require also to look at some metrical information. The complexity metric considered here calculates complexity by taking the number of symbols used for the code and adding, for each operator in the code, a certain value. This value might differ across operators, and can be adjusted later with

---

[3] https://ppw.kuleuven.be/apps/petervanderhelm/doc/pisa.html

empirical data to find the values for optimal performance of the analogy solving algorithm. Indeed, the I_{new} load does not allow for adjusting of parameters for aligning to human answers and seems somewhat unintuitive, assigning e.g., the same complexity to the codes a and $9 * (a)$.

3.2   Other Differences with PISA

This implementation relies heavily on the theoretical concepts of hyperstrings, S-graphs and A-graphs as PISA does. However, in some points we found the exact working of PISA to be unclear, and that meant that we had to fill in the blanks. The following list outlines the major differences between the two algorithms.

- The explanation of PISA in [6] mentions 'updating its database of S- and A-graphs' at the end of the first for loop. It is however not clear how this update is done. In the proposed compressor the graphs are not updated, but recreated each time.
- PISA updates the A-graphs at the *end* of the first for loop, while this compressor recreates the A-graphs at the *start* of the first for loop. A small exception to this is present in the code; at the end of each v loop, the algorithm does update the repeats of right a-graphs with the encodings of the $v \rightarrow w$ edge. This is not necessary for left a-graphs due to the algorithm encoding the string left to right.
- PISA updates the S-graphs at the *end* of the first for loop, while this compressor creates the S-graphs before the first for loop.
- PISA always returns the one code with the lowest complexity, while this compressor returns a Graph object. In this object, the edge connecting the first and last nodes also represents the edge with the lowest complexity, but other paths represent other codes, which consist of optimally encoded substrings which together form the whole string. This enables us to consider sub-optimal codes as well.

4   Results

To evaluate the proposed analogy solving algorithm, the answers generated by it will be compared against two sets of human answers obtained in distinct experiments. Furthermore, the answers generated by the proposed solver will also be compared to the answers generated by *Metacat* [13].

4.1   Murena's Dataset

Table 1 reports data published by Murena et al. [17] on human answers for analogy tests. In their experiment, 68 participants were asked to solve analogies following the template $ABC:ABD::X:?$. The left-hand side of the analogy remained the same during the experiment, but the X changed in every test. For each X, the data shows the two most common answers given by participants, as well as the percentage of

Table 1. Human answers to analogies of form $ABC{:}ABD{::}X{:}?$ from the Murena dataset 1, along with at which position the same answers were given by the solving algorithm proposed in this project (P_s) and *Metacat* (P_M).

Given X	Solutions	Selected by	P_s	P_M	Given X	Solutions	Selected by	P_s	P_M
IJK	IJL	**93%**	1	1	BCD	BCE	**81%**	2	1
	IJD	2.9%	–	–		BDE	5.9%	1	–
BCA	BCB	**49%**	3	2	IJJKKK	IJJLLL	**40%**	1	2
	BDA	43%	1	1		IJJKKL	25%	2	1
AABABC	AABABD	**74%**	1	1	XYZ	XYA	**85%**	1	–
	AACABD	12%	–	–		IJD	4.4%	–	–
IJKLM	IJKLN	**62%**	1	1	RSSTTT	RSSUUU	**41%**	1	1
	IJLLM	15%	–	–		RSSTTU	31%	2	–
KJI	KJJ	**37%**	1	1	MRRJJJ	MRRJJK	**28%**	2	1
	LJI	32%	–	2		MRRKKK	19%	1	2
ACE	ACF	**63%**	1	1					
	ACG	8.9%	–	–					

participants that chose that answer.[4] The last two columns in the Table 1 show the performances of the analogy solving algorithm proposed in this project (P_s) and *Metacat* (P_M) ins terms of the position in which that answer was generated (e.g., a 1 means it was the best answer, 2 means it was the second best, etc.). A dash indicates that the answer was not generated at all. As for speed, the lack of a built-in way to measure the time *Metacat* uses for compression made it difficult to perform an empirical speed comparison. However, when working with *Metacat*, it was clear that this method is much slower than the solver implemented here, sometimes taking more than 10 min to generate a single answer. For this reason, only two answers per question were generated using *Metacat*.

The table shows that, for this dataset, the most common answer to the problem is always generated by our solver. Furthermore, the top answer generated by the solver is always one of the two most common answers by the participants. Both of these observations are also true for *Metacat*, with the exception of the problem XYZ, for which it produced none of the answers given by participants. However, there are also answers given by human participants that the solvers did not generate. Overall, the most common human answer matched the top answer 8/11 times (72.7%), both for our solver and *Metacat*. The most common participant answer was in the top 2 generated answers 10/11 times (90.9%) for both algorithms. Answers given by participants were generated 16/22 times (72.7%) for our solver and 14/22 times (63.7%) for *Metacat*.

4.2   Our Dataset

The Murena testset is quite small and the analogies it presents follow all the same template. For this reason, a second testset was constructed on purpose for

---

[4] In the original experiments some questions were repeated to see the influence of having previously faced similar problems. Since the solving algorithm in this project runs independently of previous answers, repeated questions were omitted here.

Table 2. Human answers to analogies collected in this project experiment, along with at which position the same answers were given by the solving algorithm proposed in this project and *Metacat*.

Given problem	Solutions	Selected by	P_s	P_M
ABA:ACA::ADA:?	AEA	**97.1%**	1	1
	AFA	2.9%	–	–
ABAC:ADAE::BACA:?	DAEA	**60%**	2	–
	BCCC	28.6%	21	–
AE:BD::CC:?	DB	**68.5%**	3	1
	CC	17.1%	–	2
ABBB:AAAB::IIIJJ:?	IIJJJ	**57.1%**	1	–
	JJIII	14,3%	–	–
ABC:CBA::MLKJI:?	IJKLM	**88.6%**	1	1
	–	–	–	–
ABCB:ABCB::Q:?	Q	**100.0%**	1	–
	–	–	–	–
ABC:BAC::IJKL:?	JIKL	**54.3%**	–	–
	KIJL	14.3%	2	–
ABACA:BC::BACAD:?	AA	**57.1%**	1	–
	BCD	31.4%	–	–
AB:ABC::IJKL:?	IJKLM	**85.7%**	1	1
	IJKLMN	11.4%	–	–
ABC:ABBACCC::FED:?	FEEFDDD	**91.4%**	2	1
	–	–	–	–
ABC:BBC::IKM:?	JKM	**57.1%**	7	–
	KKM	37.1%	2	–
ABAC:ACAB::DEFG:?	DGFE	**68.6%**	2	–
	FGDE	14.3%	1	–
ABC:ABD::CBA:?	DBA	**51.4%**	1	2
	CBB	45.7%	2	1
ABAC:ADAE::FBFC:?	FDFE	**94.3%**	1	–
	FDFA	2.9%	–	–
ABCD:CDAB::IJKLMN:?	LMNIJK	**80.0%**	–	–
	–	–	–	–
ABC:AAABBBCCC::ABCD:?	AAABBBCCCDDD	**74.3%**	1	1
	AAAABBBBCCCCDDDD	17.1%	–	–
ABC:ABBCCC::ABCD:?	ABBCCCDDDD	**85.7%**	–	–
	ABBCCCDDD	8.6%	1	–
ABBCCC:DDDEEF::AAABBC:?	DEEFFF	**77.1%**	1	–
	DCCDDF	8.6%	–	–
A:AA::AAA:?	AAAAAA	**62.8%**	1	–
	AAAA	25.7%	2	1
ABBA:BAAB::IJKL:?	JILK	**71.4%**	–	–
	JIJM	11.4%	5	–

this work, consisting of 20 more complex analogies. 35 participants (18 male, 17 female, average age 26.8) were asked to solve the analogies in the testset, the results of which can be seen in Table 2. As before, the table shows the top two answers given by participants, as well as the percentage of participants that gave each answer. In some cases, only the top answer is given. This is done when either all participants gave the same answer, or when there were multiple answers tied for second which all had only one participant.

In this testset, the most common answer given by participants was generated by the solver 16/20 times (80%), whereas it was generated by *Metacat* only 7/20 times (35%). The top answer given by the solver was in the top two participant answers 13/20 times (65%), whereas the top answer generated by *Metacat* was in the top two participant answers 8/20 times (40%). The most common participant answer matched the top generated 10/20 times (50%) for the solver, and 6/20 times (30%) for *Metacat*.

4.3   Complexity Values

The complexity values or weights of iteration, symmetry and alternation operators were chosen to optimize the results of the solver on the two testsets. These variables were tested with values ranging from 0.8 to 1.2, with steps of 0.1. Each possible combination of those values was tested on how highly they ranked the participant-given answers amongst all answers. Overall, it was found that small differences in the values often did not change much about the rankings, suggesting that there was not really a risk of overfitting. On a larger scale, the following requirements seem to yield the best results: the weight of iterations should be less than 1; of symmetries less than 1; of alternation more than 1. The final weights chosen were 0.85 for iterations, 0.9 for symmetries and 1.1 for alternation.

5   Discussion

The goal of this project was to use SIT compression as the basis for an analogy solving algorithm. The analogy solving algorithm has shown promising results on the test set created by Murena et al. [17]. However, this test set is very limited, having only 11 questions, each following the same template. The lack of variety and complexity motivated the creation of a second testset.

When compared to *Metacat*, our solving algorithm has shown to achieve similar results on the first testset. This is likely because the questions in this testset share a similar structure which both solvers seem to be able to deal with. On the second testset, our solving algorithm achieves drastically better results. It should, however, be noted that *Metacat* uses randomness in its procedure to generate answers. Therefore, different runs of the algorithm on the problem could result in different, and possibly better, answers. Furthermore, for this comparison, only the first two answers generated by *Metacat* were used, but *Metacat* can often generate more answers than that. The choice to only consider the top two answers was made due to time constraints: generating a single answer using *Metacat* can, in some cases, take up to 10 min, against a few seconds for our solver.

It is important also to note that problems in the second testset were created after the implementation of the solving algorithm, and with the capabilities of this solver in mind. Because of this, for many of the questions it was predictable beforehand whether the solver would produce intuitive answers. Therefore, the percentages of correct answers should not weigh heavily in the evaluation of the algorithm. Instead, the set should be used as a showcase of what types of analogies the algorithm can and cannot deal with.

Answers of the solver are ranked by the complexities of the codes they originate from, e.g., answers such as $BCCC$ (28.6%) to $ABAC{:}ADAE{::}BACA{:}?$, DB (68.5%) to $AE{:}BD{::}CC{:}?$, JKM (57.1%) to $ABC{:}BBC{::}IKM{:}?$ and $JIJM$ (11.4%) to $ABBA{:}BAAB{::}IJKL{:}?$. Despite these answers being chosen by (fairly) significant percentages of the participants, they do not rank highly amongst the answers generated by the solver. This results hints that there exist better strategies not adequately taken into account. The reasoning behind these answers (most likely) relies on applying positional distances in the left-hand side of the analogy to the right-hand side. The most significant case of this is the answer $BCCC$ to $ABAC{:}ADAE{::}BACA{:}?$, which the solver ranks lower than 20 other solutions, despite being picked by over a quarter of the participants. Future work on this project could look at alternate ways which could, either in combination with complexity or on their own, rank answers generated by the solver in a way that corresponds better to human answers.

The answer $LMNIJK$ (80.0%) to $ABCD{:}CDAB{::}IJKLMN{:}?$ might tell us something the cognitive equivalent of what in this project is called chunking (Sect. 2.3). It seems that the structure that best corresponds to participants' interpretation of this problem is $S[(ab)(cd)]$, which essentially represents a swapping of ab and cd in part A to get part B. The same structure in the right-hand side of the analogy that corresponds to the top answer is $S[(ijk)(lmn)]$. This way of symbol substitution corresponds to *chunking element matching*, described in Sect. 2.3; whereas the method used in this project tries to keep as many elements of the chunking as possible at the same length (which results in structures like $S[(ij)(klmn)]$ or $S[(ijkl)(mn)]$), the 3-3 division suggests a preference to maintain the same ratio between the chunking elements.

Finally, other answers that cannot be solved by the algorithm are the ones discussed in Sect. 2.4, where there are relationships between iteration parameters at different levels. In the test, such relationships are (most likely) used for answer $AAAABBBBCCCCDDDD$ (17.1%) to problem $ABC{:}AAABBBCCC{::} ABCD{:}?$, and answer $ABBCCCDDDD$ (85.7%) to problem $ABC{:}ABBCCC{::} ABCD{:}?$. These answers suggest that such relationships are indeed understood and used by participants, although this begs the question of how complex these relationships can be before participants will no longer base their answer on them.

6   Future Developments

Structural Information Theory has shown itself to be a useful tool for analogy solving, although it cannot do this on its own. The lack of metrical information, or a way to define relationships between symbols, resulted in the need for a way of defining symbols as distances from other symbols, as well as a way of choosing which symbol to calculate from. Similarly, the necessity to apply structure from one part of an analogy to another entailed the need for a method for symbol substitution. In this work we introduced with some success different intuitive heuristics/strategies for these two aspects, but a general, unifying theory is needed. Additionally, test data confirms that, sometimes, the structure of the symbols has structure itself (Sect. 2.4). A unifying theory based on Kolmogorov complexity might predict that further depth is considered only if yields a reduction of complexity, and this is a required focus for future works.

References

1. Dastani, M., Indurkhya, B., Scha, R.: Analogical projection in pattern perception. J. Exp. Theor. Artif. Intell. **15**(4), 489–511 (2003)
2. Dessalles, J.-L.: From conceptual spaces to predicates. In: Zenker, F., Gärdenfors, P. (eds.) Applications of Conceptual Spaces. SL, vol. 359, pp. 17–31. Springer, Cham (2015). https://doi.org/10.1007/978-3-319-15021-5_2
3. Evans, T.G.: A program for the solution of a class of geometric-analogy intelligence-test questions. Technical report, Air Force Cambridge Research Labs (1964)
4. Gentner, D.: Structure-mapping: a theoretical framework for analogy. Cogn. Sci. **7**(2), 155–170 (1983)
5. van der Helm, P.A., van Lier, R.J., Leeuwenberg, E.L.J.: Serial pattern complexity: irregularity and hierarchy. Perception **21**(4), 517–544 (1992)
6. Van der Helm, P.A.: Simplicity in Vision: A Multidisciplinary Account of Perceptual Organization. Cambridge University Press, Cambridge (2014)
7. van der Helm, P.A.: Transparallel mind: classical computing with quantum power. Artif. Intell. Rev. **44**(3), 341–363 (2015). https://doi.org/10.1007/s10462-015-9429-7
8. Hofstadter, D.R.: Analogy as the core of cognition. In: The Analogical Mind: Perspectives from Cognitive Science, pp. 499–538 (2001)
9. Hummel, J.E., Holyoak, K.J.: LISA: a computational model of analogical inference and schema induction. In: Proceedings of the Cognitive Science Society, pp. 352–357. Lawrence Erlbaum Associates, Hillsdale (1996)
10. Itkonen, E.: Analogy as Structure and Process: Approaches in Linguistics, Cognitive Psychology and Philosophy of Science, vol. 14. John Benjamins Publishing, Amsterdam (2005)
11. Leeuwenberg, E., Van der Helm, P.A.: Structural Information Theory: The Simplicity of Visual Form. Cambridge University Press, Cambridge (2013)
12. Li, M., Chen, X., Li, X., Ma, B., Vitányi, P.M.: The similarity metric. IEEE Trans. Inf. Theory **50**(12), 3250–3264 (2004)
13. Marshall, J.B.: Metacat: a self-watching cognitive architecture for analogy-making. In: Proceedings of the Cognitive Science Society, vol. 24 (2002)

14. Mikolov, T., Sutskever, I., Chen, K., Corrado, G., Dean, J.: Distributed representations of words and phrases and their compositionality. In: Advances in Neural Information Processing Systems (NIPS 2013), vol. 26, pp. 3111–3119 (2013)
15. Mitchell, M., Hofstadter, D.R.: The emergence of understanding in a computer model of concepts and analogy-making. Physica D **42**(1–3), 322–334 (1990)
16. Morrison, R.G., Doumas, L.A., Richland, L.E.: A computational account of children's analogical reasoning: balancing inhibitory control in working memory and relational representation. Dev. Sci. **14**(3), 516–529 (2011)
17. Murena, P.A., Dessalles, J.L., Cornuéjols, A.: A complexity based approach for solving Hofstadter's analogies. In: ICCBR Workshops, pp. 53–62 (2017)
18. Rogers, A., Drozd, A., Li, B.: The (too many) problems of analogical reasoning with word vectors. In: *SEM 2017–Proceedings of the 6th Joint Conference on Lexical and Computational Semantics, pp. 135–148 (2017)
19. Shen, A., Uspensky, V.A., Vereshchagin, N.: Kolmogorov Complexity and Algorithmic Randomness, vol. 220. American Mathematical Society, Providence (2017)
20. Sileno, G., Bloch, I., Atif, J., Dessalles, J.-L.: Similarity and contrast on conceptual spaces for pertinent description generation. In: Kern-Isberner, G., Fürnkranz, J., Thimm, M. (eds.) KI 2017. LNCS (LNAI), vol. 10505, pp. 262–275. Springer, Cham (2017). https://doi.org/10.1007/978-3-319-67190-1_20
21. Zachos, K., et al.: Digital creativity in dementia care support. Int. J. Creative Comput. **1**(1), 35–56 (2013)

A Semantic Tableau Method
for Argument Construction

Nico Roos[(⊠)]

Data Science and Knowledge Engineering, Maastricht University,
Maastricht, Netherlands
roos@maastrichtuniversity.nl
https://dke.maastrichtuniversity.nl/nico.roos/

Abstract. A semantic tableau method, called an argumentation tableau,
that enables the derivation of arguments, is proposed. First, the derivation
of arguments for standard propositional and predicate logic is addressed.
Next, an extension that enables reasoning with defeasible rules is presented. Finally, reasoning by cases using an argumentation tableau is
discussed.

Keywords: Semantic tableau · Argumentation system · Reasoning by
cases

1 Introduction

The semantic tableau method is used for (automated) reasoning with different
logics such as the standard propositional and predicate logic [6], several modal
logics, description logics, etc. Although a semantic tableau proof can be viewed
as an argument for a claim/conclusion, it is not similar to arguments studied
in argumentation systems; see for instance: [4,5,15,17–20,24,25,27,31,32]. This
raises the question whether the semantic tableau method can be used to derive
proper arguments for claims/conclusions.

We will address this question by first investigating a semantic tableau
method, called an argumentation tableau, for the derivation of arguments in
standard propositional and predicate logic. The use of arguments becomes more
interesting when dealing with defeasible information. That is, we consider information that need not be valid in the context of other information. We will address
the handling of defeasible information, specifically propositional and predicate
logic extended with defeasible rules. Defeasible rules are special rules without
contraposition that allow for exceptions in specific situations.

Reasoning by cases is a problem for many argumentation systems that
use an underlying language that allows for disjunctive information. Moreover,
approaches that support reasoning by cases, do not agree on how rebutting
attacks should be handled within a case [3,7,17,18,25]. We also will investigate
reasoning by cases using an argumentation tableau.

© Springer Nature Switzerland AG 2021
M. Baratchi et al. (Eds.): BNAIC/Benelearn 2020, CCIS 1398, pp. 122–140, 2021.
https://doi.org/10.1007/978-3-030-76640-5_8

The remainder of the paper is organized as follows: The next section introduces the argumentation system that will be used in the paper. Section 3 presents the argumentation tableau for standard propositional and predicate logic. Section 4 describes an argumentation tableau for propositional and predicate logic extended with defeasible rules. Section 5 discusses reasoning by cases using an argumentation tableau, and Sect. 6 concludes the paper.

2   Preliminaries

This section presents the notion of an argument that will be used in the discussion of the argumentation tableau that is proposed in this paper.

We assume a standard logic such as propositional or predicate logic. The language of the logic will be denoted by $\mathcal{L}$. We also assume that the language $\mathcal{L}$ contains the symbols $\top$ denoting *true*, and $\bot$ denoting *false*. In case of predicate logic, the set of ground terms is denoted by $\mathcal{G}$.

Since this paper focuses on argumentation, we need a definition of an argument. Toulmin [29] views an argument as a support for some *claim*. The support is grounded in *data*, and the relation between the data and the claim is the *warrant*. Here, we use the following definition.

Definition 1. *A couple $A = (\mathcal{S}, \varphi)$ is called an argument where φ is said to be its conclusion, and $\mathcal{S}$ is a set said to be its support; its elements are called supporting elements. It is worthwhile observing here that this definition is very general and a many couples might be qualified as arguments.*

In case of propositional and predicate logic, the support $\mathcal{S}$ is a set of propositions from the language $\mathcal{L}$. Generally, $\mathcal{S}$ contains the set of premises used to derive the supported proposition φ. So, $\mathcal{S} \vdash \varphi$. In special applications, such as Model-Based Diagnosis, we may restrict $\mathcal{S}$ to assumptions about the normal behavior of components.

We may extend a standard logic with a set of defeasible rules. Defeasible rules are of the form:

$$\varphi \rightsquigarrow \psi$$

in case of propositional logic, and of the form:

$$\varphi(\mathbf{x}) \rightsquigarrow \psi(\mathbf{x})$$

in case of predicate logic. Here, φ is propositions from the language $\mathcal{L}$, ψ is either a proposition from the language $\mathcal{L}$ or a negated defeasible rule of the form: $\mathbf{not}(\eta \rightsquigarrow \mu)$, and $\mathbf{x}$ is a sequence of free variables. The free variables denote a set of ground instances of the defeasible rule $\varphi(\mathbf{x}) \rightsquigarrow \psi(\mathbf{x})$. We do not use the universal quantifier because the rule is not a proposition that belongs to the language $\mathcal{L}$. It is an additional statement about preferences that need not be valid for every ground instance.

The defeasible rules $\varphi \rightsquigarrow \mathbf{not}(\eta \rightsquigarrow \mu)$ and $\varphi(\mathbf{x}) \rightsquigarrow \mathbf{not}(\eta(\mathbf{x}) \rightsquigarrow \mu(\mathbf{x}))$ are called *undercutting defeaters* [16]. These undercutting defeaters specify the conditions φ and $\varphi(\mathbf{x})$ under which the defeasible rules $\eta \rightsquigarrow \mu$ and $\eta(\mathbf{x}) \rightsquigarrow \mu(\mathbf{x})$ respectively, are not applicable.

We use $\Sigma \subseteq \mathcal{L}$ to denote the set of available information and we use D to denote the set of available rules. Moreover, we use $\overline{D} = \{\varphi(\mathbf{t}) \rightsquigarrow \psi(\mathbf{t}) \mid \varphi(\mathbf{x}) \rightsquigarrow \psi(\mathbf{x}) \in D, \mathbf{t} \in \mathcal{G}^n\}$ to denote the set of ground instances of the defeasible rules with n free variables in case of predicate logic, and $\overline{D} = D$ in case of propositional logic.

Defeasible rules are used in the construction of arguments. Whenever we have a support $\mathcal{S}'$ for the antecedent φ of a defeasible rule $\varphi \rightsquigarrow \psi$, we can create a supporting element $(\mathcal{S}', \varphi \rightsquigarrow \psi)$, which can be used to support ψ. The arguments that can be constructed are defined as:

Definition 2. *Let $\Sigma \subseteq \mathcal{L}$ be the initial information and let D be a set of defeasible rules. An argument $A = (\mathcal{S}, \psi)$ with premises $\bar{A}$, defeasible rules $\tilde{A}$, last defeasible rules $\vec{A}$, supported proposition (claim/conclusion) $\hat{A}$, and supporting propositions $\hat{S}$ of $\hat{A}$, is recursively defined as:*

- *If $\psi \in \Sigma$, then $A = (\{\psi\}, \psi)$ is an argument.*
  $\bar{A} = \{\psi\}. \quad \tilde{A} = \varnothing. \quad \hat{A} = \psi. \quad \hat{S} = \{\psi\}.$
- *If $A_1 = (\mathcal{S}_1, \varphi_1), \ldots, A_k = (\mathcal{S}_k, \varphi_k)$ are arguments and $\{\varphi_1, \ldots, \varphi_k\} \vdash \psi$, then $A = (\mathcal{S}_1 \cup \cdots \cup \mathcal{S}_k, \psi)$.*
  $\bar{A} = \bar{A}_1 \cup \cdots \cup \bar{A}_k. \quad \tilde{A} = \tilde{A}_1 \cup \cdots \cup \tilde{A}_k. \quad \vec{A} = \vec{A}_1 \cup \cdots \cup \vec{A}_k. \quad \hat{A} = \psi.$
  $\hat{S} = \hat{S}_1 \cup \cdots \cup \hat{S}_k.$
- *If $A' = (\mathcal{S}', \varphi)$ is an argument and $\varphi \rightsquigarrow \psi \in \overline{D}$ is a defeasible rule, then $A = (\{(\mathcal{S}', \varphi \rightsquigarrow \psi)\}, \psi)$ is an argument.*
  $\bar{A} = \bar{A}'. \quad \tilde{A} = \{\varphi \rightsquigarrow \psi\} \cup \tilde{A}'. \quad \vec{A} = \{\varphi \rightsquigarrow \psi\}. \quad \hat{A} = \psi. \quad \hat{S} = \{\psi\}.$

$A = (\mathcal{S}, \psi)$ *is a minimal argument iff (1) $\mathcal{S}$ is a minimal set such that $\hat{S} \vdash \psi$, and (2) for every $(\mathcal{S}', \alpha \rightsquigarrow \beta) \in \mathcal{S}$, $(\mathcal{S}', \alpha)$ is a minimal argument.*

This abstract representation of arguments is based on the representation of arguments proposed in [24,25]. Note that for every argument, there exists a corresponding minimal argument supporting the same conclusion.

We will use a graphical representation of an argument for human readability. The argument for an inconsistency:

$$A = (\{(\{(\{p \vee q, \neg q\}, p \rightsquigarrow r), (\{s\}, s \rightsquigarrow t)\}, r \wedge t \rightsquigarrow u),$$
$$(\{v\}, v \rightsquigarrow w), \neg(u \wedge w)\}, \bot)$$

is graphically represented as:

$$A: \quad \begin{array}{l} p \vee q \\ \neg q \end{array} \Big| \begin{array}{l} p \rightsquigarrow r \\ \\ s \vdash s \rightsquigarrow t \end{array} \Big| \begin{array}{l} r \wedge t \rightsquigarrow u \\ \\ \\ v \vdash v \rightsquigarrow w \\ \neg(u \wedge w) \end{array} \Big| \; \bot$$

Here, $\hat{A} = \bot$, $\vec{A} = \{r \wedge t \rightsquigarrow u, v \rightsquigarrow w\}$, $\tilde{A} = \{p \rightsquigarrow r, s \rightsquigarrow t, r \wedge t \rightsquigarrow u, v \rightsquigarrow w\}$, $\bar{A} = \{p \vee q, \neg q, s, v, \neg(u \wedge w)\}$ and $\hat{S} = \{u, w, \neg(u \wedge w)\}$ with $A = (\mathcal{S}, \bot)$.

When an argument for an inconsistency is derived[1], one of the defeasible rules is not applicable in the current context. If no defeasible rule is involved in the argument for the inconsistency, one of the premises is invalid. In both cases we will use a strict partial order $<$ on the defeasible rules D and on the information in Σ to determine the rule and premise that is invalid, respectively. Following [22–25], we formulate an *undercutting* argument for the culprit. That is, an argument attacking every argument that uses the culprit.[2]

Definition 3. *Let $A = (\mathcal{S}, \bot)$ be an argument for an inconsistency. Moreover, let $< \subseteq (\Sigma \times \Sigma) \cup (D \times D)$ be a strict partial order over the information Σ and over the defeasible rules D. Finally, let $A' = (\mathcal{S}', \mathbf{not}(\varphi \rightsquigarrow \psi))$ and $A' = (\mathcal{S}', \mathbf{not}(\sigma))$ denote the arguments for an undercutting attack of a defeasible rule in $\overline{D}$ and a proposition in Σ respectively.*

- *If $\tilde{A} \neq \varnothing$, **defeat the weakest last rule**. For every $\varphi \rightsquigarrow \psi \in min_<(\tilde{A})$ with $(\mathcal{S}'', \varphi \rightsquigarrow \psi) \in \mathcal{S}$, $A' = (\mathcal{S} \backslash (\mathcal{S}'', \varphi \rightsquigarrow \psi), \mathbf{not}(\varphi \rightsquigarrow \psi))$ is an undercutting argument of $\varphi \rightsquigarrow \psi \in D$.*
- *If $\tilde{A} = \varnothing$, **defeat the weakest premise**. For every $\sigma \in min_<(\bar{A})$, $A' = (\mathcal{S} \backslash \sigma, \mathbf{not}(\sigma))$ is an undercutting argument of $\sigma \in \Sigma$.*

Note that $min_<(\cdot)$ need not be unique because $<$ is a strict partial order. Also note that $\mathcal{S} \backslash (\mathcal{S}', \varphi \rightsquigarrow \psi)$ is an argument for $\neg \psi$, and that $\mathcal{S} \backslash \sigma$ is an argument for $\neg \sigma$.

The undercutting arguments define an attack relation over the arguments. We denote the attack relation over a set of arguments $\mathcal{A}$ by $\longrightarrow \subseteq \mathcal{A} \times \mathcal{A}$. An undercutting argument $A = (\mathcal{S}, \mathbf{not}(\varphi \rightsquigarrow \psi))$ attacks every argument A' for which $\varphi \rightsquigarrow \psi \in \tilde{A}'$ holds. Moreover, an undercutting argument $A = (\mathcal{S}, \mathbf{not}(\sigma))$ attacks every argument A' for which $\sigma \in \bar{A}'$ holds. We denote the attack of A on A' by $A \longrightarrow A'$. The set of all derived arguments $\mathcal{A}$ and the attack relation over the arguments $\longrightarrow \subseteq \mathcal{A} \times \mathcal{A}$ determine an instance of an argumentation framework $(\mathcal{A}, \longrightarrow)$ as defined by Dung [10]. We can use one the semantics for argumentation frameworks to determine sets of valid arguments; i.e., the argument extensions. See for instance: [2,8–10,12,13,26,30].

3   Basic Argumentation Tableau

A semantic tableau method is a proof system developed by Beth [6]. In the modern version of the method, the semantic tableau for propositional and predicate logic is a tree where each node is labeled by a set of propositions. The set of

---

[1] Arguments for inconsistencies cover rebutting attacks.

[2] Note the difference between an undercutting argument and an undercutting defeater. The former is an argument for not using a proposition or a defeasible rule, and the latter is a defeasible rule specifying a condition under which another defeasible rule should not be used [16].

propositions that labels a node of the tree is satisfiable if and only if the set of propositions that labels one of its child nodes, is satisfiable. For convenience we will use Γ to denote a node of the semantic tableau as well as the set of propositions that labels the node.

We are interested in arguments, which are propositions and their supports. Therefore we introduce an *argumentation tableau* of which each node Γ is a set of arguments.

Definition 4. *Let T be an argumentation tableau. T is a tree of which each node Γ is of a set of arguments.*

The tableau rules of an argumentation tableau are similar to the rules of a traditional semantic tableau. The only difference is the supports for the propositions. In the remainder of the paper, we will focus on the tableaux for propositional and predicate logic. However, the results are not limited to these logic. The approach can also be applied to semantic tableaux for several modal logics [14], dynamic logic [1], etc. The tableau rules for propositional logic arguments are:

$$\frac{(\mathcal{S}, \varphi \wedge \psi)}{(\mathcal{S}, \varphi), (\mathcal{S}, \psi)} \qquad \frac{(\mathcal{S}, \varphi \vee \psi)}{(\mathcal{S}, \varphi) \mid (\mathcal{S}, \psi)}$$

$$\frac{(\mathcal{S}, \varphi \rightarrow \psi)}{(\mathcal{S}, \neg\varphi) \mid (\mathcal{S}, \psi)} \qquad \frac{(\mathcal{S}, \varphi \leftrightarrow \psi)}{(\mathcal{S}, \varphi \rightarrow \psi), (\mathcal{S}, \psi \rightarrow \varphi)}$$

$$\frac{(\mathcal{S}, \neg(\varphi \vee \psi))}{(\mathcal{S}, \neg\varphi), (\mathcal{S}, \neg\psi)} \qquad \frac{(\mathcal{S}, \neg(\varphi \wedge \psi))}{(\mathcal{S}, \neg\varphi) \mid (\mathcal{S}, \neg\psi)}$$

$$\frac{(\mathcal{S}, \neg(\varphi \rightarrow \psi))}{(\mathcal{S}, \varphi), (\mathcal{S}, \neg\psi)} \qquad \frac{(\mathcal{S}, \neg(\varphi \leftrightarrow \psi))}{(\mathcal{S}, \neg(\varphi \rightarrow \psi)) \mid (\mathcal{S}, \neg(\psi \rightarrow \varphi))}$$

$$\frac{(\mathcal{S}, \neg\neg\varphi)}{(\mathcal{S}, \varphi)} \qquad \frac{(\mathcal{S}, \varphi), (\mathcal{S}', \neg\varphi)}{(\mathcal{S} \cup \mathcal{S}', \bot)}$$

There are three aspects to note:

- The right rule on the last line specifies the support for the closure of a branch of the semantic tableau,
- More than one support for the closure of a branch may be derived. Here, we are interested in every support for a branch closure.
- For an element $(\mathcal{S}, \varphi)$ of a tableau node, unlike an argument defined by Definition 2, $\hat{\mathcal{S}} \models \varphi$ need not hold.

Four additional tableau rules are used for predicate logic.

$$\frac{(\mathcal{S}, \forall x \ \varphi)}{(\mathcal{S}, \varphi[^x/_t])} \qquad \frac{(\mathcal{S}, \exists x \ \varphi)}{(\mathcal{S}, \varphi[^x/_c])}$$

$$\frac{(\mathcal{S}, \neg(\forall x \ \varphi))}{(\mathcal{S}, \neg\varphi[^x/_c])} \qquad \frac{(\mathcal{S}, \neg(\exists x \ \varphi))}{(\mathcal{S}, \neg\varphi[^x/_t])}$$

Here, t can be any term that occurs in the current node, and c must be a new constant not yet occurring the current node of the argumentation tableau. Since t can be any term that occurs in the current node, the corresponding rule can be applied more than once for the same proposition.

If an argumentation tableau closes, we can determine the support(s) for the closure.

Definition 5. *Let an argumentation tableau T with n leaf nodes: $\Lambda_1, \ldots, \Lambda_n$.*

- *The argumentation tableau is closed iff for every leaf Λ_i there is an argument $(\mathcal{S}_i, \perp) \in \Lambda_i$.*
- *A support for a tableau closure is defined as:*
  $\mathcal{S} = \bigcup_{i=1}^{n} \mathcal{S}_i$ *where $(\mathcal{S}_i, \perp) \in \Lambda_i$.*

Note that a leaf of a closed tableau may contain more than one argument of the form $(\mathcal{S}', \perp)$. Therefore, there can be multiple supports for the closure of the tableau. In order to determine every possible $(\mathcal{S}', \perp)$, the leafs of the closed tableau must also be saturated. A leaf node is *saturated* if and only if there are no tableau rules that can be applied. It may be impossible to determine saturated leafs in case of predicate logic.

Proposition 1. *Let $\mathcal{L}$ be the language of propositional or predicate logic, let the $\Sigma \subseteq \mathcal{L}$, and let T be an argumentation tableau. Then,*

1. *If $\mathcal{S}$ is a support for the closure of the tableau T with root node $\Gamma_0 = \{(\{\sigma\}, \sigma) \mid \sigma \in \Sigma\}$, then $\mathcal{S} \subseteq \Sigma$ is inconsistent.*
2. *If $\mathcal{S} \subseteq \Sigma$ is a minimal inconsistent set, then there exists a tableau T' which extends the tableau T and $\mathcal{S}$ is a support for the closure of T'.*

Proof. We can prove that an interpretation entails the root of the tableau iff it entails all nodes on a branch from the root to a leaf. The proof is similar to the proof for a standard semantic tableau. We only have an argument $(\mathcal{S}_i, \perp)$ in a leaf node Λ_i iff the branch containing Λ_i closes. Therefore, the argumentation tableau is *closed* iff for every leaf Λ_i there is an argument $(\mathcal{S}_i, \perp) \in \Lambda_i$.

1. Let $\mathcal{S}$ be the support of the closure of the tableau T. We can remove from every node, the arguments $(\mathcal{S}', \sigma)$ such that $\mathcal{S}' \not\subseteq \mathcal{S}$. This may result in some nodes Γ having children that are all equal to Γ. The following holds for the resulting tableau T':
   - The tableau T' has a root $\Gamma_0' = \{(\{\sigma\}, \sigma) \mid \sigma \in \mathcal{S}\}$.
   - There is an interpretation entailing the root iff it entails every node on a branch from the root to a leaf.
   - The tableau T' still closes with $\mathcal{S}$ being the support of the closure.
   Hence, $\mathcal{S}$ is an inconsistent set of propositions.
2. Let $\mathcal{S}$ be a minimal inconsistent subset of Σ. Then there exists a finite argumentation tableau T'' that closes. We can extend the tableau T by replacing every leaf Λ of T by T'' after adding Λ of every node in T''. A rewriting step can occur twice in a branch of the resulting tableau. Since we normally

do not have duplicate rewriting steps, we can remove the duplicate rewriting steps in T'', and if a rewriting step resulted in two or more children, we can remove all branches except one. The resulting tableau is T'.

Since the tableau T'' is closed, so is T'. Next, we remove from every node, the arguments (S'', σ) such that $S'' \not\subseteq S$. This will result in some nodes Γ having children that are all equal to Γ. Clearly, T' is still closed because of the extension of every leaf with T''. The support S' of the closure satisfies $S' \subseteq S$. Since S is a minimal inconsistent set, according to the first item of his proposition, $S' = S$.   □

A standard semantic tableau uses refutation to prove a conclusion. The support S for a closure of an argumentation tableau can be used for the same purpose. Since S is inconsistent for any $\sigma \in S$, $S \backslash \sigma \models \neg\sigma$. Hence, to prove φ and identify a corresponding argument, we add $(\{\neg\varphi\}, \neg\varphi)$ to the root Γ_0 of the tableau. If the tableau closes and if the support S of an inconsistency contains $\neg\varphi$, then we can construct an argument $(S \backslash \neg\varphi, \varphi)$. To keep track of the proposition we try to refute, we put a question-mark behind the proposition in the support $(\{\neg\varphi?\}, \neg\varphi)$. The element $(\{\neg\varphi?\}, \neg\varphi)$ that we add to the root node, is called a *test*. It is a special supporting element, which has no effect on the application of the tableau rules.

Corollary 1. *Let $\Sigma \subseteq \mathcal{L}$ be the initial information and let $\varphi \in \mathcal{L}$ be the proposition for which we search supporting arguments. Moreover, let S be the support for a tableau closure of a tableau T with root $\Gamma_0 = \{(\{\sigma\}, \sigma) \mid \sigma \in \Sigma\} \cup (\{\neg\varphi?\}, \neg\varphi)$.*

1. *If S is the support for a tableau closure of a tableau T and S contains a single test $\neg\varphi?$, then $S \backslash \neg\varphi? \vdash \varphi$.*
2. *If $S' \subseteq \Sigma$ is a minimal set such that $S' \vdash \varphi$, then there exists a tableau T' which extends the tableau T and $S' \cup \{\varphi?\}$ is a support of its closure.*

It can be beneficial if we can derive multiple conclusions simultaneously. The argumentation tableau offers this possibility by simply adding several tests to the root node. After deriving a support S for a tableau closure, we check whether the support contains multiple tests. If it does, it can be ignored. We are interested in supports with zero or one test. The latter provides arguments for conclusion of interest, and the former enables us to handle with inconsistencies in the initial information. For instance Roos [21–23] proposes to resolve the inconsistencies by formulating undercutting arguments for the least preferred propositions in S given a partial preference order $<$ (which can be empty).

Definition 6. *Let S be a support without tests for the tableau closure.*
For every $\sigma \in \min_< S$, $(S \backslash \sigma, \mathbf{not}\ \sigma)$ is an undercutting argument of σ.

Other names that can be found in the literature for this form of undercutting attack are: *premise attack* and *undermining* [20]. The derivation of arguments for conclusions and undercutting arguments to resolve inconsistencies is related to [4, 5, 11, 23, 28].

4   Defeasible Rules

The argumentation tableau presented in the previous section enables us to derive deductive arguments. It does not support arguments containing defeasible rules. Here, we will extend the argumentation tableau in order to derive arguments as defined in Definition 2.

The support of the argument defined in Definition 2 is a tree consisting of alternating deductive and defeasible transitions. The root of the tree is the conclusion/claim supported by the argument. For instance,

$$A: \begin{array}{c|} p \vee q \\ \hline \neg q \end{array} \vdash p \leadsto r \vdash r \leadsto s \vdash s$$

The support of the deductive transitions can be determined by the basic argumentation tableau described in the previous section by adding the antecedent of a defeasible rule as a test to the root of the argumentation tableau. Since we do not know which antecedents of defeasible rules will be supported, we add all of them as tests to the root Γ_0.

Next, we extend every node of the tableau with the consequent of a defeasible rule after determining a support for its antecedent from a tableau closure. In the graphical representation of a tableau in Figs. 1 and 2, this corresponds to extending the root of the tableau with the consequent of a defeasible rule after determining a support for its antecedent from a tableau closure.

Definition 7. *Let T be a tableau with root Γ_0. Moreover, let S be the support for the antecedent φ of the rule $\varphi \leadsto \psi \in \overline{D}$ determined by the tableau T where $(\{\neg\varphi?\}, \neg\varphi) \in \Gamma_0$.*

Then we extend every node Γ of T with the argument $(\{(S, \varphi \leadsto \psi)\}, \psi)$.

To give an illustration, consider the initial information $\Sigma = \{p \vee q, \neg q\}$ and the defeasible rules $D = \{p \leadsto r, r \leadsto s\}$. We are interested in an argument for the conclusion s. We start constructing the tableau shown on the left in Fig. 1. The support for the closure of this tableau is: $\{p \vee q, \neg q, \neg p?\}$ implying the argument $(\{p \vee q, \neg q\}, p)$. We may therefore add the consequence r of the defeasible rule $p \leadsto r$ with the support $\{(\{p \vee q, \neg q\}, p \leadsto r)\}$ to the root of the tableau and continue rewriting the tableau. This results in the tableau shown on the right in Fig. 1.

The support for the new closure of the tableau shown on the right in Fig. 1 is: $\{(\{p \vee q, \neg q\}, p \leadsto r), \neg r?\}$ implying the argument $(\{(\{p \vee q, \neg q\}, p \leadsto r)\}, r)$. We may therefore add the consequence s of the defeasible rule $r \leadsto s$ with the support $\{(\{(\{p \vee q, \neg q\}, p \leadsto r)\}, r \leadsto s)\}$ to the root of the tableau and continue rewriting the resulting tableau as shown in Fig. 2. The support for the closure of the tableau as shown in Fig. 2 is:

$$\{(\{(\{p \vee q, \neg q\}, p \leadsto r)\}, r \leadsto s), \neg s?\}$$

implying the desired argument:

$$(\{(\{(\{p \vee q, \neg q\}, p \leadsto r)\}, r \leadsto s)\}, s)$$

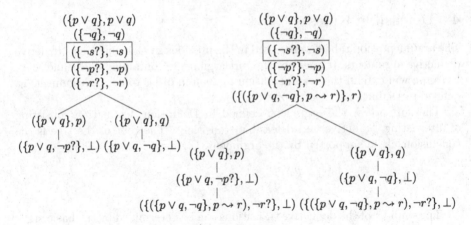

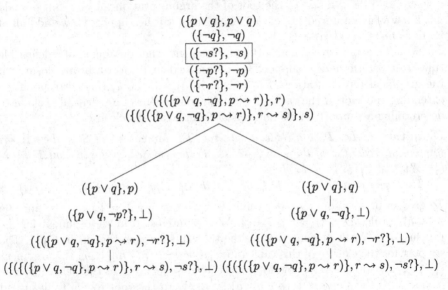

Fig. 1. Deriving defeasible arguments 1

Fig. 2. Deriving defeasible arguments 2

4.1   Predicate Logic

The construction of an argumentation tableau for predicate logic extended with defeasible rules is the same as the above described argumentation tableau for propositional logic with defeasible rules. We should in principle add every ground instance of the negated antecedent of each rule $\varphi(\mathbf{t}) \leadsto \psi(\mathbf{t}) \in \overline{D}$ as a test to the root of the tableau. That is, we should add the set of tests

$$\{(\{\neg\varphi(\mathbf{t})?\}, \neg\varphi(\mathbf{t})) \mid \varphi(\mathbf{t}) \leadsto \psi(\mathbf{t}) \in \overline{D}, \mathbf{t} \in \mathcal{G}\}$$

to the root of the tableau. If functions are used, this set of tests will be infinite, and therefore adding all ground instances is not practically feasible. Instead, we may limit ourselves to the ground instances that are present in the current tableau. So, while expanding the tableau, more ground instance may be added.

4.2   Correctness and Completeness

We can proof that the argumentation tableau determines exactly the same set of arguments as those defined in Definition 2. First, we prove a proposition similar to Proposition 1

Proposition 2. *Let $\mathcal{L}$ be the language of propositional or predicate logic, let the $\Sigma \subseteq \mathcal{L}$, let D be a set of defeasible rules over $\mathcal{L}$, and let $\Gamma_0 = \{(S_i, \psi_i)\}_{i=1}^{n}$ be the root node of the tableau $\mathcal{T}$ and let $\Psi = \{\psi \mid (S, \psi) \in \Gamma_0\}$. Then,*

1. *If S is a support for the closure of the tableau $\mathcal{T}$, then $\hat{S} \subseteq \Psi$ is inconsistent.*
2. *If $\hat{S} \subseteq \Psi$ is a minimal inconsistent set, then S is a support for the closure of the tableau $\mathcal{T}$.*

Proof. Since $\hat{S}$ is a subset of $\mathcal{L}$, the proof is similar to the proof of Proposition 1. □

Theorem 1. *If A is a minimal argument according to Definition 2, then A can be derived by an argumentation tableau. If the argument A can be derived by an argumentation tableau, then A is an argument according to Definition 2.*

Proof. We prove the theorem by induction on the construction of an argument. *Initialization step:* Let $\sigma \in \Sigma$. Clearly, $A = (\{\sigma\}, \sigma)$ is an argument according to Definition 2 iff the tableau with test $(\{\neg\sigma?\}, \neg\sigma)$ closes with support $\{\sigma, \neg\sigma?\}$. *Induction step:*

- Let $A = (S, \varphi)$ with $\hat{S} \vdash \varphi$ be a minimal argument according to Definition 2. Then, $\hat{S} \cup \{\neg\varphi\}$ is a minimal inconsistent set. Therefore, according to Proposition 2, $S \cup \{(\{\neg\varphi?\}, \neg\varphi)\}$ supports a tableau closure, and $A = (S, \varphi)$ can be derived by an argumentation tableau.
  Let $A = (S, \varphi)$ be an argument that can be derived by an argumentation tableau. Then $S \cup \{(\{\neg\varphi?\}, \neg\varphi)\}$ supports a tableau closure, and according to Proposition 2, $\hat{S} \vdash \varphi$. So, $A = (S, \varphi)$ is an argument according to Definition 2.
- Let $A = (\{(S, \varphi \rightsquigarrow \psi)\}, \psi)$ be a minimal argument according to Definition 2. Then $\hat{S} \vdash \varphi$ and there exists an argument $A' = (S, \varphi)$. According to the previous item, $S \cup \{(\{\neg\varphi?\}, \neg\varphi)\}$ supports a tableau closure. Therefore, $(\{(S, \varphi \rightsquigarrow \psi)\}, \psi)$ can be added to the root of the tableau. Hence, $A = (\{(S, \varphi \rightsquigarrow \psi)\}, \psi)$ is an argument that can be derived by an argumentation tableau.
  Let $A = (\{(S, \varphi \rightsquigarrow \psi)\}, \psi)$ be an argument that can be derived by an argumentation tableau. Then $S \cup \{(\{\neg\varphi?\}, \neg\varphi)\}$ supports a tableau closure. So, $\hat{S} \vdash \varphi$, and $A = (\{(S, \varphi \rightsquigarrow \psi)\}, \psi)$ is an argument according to Definition 2. □

5 Reasoning by Cases

Reasoning by cases addresses the derivation of conclusions in the context of uncertainty. Uncertainty described by disjunctions results in multiple cases. Each case is a possible description of the world. If the same conclusion is derived in each case, then that conclusion will certainly hold in the case describing the world. The use of defeasible rules to derive new conclusions in a case should make no difference despite that the arguments supporting the conclusions might defeat other arguments.

5.1 Cases in an Argumentation Tableau

If we ignore the *tests* that we add to the root of an argumentation tableau, then the construction of a tableau can be viewed as the construction of all cases implied by the available information. Ignoring the tests, each open branch describes one case implied by the available disjunctive information. If a case describes the world, additional information may eliminate all other cases and a defeasible rule should be applied as described in the previous section.

The use of defeasible rules in a case implies that we should extend a leaf of the argumentation tableau with the consequence of a defeasible rule whenever the leaf entails the antecedent this rule. We cannot test whether a leaf entails the antecedent of a defeasible rule by adding the antecedent as a test to the root of the tableau. We should add the antecedent to the leaf. Preferably the leaf is saturated because a possibly successful test may fail if we add it too early. To give an illustration, consider $\Sigma = \{p \vee q\}$ and $D = \{p \rightsquigarrow r, q \rightsquigarrow r\}$. If we add the tests $(\{\neg p?\}, \neg p)$ and $(\{\neg q?\}, \neg q)$ to the root of the tableau, both tests will fail because there is no support for a tableau closure with only one test. If however we first rewrite $p \vee q$ and then add the tests to the resulting leafs, in each branch we will derive a support for a closure that enables us to add the consequence of the corresponding rule. The two cases are illustrated by the two tableaux in Fig. 3.

The example illustrates that adding the tests is a strategic choice, which can be dealt with through search. We add a test for the negated antecedent of a rule to a current leaf and try to close all resulting branches starting from the leaf. If we cannot close all these branches, we backtrack to the leaf and remove the test. Using such a search process is of course not a very efficient solution.

Instead of adding tests for the antecedents of defeasible rules, we can check whether the current leaf of a branch of a tableau entails the antecedent. This works fine for propositional logic but raises a problem for predicate logic. If the antecedent of a rule contains a universal claim; i.e., a universally quantified proposition that must be true or an existentially quantified proposition that must be false, then entailment is not decidable because we do not know all the objects over which we have to quantify. So, we should restrict the defeasible rules to those that do not contain universal claims in the antecedent. This restriction implies that we cannot state that *a Student that Passes all Exams normally*

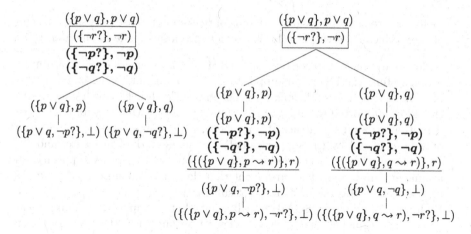

Fig. 3. Reasoning by cases.

receives a Diploma: $S(x) \wedge \forall[E(y) \rightarrow P(x,y)] \rightsquigarrow D(x)$. This even holds if the exams have been specified explicitly: $\forall y[E(y) \leftrightarrow y = e_1 \vee \cdots \vee y = e_n]$.

A possible solution for this restriction is a first order logic that uses binary quantifiers in combination with a special specification of the ground terms for which a predicate is true: $E = \{e_1 \ldots e_n\}$ and $S(x) \wedge \forall E(y)[P(x,y)] \rightsquigarrow D(x)$. However, if we wish to stay in the domain of standard predicate logic, we should rely on the above described search process.

5.2   How to Reason by Cases with Defeasible Information

There have been a few proposals how to introduce reasoning by cases in argumentation systems [3,7,18,25]. Unfortunately, there is no consensus on the correct conclusion(s) when reasoning by cases using defeasible information. Here, we propose that *the (defeasible) conclusions supported in a case by defeasible information must be the same as when uncertainty is eliminated by additional information*. This principle implies that we only eliminate alternative cases (through additional information) in which the antecedent of a defeasible rule does not hold. Note that a case can therefore have sub-cases. To give an illustration, consider the information $\Sigma = \{\neg(p \wedge q), r \vee s, t\}$ and the defeasible rules $D = \{r \rightsquigarrow p, t \rightsquigarrow q\}$. The defeasible rule $r \rightsquigarrow p$ is applicable in the case $\{\neg(p \wedge q), r, t\}$. This case has two sub-cases, $\{\neg p, r, t\}$ and $\{\neg q, r, t\}$. An inconsistency can be derived in the case $\{\neg(p \wedge q), r, t\}$ and the set of last rules involved in the inconsistency is: $\{r \rightsquigarrow p, t \rightsquigarrow q\}$.

Before addressing the technical details of reasoning be cases in using an argumentation tableau, we will first briefly review proposals made in the literature.

- Pollock's argumentation system OSCAR [17,18] is an example of an argumentation system that allows for suppositional reasoning, and is therefore capable of reasoning by cases. Pollock does not explicitly discuss which conclusions should be supported when using reasoning by cases with defeasible rules. His definition of rebutting attack [17] implies that a suppositional argument can only be defeated by (1) suppositional arguments of the same case, and (2) by arguments that do not depend on the considered cases. A suppositional argument cannot defeat an argument that does not depend on any case. As argued in [25], this restriction may result in incorrect conclusions.
- Bodanza [7] adapts OSCAR by allowing that a suppositional argument defeats an argument that does not depend on any case. However, Bodanza changes the interpretation of the $\neg$-operator. $\neg\alpha$ is interpreted as: "α is not an alternative" when reasoning by cases.
- Recently, the framework for structured argumentation ASPIC$^+$ [15,20] has been extended in order to enable reasoning by cases [3]. The authors introduce hypothetical sub-arguments to handle the cases. An argument can attack a hypothetical sub-argument but not vice versa. Hypothetical sub-arguments can only attack other hypothetical sub-arguments.

The first and the last approach above result in counter-intuitive conclusions in the following example.

Harry and Draco are involved in a fight and therefore are punishable. However, if someone involved in a fight, acted in self-defense, then he or she is not punishable. Witnesses state that either Harry or Draco acted in self-defense.

The first and last approach above support the conclusion that both Harry and Draco are punishable, while we would expect that only one of them is punishable. Our proposal that *conclusions supported in a case by defeasible information must be the same as when uncertainty is eliminated by additional information* avoids the counter-intuitive conclusion. However, it introduces a technical issue, which will be discussed in the next subsection.

5.3   Local Tableau Closures

Reconsider the above example with information $\Sigma = \{\neg(p \wedge q), r \vee s, t\}$ and defeasible rules $D = \{r \rightsquigarrow p, t \rightsquigarrow q\}$. We can use the information and the rules to construct the tableau in Fig. 4. If we eliminate the right most branch by adding the information $\neg s$, we get a tableau as described in Sect. 4, and the set of last rules for the derived inconsistency is: $\{r \rightsquigarrow p, t \rightsquigarrow q\}$. It is not difficult to determine the same inconsistency in the tableau in Fig. 4.

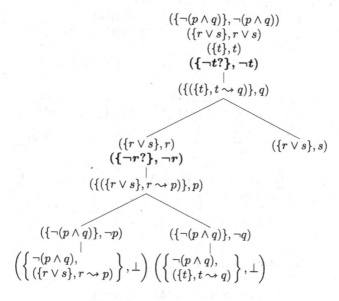

Fig. 4. Local tableau closure 1.

It is also possible to construct the tableau in Fig. 5 using the same information. Here, it is more difficult to determine the set of last rules involved in the
inconsistent case.

The proposition $r \lor s$ in the above example specifies two cases: r and s. If
we eliminates the case s, we get an argumentation tableau as described in the
previous section. Eliminating the case corresponds to eliminating the right most
branch in Fig. 4 and corresponds to eliminating the middle branch in Fig. 5. All
remaining branches are closed, implying that the case r results in a closure. Such
a closure of a case will be called a *local tableau closure*.

The key to identify an inconsistent case, i.e., a local tableau closure, is by
checking whether all alternatives implied by the propositions $\hat{S}$ of a closed branch
with support S for the closure, are also closed. Consider the closed left branch
in Figs. 4 and 5. The support $S = \{\neg(p \land q), (\{r \lor s\}, r \leadsto p)\}$ for the closure
is based on one of the two cases implied by $\neg(p \land q)$, namely the case in which
$\neg p$ holds. It is possible that the other case in which $\neg q$ holds, is consistent. The
case r implied by $r \lor s$ can only be inconsistent if both sub-case p and q are
inconsistent.

To determine whether a case is inconsistent; i.e., whether we have a local
tableau closure, we need to consider all cases implied by a set of propositions $\hat{S}$
where S is the support of a branch closure. Since these cases can be spread over
the whole tableau, we will propagate the support for branch closures towards
the root of the tableau. Cases are the result of applying tableau rules that create
more than one child node. We can therefore combine the supports for closures
of sub-cases at nodes with more than one child node while propagating the

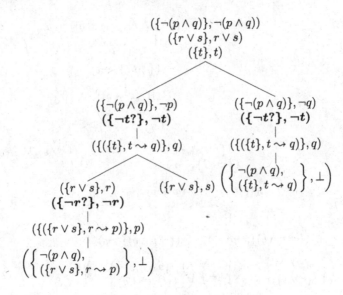

Fig. 5. Local tableau closure 2.

supports for branch closures towards the root. This procedure enables us to check for the propositions involved in a leaf closure whether all cases implied by these propositions are closed.

Definition 8. *Let $\mathcal{T}$ be an argumentation tableau with root Γ_0 and with leaf nodes: $\Lambda_1, \ldots, \Lambda_n$. Moreover, let $\Lambda_{i_1}, \ldots, \Lambda_{i_k}$ be the closed leaf nodes. We propagate the support for the closure of a leaf toward the root of the tableau.*

- *If the argument $(\mathcal{S}, \eta)$ was rewritten in a node Γ and resulted in one child node Γ', then add every $(\mathcal{S}', \perp) \in \Gamma'$ to Γ.*
- *If the argument $(\mathcal{S}, \eta)$ was rewritten in a node Γ and resulted in more than one child node $\Gamma_1, \ldots, \Gamma_m$, then add every $(\bigcup_{i=1}^{m} \mathcal{S}_i, \perp)$ with $(\mathcal{S}_i, \perp) \in \Gamma_i$ and $\mathcal{S} \subseteq \mathcal{S}_i$, to Γ.*
- *If the argument $(\mathcal{S}, \eta)$ was rewritten in a node Γ and resulted in more than one child node $\Gamma_1, \ldots, \Gamma_m$, then add every $(\mathcal{S}_i, \perp) \in \Gamma_i$ such that $\mathcal{S} \not\subseteq \mathcal{S}_i$, to Γ.*

Every $(\mathcal{S}, \perp) \in \Gamma_0$ represents a local tableau closure.

When we apply the procedure in this definition to the above example, we get the tableau shown in Fig. 6. The tableau supports the local closure that we expect.

$$(\{\neg(p \wedge q)\}, \neg(p \wedge q))$$
$$(\{r \vee s\}, r \vee s)$$
$$(\{t\}, t)$$
$$\left(\left\{\begin{array}{l} \neg(p \wedge q), \\ (\{r \vee s\}, r \rightsquigarrow p), \\ (\{t\}, t \rightsquigarrow q) \end{array}\right\}, \perp\right)$$

$$(\{\neg(p \wedge q)\}, \neg p)$$
$$(\{\neg t?\}, \neg t)$$
$$\left(\left\{\begin{array}{l} \neg(p \wedge q), \\ (\{r \vee s\}, r \rightsquigarrow p) \end{array}\right\}, \perp\right)$$

$$(\{\neg(p \wedge q)\}, \neg q)$$
$$(\{\neg t?\}, \neg t)$$
$$\left(\left\{\begin{array}{l} \neg(p \wedge q), \\ (\{t\}, t \rightsquigarrow q) \end{array}\right\}, \perp\right)$$

$$(\{(\{t\}, t \rightsquigarrow q)\}, q)$$
$$\left(\left\{\begin{array}{l} \neg(p \wedge q), \\ (\{r \vee s\}, r \rightsquigarrow p) \end{array}\right\}, \perp\right)$$

$$(\{(\{t\}, t \rightsquigarrow q)\}, q)$$
$$\left(\left\{\begin{array}{l} \neg(p \wedge q), \\ (\{t\}, t \rightsquigarrow q) \end{array}\right\}, \perp\right)$$

$$(\{r \vee s\}, r)$$
$$(\{\neg r?\}, \neg r)$$
$$\left(\left\{\begin{array}{l} \neg(p \wedge q), \\ (\{r \vee s\}, r \rightsquigarrow p) \end{array}\right\}, \perp\right)$$

$$(\{r \vee s\}, s)$$

$$\left(\left\{\begin{array}{l} \neg(p \wedge q), \\ (\{t\}, t \rightsquigarrow q) \end{array}\right\}, \perp\right)$$

$$(\{(\{r \vee s\}, r \rightsquigarrow p)\}, p)$$
$$\left(\left\{\begin{array}{l} \neg(p \wedge q), \\ (\{r \vee s\}, r \rightsquigarrow p) \end{array}\right\}, \perp\right)$$

$$\left(\left\{\begin{array}{l} \neg(p \wedge q), \\ (\{r \vee s\}, r \rightsquigarrow p) \end{array}\right\}, \perp\right)$$

Fig. 6. The support for a local tableau closure.

We can prove that Definition 8 guarantees that supports for local closures represent inconsistent cases.

Proposition 3. *If S is the support for the local closures of a tableau, then $\hat{S} \vdash \perp$.*

Proof. Let $(S_1, \perp), \ldots, (S_k, \perp)$ be the closures of the leafs $\Lambda_1, \ldots, \Lambda_k$ that resulted in the support S according to Definition 8. Consider the propagation of $(S_1, \perp), \ldots, (S_k, \perp)$ towards the root of the tableau.

- Each time the third item of Definition 8 was applied, remove all branches except for the current branch over which we propagate the closure. The removed side branches do not contribute to the support S.
- Next, remove from all nodes, the elements (S', η) for which $S' \not\subseteq S$.
- Finally, add $\{(\{(S', \varphi \rightsquigarrow \psi)\}, \psi) \mid (S', \varphi \rightsquigarrow \psi) \in S\}$ to every node of the tableaux to get a proper argumentation tableau. Note that some nodes Γ may have children that are all equal to Γ.

The following holds for the resulting tableau T':

- The tableau T' has a root $\Gamma_0 = \{(\{\sigma\}, \sigma) \mid \sigma \in S \cap \mathcal{L}\} \cup \{(\{(S', \varphi \rightsquigarrow \psi)\}, \psi) \mid (S', \varphi \rightsquigarrow \psi) \in S\}$.
- There is an interpretation entailing the root iff it entails every node on a branch from the root to a leaf.

– The tableau $\mathcal{T}'$ still closes with $\mathcal{S}$ being the support of a tableau closure according to Definition 5.

Hence, $\hat{\mathcal{S}}$ is an inconsistent set of propositions.   □

We can also prove that inconsistent cases can be identified through supports for local tableau closures.

Proposition 4
Let $\{(\{\sigma_1\}, \sigma_1), \ldots, (\{\sigma_m\}, \sigma_m), (\mathcal{S}_1, \eta_1 \rightsquigarrow \mu_1), \ldots, (\mathcal{S}_n, \eta_n \rightsquigarrow \mu_n)\}$ be a minimal inconsistent case.
Then $\mathcal{S} = \{(\{\sigma_1\}, \sigma_1), \ldots, (\{\sigma_m\}, \sigma_m), (\mathcal{S}_1, \eta_1 \rightsquigarrow \mu_1), \ldots, (\mathcal{S}_n, \eta_n \rightsquigarrow \mu_n)\}$ is a support for a local closure.

Proof. Since $\{\sigma_1, \ldots, \sigma_m, \mu_1, \ldots, \mu_n\}$ is a minimal inconsistent set, each branch containing an element of $\mathcal{S}$ can be closed by extending the tableau. The support for each closure of the branches is a subset of $\{(\{\sigma_1\}, \sigma_1), \ldots, (\{\sigma_m\}, \sigma_m), (\mathcal{S}_1, \eta_1 \rightsquigarrow \mu_1), \ldots, (\mathcal{S}_n, \eta_n \rightsquigarrow \mu_n)\}$. We can propagate the supports towards the root as specified by Definition 8. Since all sub-cases are closed, the propagation will be successful and the root will have a support $\mathcal{S}'$ for the local closure.

Suppose that $\mathcal{S}' \neq \mathcal{S}$. Then $\mathcal{S}' \subset \mathcal{S}$ and according to Proposition 3, $\hat{\mathcal{S}}'$ is an inconsistent set implying that $\hat{\mathcal{S}}$ is not a minimal inconsistent set. Contradiction.

Hence, $\mathcal{S}$ is a support for a local tableau closure.   □

5.4   Mutually Exclusive Cases

There is one last issue concerning reasoning by cases. The tableau rule $\frac{(\mathcal{S}, \varphi \vee \psi)}{(\mathcal{S}, \varphi) | (\mathcal{S}, \psi)}$ does not guarantee that cases are mutually exclusive.[3] The applying this tableau rule results in two children representing two cases. Both cases may support a conclusion η. This conclusion is not justified if η does not hold when both φ and ψ are true. As an illustration, suppose that a party will be great if Harry or Ron will attend it, but not if both will attend (because Harry and Ron have a quarrel). Here, the case that Harry attends the party and whether Ron attends is unknown, is not the same as drawing a conclusion in the absence of more specific information. The disjunction implies that Ron might attend the party too. The solution to this issue is to ensure that the tableau only contains cases that are mutually exclusive. We address this problem by adapting three tableau rules.

$$\frac{(\mathcal{S}, \varphi \vee \psi)}{(\mathcal{S}, \varphi \wedge \neg\psi) \mid (\mathcal{S}, \varphi \wedge \psi) \mid (\mathcal{S}, \neg\varphi \wedge \psi)} \qquad \frac{(\mathcal{S}, \varphi \rightarrow \psi)}{(\mathcal{S}, \neg\varphi \wedge \neg\psi) \mid (\mathcal{S}, \neg\varphi \wedge \psi) \mid (\mathcal{S}, \varphi \wedge \psi)}$$

$$\frac{(\mathcal{S}, \neg(\varphi \wedge \psi))}{(\mathcal{S}, \neg\varphi \wedge \psi) \mid (\mathcal{S}, \neg\varphi \wedge \neg\psi) \mid (\mathcal{S}, \varphi \wedge \neg\psi)}$$

---

[3] Note that the goal is not to define a tableau rule for an 'exclusive or' but for a standard 'or', which can be viewed as describing three mutually exclusive cases.

Using these adapted tableau rules we will consider three mutually exclusive cases given the information that Harry or Ron will attend the party. In two cases the party will be great and in one case it will not.

6   Conclusion

This paper investigated the possibility of using the semantic tableau method to derive arguments for claims/conclusions. We conclude that it is possible to define an argumentation tableau that provides the arguments supporting conclusions in case of propositional and predicate logic. If the initial information is inconsistent, undercutting arguments can also be derived for resolving the inconsistencies. We further conclude that an argumentation tableau can provide arguments supporting conclusions if propositional and predicate logic are extended with defeasible rules. Arguments for inconsistencies, covering rebutting attacks, can be resolved by deriving undercutting arguments for defeasible rules. Our last conclusion is that an argumentation tableau enables reasoning by cases and that conclusions supported by reasoning by cases are intuitively plausible.

Further research can be done on (*i*) efficiently implementing an argumentation tableau, and (*ii*) adapting the argumentation tableau to other logics.

References

1. Baader, F., Sattler, U.: An overview of tableau algorithms for description logics. Studia Logica 5–40 (2001). https://doi.org/10.1023/A:1013882326814
2. Baroni, P., Giacomin, M., Guida, G.: SCC-recursiveness: a general schema for argumentation semantics. Artif. Intell. **168**, 162–210 (2005)
3. Beirlaen, M., Heyninck, J., Straßer, C.: Reasoning by cases in structured argumentation. In: Proceedings of the Symposium on Applied Computing, pp. 989–994. SAC 2017 (2017)
4. Besnard, P., Hunter, A.: Practical first-order argumentation. In: Proceedings of the Twentieth National Conference on Artificial Intelligence (AAAI), pp. 590–595 (2005)
5. Besnard, P., Hunter, A.: Argumentation based on classical logic. In: Simari, G., Rahwan, I. (eds) Argumentation in Artificial Intelligence, pp. 133–152. Springer, Boston (2009). https://doi.org/10.1007/978-0-387-98197-0_7
6. Beth, E.W.: Formal methods: an introduction to symbolic logic and to the study of effective operations in arithmetic and logic. Synthese library. D. Reidel Publ. Comp
7. Bodanza, G.: Disjunctions and specificity in suppositional defeasible argumentation. Logic J. IGPL **10**(1), 23–49 (2002)
8. Caminada, M.: Semi-stable semantics. In: Proceedings of the 1st Conference on Computational Models of Argument (COMMA 2006), Frontiers in Artificial Intelligence and Applications, vol. 144. IOS Press (2006)
9. Cramer, M., vab der Torre, L.: SCF2 - an argumentation semantics for rational human judgments on argument acceptability. In: Proceedings of the 8th Workshop on Dynamics of Knowledge and Belief (DKB-2019) and the 7th Workshop KI & Kognition (KIK 2019), pp. 24–35 (2019)

10. Dung, P.M.: On the acceptability of arguments and its fundamental role in non-monotonic reasoning, logic programming and n-person games. Artif. Intell. **77**, 321–357 (1995)
11. Dung, P.M., Kowalski, R.A., Toni, F.: Assumption-based argumentation. In: Simari, G., Rahwan, I. (eds.) Argumentation in Artificial Intelligence, pp. 199–218. Springer, Boston (2009). https://doi.org/10.1007/978-0-387-98197-0_10
12. Dung, P., Mancarella, P., Toni, F.: Computing ideal sceptical argumentation. Artif. Intell. **171**, 642–674 (2007)
13. Dvořák, W., Gaggl, S.A.: Stage semantics and the SCC-recursive schema for argumentation semantics. J. Logic Comput. **26**(4), 1149–1202 (2016). https://doi.org/10.1093/logcom/exu006
14. Massacci, F.: Single step tableaux for modal logics: computational properties, complexity and methodology. J. Autom. Reason. **24**, 319–364 (2000)
15. Modgil, S., Prakken, H.: The ASPIC$^+$ framework for structured argumentation: a tutorial. Argument Comput. **5**, 31–62 (2014)
16. Pollock, J.L.: Defeasible reasoning. Cogn. Sci. **11**, 481–518 (1987)
17. Pollock, J.L.: A theory of defeasible reasoning. Int. J. Intell. Syst. **6**, 33–54 (1991)
18. Pollock, J.L.: How to reason defeasibly. Artif. Intell. **57**, 1–42 (1992)
19. Prakken, H., Vreeswijk, G.: Logics for defeasible argumentation. In: The Handbook of Philosophical Logic, pp. 219–318. Springer, Netherlands (2002)
20. Prakken, H.: An abstract framework for argumentation with structured arguments. Argument Comput. **1**(2), 93–124 (2010)
21. Roos, N.: A preference logic for non-monotonic reasoning. Technical Report 88–94, Delft University of Technology, Faculty of Technical Mathematics and Informatics (1988)
22. Roos, N.: Preference logic: a logic for reasoning with inconsistent knowledge. Technical Report 89–53, Delft University of Technology, Faculty of Technical Mathematics and Informatics (1989)
23. Roos, N.: A logic for reasoning with inconsistent knowledge. Artif. Intell **57**, 69–103 (1992)
24. Roos, N.: On resolving conflicts between arguments. Technical report, TR-CTIT-97-37 Centre for Telematics and Information Technology, University of Twente, Enschede (1997)
25. Roos, N.: On resolving conflicts between arguments. Comput. Intell. **16**, 469–497 (2000)
26. Roos, N.: Preferential model and argumentation semantics. In: Proceedings of the 13th International Workshop on Non-Monotonic Reasoning (NMR 2010) (2010)
27. Simari, G.R., Loui, R.P.: A mathematical treatment of defeasible reasoning and its implementation. Artif. Intell. **53**, 125–157 (1992)
28. Toni, F.: A tutorial on assumption-based argumentation. Argument Comput. **5**(1), 89–117 (2014)
29. Toulmin, S.: The uses of argument. Cambridge University Press (1958)
30. Verheij, B.: Two approaches to dialectical argumentation: admissible sets and argumentation stages. In: In Proceedings of the Biannual International Conference on Formal and Applied Practical Reasoning (FAPR) Workshop, pp. 357–368 (1996)
31. Vreeswijk, G.: Abstract argumentation systems. Artif. Intell **90**, 225–279 (1997)
32. Yun, B., Oren, N., Croitoru, M.: Efficient construction of structured argumentation systems. In: Prakken, H., Bistarelli, S., Santini, F., Taticchi, C. (eds.) COMMA. Frontiers in Artificial Intelligence and Applications, vol. 326, pp. 411–418. IOS Press (2020). https://doi.org/10.3233/FAIA200525

'Thy Algorithm Shalt Not Bear False Witness': An Evaluation of Multiclass Debiasing Methods on Word Embeddings

Thalea Schlender$^{(\boxtimes)}$ and Gerasimos Spanakis

Department of Data Science and Knowledge Engineering, Maastricht University, Maastricht, Netherlands

Abstract. With the vast development and employment of artificial intelligence applications, research into the fairness of these algorithms has been increased. Specifically, in the natural language processing domain, it has been shown that social biases persist in word embeddings and are thus in danger of amplifying these biases when used. As an example of social bias, religious biases are shown to persist in word embeddings and the need for its removal is highlighted. This paper investigates the state-of-the-art multiclass debiasing techniques: Hard debiasing, SoftWEAT debiasing and Conceptor debiasing. It evaluates their performance when removing religious bias on a common basis by quantifying bias removal via the Word Embedding Association Test (WEAT), Mean Average Cosine Similarity (MAC) and the Relative Negative Sentiment Bias (RNSB). By investigating the religious bias removal on three widely used word embeddings, namely: Word2Vec, GloVe, and ConceptNet, it is shown that the preferred method is ConceptorDebiasing. Specifically, this technique manages to decrease the measured religious bias on average by 82.42%, 96.78% and 54.76% for the three word embedding sets respectively.

Keywords: Natural language processing · Word embeddings · Social bias

1 Introduction

In recent years, there have been rapid advances in artificial intelligence and the accompanying development of machine learning applications. With the increased widespread (commercial) employment of such applications it has become increasingly more vital to ensure their transparency, fairness and equality. Recent investigations of various application domains have shown that many of these applications exhibit several social biases endangering their fairness [16]. Social biases describe the discrimination of certain identity groups based on, for example, their gender, race or religion. When social biases persist in machine learning applications, they run the danger of amplifying these biases. For instance, regarding social bias against discriminated groups, e.g. minorities, it was found that these

© Springer Nature Switzerland AG 2021
M. Baratchi et al. (Eds.): BNAIC/Benelearn 2020, CCIS 1398, pp. 141–156, 2021.
https://doi.org/10.1007/978-3-030-76640-5_9

were recognized considerably less in face/voice recognition [6]. To illustrate the real-world consequences which originate from these biased algorithms, consider the use of these face/voice applications in sensitive areas such as the justice system or medical diagnosis. In the first case, less recognition of minorities could lead to biased information "the use of [which] could entail an extended and undeserved period of incarceration" [6, p. 7]. In a medical domain, less recognition of minorities could result in "a revolutionary test for skin cancer that does not work on African Americans" [14, 1].

Biases inherent in our society are, thus, perpetuated in the machine learning models, recorded by the model's outcomes and, hence, threaten to treat various groups differently. To rectify the unequal treatment, the origin of biases in artificial intelligence needs to be examined and, consequently, removed. These biases in data driven applications may have myriad causes. One cause is the gathering of the data that is primarily done or planned by humans, which causes the data to be subject to similar biases as humans have. Moreover, the gathering process favours easily accessible and quantifiable data [15], which may favour certain societal groups over others. Further, biases are captured in the under-/over-representation of societal groups in the dataset, which makes the complete data not representative of the end users anymore [15]. Another origin of bias is data directly containing sensitive attributes, such as race or religion, or any proxy features for these. These proxy features may be well hidden, for instance a societal group may be represented in the post codes of communities. With the encoding of sensitive information, an algorithm can learn wrong causal inferences concerning these which can be hard to identify [15].

The origins of bias mentioned above can be present in many representations of data. To provide an elaborate analysis, this paper will henceforth tend to textual data solely. To process textual data for an application, the data must be represented numerically. This is done via word embeddings, which attempt to capture the meaning and semantic relationships of a word and translate these to a real valued vector. Since word embeddings are learnt from possibly biased data, word embeddings themselves may contain biases, which could ripple through an application. Having outlined why the mitigation of these biases is vital and having introduced the domain of biased word embeddings, this paper will review work on analysis and mitigation of biased word embeddings, before presenting and evaluating various state-of-the-art post processing approaches to the mitigation of the found biases. Specifically, the attempted removal of multiclass social biases in three word embeddings is quantified on geometrical as well as on downstream evaluation metrics.

In order to highlight the results, the problem of religious bias is taken as a novel example for multi-class social bias. By doing so this paper aims to answer following research questions:

- To what extent are Religious biases, as an example for social bias, present in widely used word embeddings?
- How do state-of-the-art multiclass debiasing techniques compare geometrically?

– How do state-of-the-art multiclass debiasing techniques compare considering the discrimination of a downstream application?

To address which state-of-the-art debiasing technique performs religious debiasing the best, an extensive background on social biases in word embeddings is given. The evaluation metrics this paper uses are explained, before the debiasing techniques examined are illustrated. This paper, then, highlights the need for religious debiasing by showing its presence in a word embedding. Next, a common base for the analysis of bias removal is established to compare the debiasing methods. Finally, this paper discusses the performance of the debiasing techniques and via this evaluation, advises the use of one.

2   Background

Social biases have been found in popular, widely used word embeddings such as GloVe [18] or word2Vec [3,13]. Specifically, gender biases have been found to persist by creating simple analogies, which have led to the example "Man is to Computer Programmer as Woman is to Homemaker" [1,3]. This analogy clearly shows that the word embeddings have captured gender bias with regards to occupation, which may cause disruption in, e.g., a CV-Scanning application. Similarly, the multi-class racial bias in word embeddings has led to other biased analogies [11] being coined. Sweeney and Najafan have also shown that multi-class bias based on nationality or religion is present in word embeddings, which endangers specific identity groups to be treated differently [21].

Social biases have, therefore, been proven to likely exist within word embeddings. As mentioned before (1), biases in data driven models and, thus, word embeddings have many causes, especially related to the bias present in the data used. Papakyriakopoulos, Hegelich, Serrano, and Marco find that biases in word embeddings are closely related to the input training data [17]. In fact, even when the text used for training was written for a "formal and controlled environment like Wikipedia, [it] result[ed] in biased word embeddings" (p. 455, [17]).

A strong cause for bias in textual data is the more frequent co-occurrence of particular words to the identity terminology of one group rather than the other(s). Word embedding algorithms typically take co-occurrences as an indicator of context and semantic relationships. Thus, the word embeddings learn a stronger association between, for example, 'woman' and 'nurse' than 'man' and 'nurse'. This association, however, is an example of a stereotype, which should ideally not be captured in the artificial intelligence applications. Garg, Schiebinger, Jurafsky and Zou confirm that word embeddings "accurately capture both gender and ethnic occupation percentages" [4, 3636].

The biases within word embeddings can amplify through an application, causing unfair results, which may influence actions in the real world. This, in turn, may lead to unequal treatment based on certain sensitive attributes and actively cause discrimination. Hence, it is vital to establish mitigation methods.

Debiasing methods may tend to different categories of biases. For instance, debiasing binary biases mitigates the unequal treatment of two groups based on a sensitive feature, and joint debiasing mitigates biases based on various sensitive attributes simultaneously. This paper demonstrates a multi-class debiasing, which deals with bias across more than two groups, by considering three religious groups, namely: Christianity, Islam, Judaism. The development of debiasing techniques is novel research, yet a few state-of-the-art approaches have been proposed. Following the notion that word embedding biases are a direct result of bias in the data, Brunet, Alkalay-Houlihan, Anderson, and Zemel have proposed a technique to track which segment of data is responsible for some bias [2]. It follows naturally that this can be applied as a debiasing technique by omitting these segments when training the word embedding model. Most debiasing techniques, however, concentrate on post-processing pre-trained word embeddings.

Bolukbasi, Chang, Zou, and Saligrama propose soft and hard debiasing as binary debiasing methods [1], which Manzini, Lim, Tsvetkov, and Black transfer into the multi-class domain [11]. Popovic, Lemmerich and Strohmaier expand these debiasing techniques further into SoftWEAT and hardWEAT, which also are applicable for joint debiasing [19]. Another joint multiclass debiasing approach is the Conceptor debiasing method by Karve, Ungar and Sedoc [9].

With the increased research into debiasing methods, Gonen and Goldberg [5] provide a critical view on the effectiveness of debiasing. The removal of bias in the techniques, such as hard debiasing, relies on the definition of the bias as being the projection onto a biased subspace. Gonen and Goldberg, however, believe that this is a mere indication of the presence of bias. Thus, although the debiasing methods may eliminate the bias projections, the bias is still captured within the geometry of supposedly neutralized words [5]. Hence, it is important to consider the quantification of bias removal critically.

In this paper, the multi-class debiasing methods, all mentioned above, namely Hard debiasing, SoftWEAT debiasing and Conceptor debiasing will be evaluated on different metrics in an attempt to quantify bias removal from geometrical and downstream perspectives. Previous work comparing debiasing techniques have evaluated their performance on merely one geometric metric quantifying bias [1,9,11], whereas this paper uses two geometric metrics, in addition to utilizing a downstream bias metric.

3   Methodology

The metrics and debiasing techniques will now be introduced, before an investigation of religious bias, as an example of multiclass social bias, is conducted on a word embedding. Having established the need for religious debiasing, the bias removal will be conducted and analysed.

3.1   Terminology

To aid in the explanation of the debiasing techniques and evaluation metrics, some definitions and terminologies are introduced first.

- A class C consists of a set of protected groups defined by some criteria, like religion or race.
- A subclass S_c then refers to a particular protected group within that class, such as Judaism when considering the religion class.
- An equality set E for a class is a set containing a term for each subclass, where all terms can be considered to denote an equivalent concept within each subclass. Thus, for instance, an equality set for C = religion with S_c = (Christianity, Islam, Judaism) could be (Church, Mosque, Synagogue).
- A target set T is a set of identity terms referring to a particular sub-class, thus inherently carrying bias. For Christianity this could include: {Church, Churches, Bible, Bibles, Jesus}.
- An attribute set A contains sets of words referring to several topics, none of which should, in principle, be linked to the target set of a subclass, but that a target set of words may be associated to [19]. The aim of the debiasing methods is to remove this link. Examples for attribute sets are collections of words considered to be pleasant, or unpleasant, respectively or collections of words describing notions such as families, arts or occupations.

3.2   Bias Measurements Techniques

To quantify the bias removal, the three metrics introduced below are used. The first two metrics introduced evaluate the removal geometrically by considering the cosine distance of target and attribute sets, whereas the third highlights bias presence via a simple sentiment analysis application.

Word Embedding Association Test (WEAT). The standard evaluation of bias is the Word Embedding Association Test (*WEAT*) as established by Caliskan, Bryson, and Narayanan. It is widely used, e.g. in [1,19], and it has been expanded, for instance, to the Sentence Encoder Association Test (SEAT) [12].

WEAT tests the association between one target and attribute set, relative to the association of the other target and attribute set in order to examine the null hypothesis that both target sets are equally similar to both attribute sets and not exhibiting any bias [3].

To perform WEAT, the mean cosine similarity of the target set T_1 to attribute sets A_1 and A_2 is compared to the mean cosine similarity of the target set T_2 to A_1 and A_2. The exact calculations for the test statistic $S(T_1, T_2, A_1, A_2)$ and the effect size d of the two attribute - target set pairs is given below. Let $s(w, A_1, A_2)$ be defined as in Eq. 1, where w is a given word vector:

$$s(w, A_1, A_2) = mean_{a_1 \in A_1} \cos(\vec{w}, \vec{a_1}) - mean_{a_2 \in A_2} \cos(\vec{w}, \vec{a_2}) \qquad (1)$$

$$S(T_1, T_2, A_1, A_2) = \sum_{t \in T_1} s(t, A_1, A_2) - \sum_{t \in T_2} s(t, A_1, A_2), \qquad (2)$$

The effect size d quantifies how distant these two associations of target and attribute pairs are. The closer the effect size d is to zero, the less distant the two associations are and thus, the less bias can be found between the target and attribute sets [3]. Note that bias here is defined on the relative distances.

$$d = \frac{mean_{t \in T_1} s(t, A_1, A_2) - mean_{t \in T_2} s(t, A_1, A_2)}{std\text{-}dev_{w \in T_1 \cup T_2} s(w, A_1, A_2)} \qquad (3)$$

Mean Average Cosine Similarity (MAC). WEAT as proposed by Caliskan et al. [3] provides a geometric interpretation of the distance between two sets of target words and two sets of attribute words.

The mean average cosine similarity (MAC) uses the intuition behind WEAT and applies this notion to a multiclass domain as proposed by Manzini et al. [11]. Instead of comparing the associations of one target set T_1 and an attribute set A_1, to the association of T_2 and A_2, MAC considers the association of one target set T_1 to all attribute sets A at one time.

The MAC metric is computed by calculating the mean over the cosine distances between an element t in a target set T to each element in an attribute set A, as seen in Eq. 4, in which the cosine distance is defined as $cos_{distance}(t, a) = 1 - \cos(t, a)$. This is repeated for all elements in T to all attribute sets. The MAC then describes the average cosine distance between each target set and all attribute sets.

$$s_{MAC}(t, A_j) = \frac{1}{|A_j|} \sum_{a \in A_j} \cos_{distance}(t, a) \qquad (4)$$

Relative Negative Sentiment Bias (RNSB). The relative negative sentiment bias ($RNSB$) is an approach proposed by Sweeney and Najafan [21] in order to offer insights on the effect of biased word embeddings through downstream applications. Its framework involves training a logistic classifier to predict the positive or negative sentiment of a given word. The classifier is trained on supposedly unbiased sentiment words, which are encoded via the word embedding to be investigated. Sweeney and Najafan then encode identity terms and predict their respective negative sentiment probability. These results are used to form a probability distribution P. Intuitively, unbiased word embeddings would result in this probability distribution to be uniform, i.e., each class has equal probability of being classified as of negative sentiment. The RNSB is then defined as Kullback-Leibler divergence of P from the uniform distribution U [21].

3.3 Debiasing Techniques

These three metrics will be used to quantify the bias removal in the three debiasing techniques considered in this paper. Namely, these are Hard debaising, SoftWEAT and Conceptor debiasing.

Hard Debiasing. Bolukbasi et al. [1] established two binary debiasing methods, namely: Soft and Hard debiasing, which Manizini et al. [11] then applied to the multiclass domain. These approaches mainly rely on two steps: The identification of a bias subspace, and the subsequent removal of that bias. The main difference between these two methods is the severity of bias removal: Hard debiasing forces neutral words to zero in the bias subspace, whereas soft debiasing dampens the bias subspace components [1].

The bias subspace identification utilizes equality sets E_i. For each set, the centre of the set is computed and the distance of each term in the equality set to the centre is considered. The subspace capturing the class is then found by examining the variance of each term. Bias removal is carried out by a 'neutralize and equalize' approach. The projection of words that are declared neutral onto the bias subspace is subtracted from their word vector. The identity words, however, rely on their bias component. Thus, in the equalization step, the terms within an equality set, are centralized and are each given an equal bias component.

SoftWEAT Debiasing. Borrowing intuition from WEAT [3] and hard-/soft-debiasing [11], Popovic et al. propose debiasing techniques SoftWEAT and hard-WEAT [19], which differ in the harshness of bias removal. SoftWEAT expands the target set of each subclass by considering the n closest neighbours to all identity terms. Merely this set is then manipulated. To find the linear transformation to be applied, the attribute sets the target set of a subclass is biased against is found via WEAT and their respective null space vectors are calculated. The translation of the subclass embeddings is then taken from the null space vector, which decreases the WEAT score the most. The final transformation is scalable by hyper-parameter λ.

Conceptor Debiasing. Karve et al. developed the Conceptor debiasing post processing method [9]. The notion of this method is to generate a conceptor, as defined by Jaeger [8], to represent bias directions and to subsequently project these biased directions out of the word embeddings.

A square matrix conceptor C is a regularized identity map, which maps an input to another – in the debiasing domain, a word embedding to its bias [9]. For the exact mathematical definition of a conceptor readers can refer to [9,10]. Conceptors can be manipulated through boolean logic. Thus, to project out a bias subspace, one can apply the negated conceptor (representing the bias directions) to the word embeddings. In addition to this, through the use of boolean logic, multiple conceptors generated for various class biases can be combined, enabling joint debiasing [9]. Moreover, a conceptor provides a soft projection [8]. For debiasing this means, that the conceptor dampens the bias directions captured in it. Hence, the soft projection will alter only some components of some embeddings, leaving others largely unaltered [7].

4   Analysis of Religious Bias in Word Embeddings

This section shows the common basis on which the debiasing methods are applied. Further, it is shown that religious bias persists in a word embedding.

4.1   Data

Each of the debiasing approaches described is based on different types of data: Conceptor debiasing utilizes a set of unlabelled biased words, Hard debiasing requires equality sets, and SoftWEAT is based on the target and attribute sets of WEAT. This paper will attempt to debias against the religion class, specifically with the subclasses: Christianity, Islam, Judaism. The equality set used for religious multiclass debiasing in Manizini et al.'s paper [11] is extended by hand to include 11 equality sets, which are available for downloading[1]. The attribute sets used in this paper are inspired from Popovic et al.'s work [19].

Finally, the debiasing methods are applied on three established word embedding representations, namely: Word2Vec[2], GloVe[3] and ConceptNet[4].

4.2   Analysis

Social biases are present in the word embeddings when neutral words are more strongly associated with one subclass than another. In this section it is shown what impact these associations have more specifically to each subclass of religion.

In order to quantify captured stereotypes in word embeddings, analogies are scored, as proposed by Bolukbasi et al. [1]. The analogies are then scored via Eq. (5), where δ is the similarity threshold and $\vec{a}, \vec{b}, \vec{x}, \vec{y}$ are words as given above. The intuition behind this equation is that an analogy capturing relationships well should have directions $\vec{a} - \vec{b}$ and $\vec{x} - \vec{y}$ approach parallelism.

$$S_{(a,b)}(x,y) = \begin{cases} cos(\vec{a} - \vec{b}, \vec{x} - \vec{y}) & \text{if } ||\vec{x} - \vec{y}|| \leq \delta \\ 0, & \text{otherwise} \end{cases} \tag{5}$$

Table 1 lists high scoring examples of analogies that are established within the word2Vec embeddings. To limit the analogies scored, the tested dataset is compromised of Manzini et al.'s religious stereotype words [11] and Popovic et al.'s attribute words [19]. As a comparison, the biased analogy established by Bolukbasi et al. [1] and Manzini et al. [11], in addition to some appropriate analogies, are given with their respective scores. The stereotypical analogies given exhibit different orientations regarding the religions: for negative (positive) analogies a negative (positive) term is provided for each religion. Further, mixed

---

[1] https://github.com/thaleaschlender/An-Evaluation-of-Multiclass-Debiasing-Methods-on-Word-Embeddings.
[2] https://code.google.com/archive/p/word2vec/.
[3] https://nlp.stanford.edu/projects/glove/.
[4] http://blog.conceptnet.io/posts/2019/conceptnet-numberbatch-19-08/.

analogies are possible in which a positive a negative term are paired. Although it follows that the maximal absolute score of Eq. (5) is 1, in Table 1 one can see that established analogies like *"kitten is to cat, as puppy is to dog"*, achieve a score of 0.38. Thus, when regarding how high appropriate analogies are scored, biased analogies with an absolute score of higher than 0.15 indicate that these biased analogies are captured in the word embeddings.

An appropriate analogy concerning religion would be *"Muslim is to Islam as Christian is to Christianity"*, which describes the correct correspondence of religion and its members. However, a similarly high classified analogy is *"Christian is to judgemental as Muslim is to terrorist"*. This wrong association of religions to terrorist and judgemental is an unjust example of a captured stereotype in the word embedding. The prejudice of Muslims being more strongly associated with violence and terrorism is deeply embedded in society as proven by Sides and Gross. They hypothesize and confirm that "Americans will stereotype Muslims negatively on the warmth dimension– that is, as threatening, violent, etc." [20, p. 5].

Table 1. Examples of top scoring analogies for each Religion pair in Word2Vec. The union of all attribute set words is tested. As a reference, further analogies are shown. The analogies are categorised as appropriate, positive-positive (PP), negative-positive (NP) or negative-negative (NN).

Analogy	score	Orientation
Appropriate Analogies		
Cat is to *kitten* as *dog* is to *puppy*	.38332	Appropriate
Muslim is to *Islam* as *Christian* is to *Christianity*	.27088	Appropriate
Christian is to *Christianity* as *Jew* is to *Judaism*	.26884	Appropriate
Muslim is to *Islam* as *Jew* is to *Judaism*	.24883	Appropriate
Christianity is to *Church* as *Judaism* is to *Synagogue*	.24054	Appropriate
Analogies Exhibiting Stereotypes		
Woman is to *homemaker* as *man* is to *programmer*	.26415	NP
Black is to *criminal* as *Caucasian* is to *police*	.07325	NP
Christian is to *astronomy* as *Muslim* is to *terrorist*	.269664	PN
Christian is to *heaven* as *Muslim* is to *relatives*	.262772	PP
Christian is to *heaven* as *Muslim* is to *terrorist*	.261527	PN
Christian is to *astronomy* as *Muslim* is to *relatives*	.255617	PP
Christian is to *judgmental* as *Muslim* is to *terrorist*	.246935	NN
Jew is to *rotten* as *Christian* is to *conservative*	.254316	NN
Jew is to *hairy* as *Christian* is to *conservative*	.222221	NN
Jew is to *cousins* as *Christian* is to *trustworthy*	.219419	PP
Jew is to *hariy* as *Christian* is to *trustworthy*	.215475	NP
Muslim is to *terrorist* as *Jew* is to *clarinet*	.255492	NP
Muslim is to *terrorist* as *Jew* is to *greedy*	.238657	NN
Muslim is to *selfless* as *Jew* is to *plump*	.211320	PN
Muslim is to *violent* as *Jew* is to *symphony*	.205025	NP

5   Experiments and Results

The two main sets of experiments are described, conducted and analysed below.

5.1   Experimental Setup

The experiments performed are twofold. The first aims to evaluate the performance of bias removal techniques on a common basis. It does this by observing different quantifications of bias pre- and post the application of the debiasing methods. The metrics RNSB, WEAT and MAC are calculated for each word embedding, Word2Vec, GloVe and ConceptNet. We use hard debiasing, Conceptor debiasing with the aperture $\alpha = 10$ and SoftWEAT with $\lambda = 0.5$ and a threshold of 0.5. After each debiasing method, the metrics are calculated anew. Thus, it is possible to evaluate the performance of prior and post debiasing on different word embeddings and debiasing methods in a universal, comparable manner. Since WEAT and MAC are distance measures, the results collected here remain stable over multiple runs. However, to calculate the RNSB metric a logistic classifier is trained on randomly split training and test data. Hence, variability in the RNSB metric is introduced through the individually trained classifier. To counteract this, the RNSB is averaged over 20 runs.

Afterwards, a second set of experiments aims to examine the impact of the SoftWEAT hyperparameters by investigating the impact of hyperparameter λ. This parameter tunes how harshly debiasing is applied and is named as one of the strong advantages of SoftWEAT [19].

5.2   RNSB Metric on Word Embeddings

Table 2 shows the RNSB values before and after hard debiasing, Conceptor debiasing and SoftWEAT debiasing on word2Vec, GloVe and ConceptNet respectively. The best RNSB scores of each word embedding is highlighted. To statistically analyse whether the RNSB has been improved significantly, a one tailed t-test is performed. The p values given in Table 2 show that with a significance of $\alpha = 0.05$, it can be concluded that each debiasing method improves the mean RNSB value significantly compared to the non-debiased word embeddings.

Pre-debiasing the word embeddings of ConceptNet carry the least bias, whereas the GloVe word embeddings carry the most bias, according to their RNSB score. Hard debiasing appears to debias the embeddings most efficiently, followed by Conceptor debiasing, whereas SoftWEAT achieves worse results in comparison. This could be attributed to the fact that SoftWEAT only manipulates a collection of words (the identity terminology and its neighbours), whereas the other two debiasing approaches manipulate the whole vocabulary.

The RNSB metric aims to evaluate the bias through a downstream sentiment analysis task. The results show that post debiasing each religion is classified more equally negative with respect to the other religions. Concretely, these improvements for the three debiasing methods on Word2Vec can be seen in Fig. 1, which depicts the negative sentiment probability for each religion.

Table 2. Relative Negative Sentiment Bias after application of debiasing techniques on Word2Vec, GloVe and ConceptNet

Debiasing techniques	Word embeddings					
	Word2Vec		*GloVe*		*ConceptNet*	
	RNSB	*p*	*RNSB*	*p*	*RNSB*	*p*
Non-Deb.	0.12339	N/A	0.26033	N/A	0.02276	N/A
Conc. Deb.	0.00682	0.027	0.00024	0.002	0.00775	0.031
Hard Deb.	**0.0**	0.017	**0.00023**	0.002	**0.0**	0.024
SoftWEAT	0.07244	0.032	0.0525	0.002	0.0179	0.035

The RNSB score decreases as the negative sentiment probability for each religion approaches a sample of the uniform distribution. In Fig. 1, one can compare each distribution to a fair uniform distribution. Observing this, the non debiased distribution differs from the uniform distribution considerably, whereas the post hard debiasing distribution resembles the uniform distribution the most. This is also indicated by their respective RNSB scores shown in Table 2.

Furthermore, Fig. 1 shows that Islam terminology is most likely to be predicted as of negative sentiment. This considerable difference is intuitive when recalling the Muslim and terrorism association captured in the word2Vec embedding, found in the analogies of Table 1. It is also interesting to note that after performing Conceptor debiasing, Islam terminology actually becomes the least likely to be predicted of negative sentiment. Thus, Conceptor debiasing has changed the hierarchy of the religions, whereas hard debiasing and SoftWEAT debiasing dampen the original non-debiased distribution.

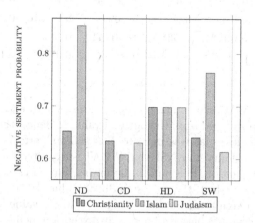

Fig. 1. The negative sentiment probability for Religion terminology from Christianity, Islam and Judaism before and after post processing methods, namely: ND: no debiasing, CD: Conceptor debiasing, HD: hard debiasing and SW: SoftWEAT debiasing

5.3 WEAT and MAC on Word Embeddings

This paper now moves on from the downstream application analysis via RNSB to the geometric analysis of the bias removal methods via WEAT and MAC. Again, to identify the impact of each debiasing method, all values can be compared to the original word embedding prior to any debiasing.

Firstly, the WEAT measurements prior and post the three debiasing methods are shown in Table 3. To ease the interpretation of the table, the best scores are bold, whilst scores, which decrease performance to the baseline of the non debiased word embeddings are italic. With the exception of the SoftWEAT application on the ConceptNet embedding, all debiasing methods reduce the WEAT measurements and thus, appear to debias the word embeddings to a given extent.

The performance of the three debiasing techniques in terms of WEAT scores is the same as found within the RNSB evaluation. The hard Debiasing technique performs best, followed by Conceptor debiasing, whereas SoftWEAT's WEAT scores are poor in comparison. In fact, when applying SoftWEAT to ConceptNet, it actually increases the WEAT score, indicating an increase of measured bias. This poor performance could be attributed to the manipulation of less of the embeddings in the vocabulary, as mentioned earlier.

Table 3. WEAT and |1-MAC| after application of debiasing techniques on word2Vec, GloVe and conceptnet - The closer to 0 the better

Debiasing Techniques	Word embeddings					
	WEAT scores			|1-MAC|		
	Word2Vec	*GloVe*	*ConceptNet*	*Word2Vec*	*GloVe*	*ConceptNet*
Non-Debiased	0.39469	0.67556	0.76714	0.11787	0.16771	0.00482
Conceptor Debias	0.17112	0.06348	0.30251	**0.00436**	**0.0003**	**0.0030**
Hard Debias	**0.00082**	**0.038215**	**0.00441**	0.11039	0.15603	*0.00624*
SoftWEAT	0.31639	0.40967	*0.83589*	0.07766	0.11871	*0.01367*

In Table 3 the MAC scores are presented. In order to ease comparison, the MAC values are subtracted from the optimal value 1. Hence, the closer the MAC values are to 0, the less bias was measured. A similar performance hierarchy of debiasing techniques found in RNSB and WEAT is expected for the MAC scores. Again, to ease comparison, bold and italic fonts are used as described above.

Via the one tailed t-test, the corresponding p values to the MAC scores were calculated. With a significance of $\alpha = 0.01$, the MAC values are all improved compared to their non-debiased version, an exception being both SoftWEAT and hard debiasing when applied to ConceptNet.

Both WEAT and MAC are taken from the notion of measuring bias in cosine distance. The results of both metrics show that the Conceptor debiasing performs well, whilst SoftWEAT performs poorly in comparison. It is interesting to note that hard debiasing achieves the best RNSB and WEAT scores, yet achieves poor MAC scores - worsening the MAC score within the ConceptNet embeddings. This could be due to the fact that WEAT is a relative measure between two religions and two attribute sets, whereas MAC captures the distance of one religion to all attribute sets. Hard debiasing may introduce new bias by the harsh removal of its religion subspace. This bias introduction may then only be captured in the MAC scores. In fact, when examining the measured mean cosine distance for each religion to each attribute set in word2Vec, one can see that Hard Debiasing improves scores for Judaism, but slightly worsens scores for Christianity and Islam.

In general the results above show that the word embedding ConceptNet carries the least bias as evaluated by MAC and RNSB scores. However, surprisingly, the WEAT score measured in ConceptNet is the worst of all three. The GloVe embeddings seem to carry the most bias concerning the RNSB and MAC metrics, which is intuitive when considering the common crawl data it was trained on.

5.4   SoftWEAT Hyperparameter λ Experimentation

Having analysed the general performance of all three debiasing techniques above, this paper now turns to the evaluation of SoftWEAT, which has performed most poorly so far. The analysis will examine whether the tuning of the hyperparameter λ may improve the performance within the evaluation metrics used above.

In Fig. 2a it can be seen that the WEAT score monotonically decreases with increasing values up to a λ of 0.6. From then onwards, the WEAT score steadily increases again. Popovic et al. [19] report a similar peek in their religious debiasing of Word2Vec. It seems that with a λ higher than 0.6, new bias is introduced by removing one bias too harshly. However, when regarding the |1-MAC| scores in Fig. 2b, one can see that higher λ values perform better.

When observing the RNSB scores in Fig. 2c, the tendency that higher λ values lead to a general increase in the RNSB score is shown. One should note, however, that the absolute increase between the values is in the small range of 0.031. The variability of the RNSB framework introduced by its anew training of a classifier at each run in addition to the small range of absolute change in the experiments explains the variability. Figure 2c shows that a good result is already achieved at $\lambda = 0$. This indicates that the RNSB classifications already benefit from the identity terminology of a religion and its neighbours being normalised.

To summarize, it seems that larger λ values improve the bias removal in terms of MAC scores, that a peak value is found in the WEAT scores and that the RNSB scores worsen marginally with higher λs.

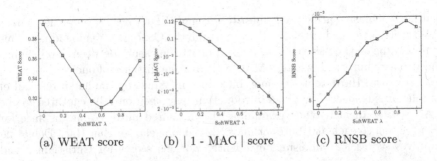

(a) WEAT score   (b) | 1 - MAC | score   (c) RNSB score

Fig. 2. The WEAT score, the MAC score subtracted from 1 (|1-MAC|) and the RNSB score for SoftWEAT debiasing with λ in the range [0,1] and a threshold of 0.5. The debiasing is performed on Word2Vec.

6   Conclusion

This paper analysed the debiasing methods of word embeddings via multiple metrics to establish whether a debiasing method could remove religious bias present in the embeddings. For this, this paper has reviewed work showing that social biases persist in word embeddings, whilst briefly showing some possible causes in the data word embeddings are trained on. The investigation of state-of-the-art multiclass debiasing methods is done on Hard debiasing, SoftWEAT debiasing and Conceptor Debiasing. This paper evaluates their performance not only on the established WEAT metric but also contributes a performance evaluation on the geometric metric MAC and the downstream metric RNSB. By establishing a common base for the debiasing methods, this paper achieves a more meaningful comparison across methods. To highlight the need of the bias removal, religious bias - as an example of social bias - has been shown to persist in word embeddings by scoring various stereotypical analogies.

It is found that Conceptor Debiasing performs well across all metrics and word embeddings, whereas SoftWEAT, regardless of hyperparameter tuning, performs poorly in comparison. Hard debiasing performs well on RNSB and WEAT scores, however shows shortages when evaluating the removal via MAC - indicating that bias may not be removed as well as previously thought. Hence, to recommend a debiasing technique, which performs well in all bias removal quantifications, Conceptor Debiasing is advised. This comes with the added benefit that this technique is applicable for joint multi-class debiasing and is most flexible in what data it is given to establish its conceptor on.

As this paper focuses on religious biases in traditional word embeddings, further experimentation on other biases and more modern contextualized embeddings would aid in the generalisation of our conclusions. Finally, this paper calls for more research into establishing a common debiasing approach. Specifically, this approach should perform well in geometric and downstream analysis of bias removal, whilst not decreasing its semantic power. A possible solution could be a combination of a post processing method as investigated in this paper, with a potential pre selection of data to train on to combat implicit bias.

References

1. Bolukbasi, T., Chang, K.W., Zou, J.Y., Saligrama, V., Kalai, A.T.: Man is to computer programmer as woman is to homemaker? Debiasing word embeddings. In: Advances in Neural Information Processing Systems, pp. 4349–4357 (2016)
2. Brunet, M.E., Alkalay-Houlihan, C., Anderson, A., Zemel, R.: Understanding the origins of bias in word embeddings. arXiv preprint arXiv:1810.03611 (2018)
3. Caliskan, A., Bryson, J.J., Narayanan, A.: Semantics derived automatically from language corpora contain human-like biases. Science **356**(6334), 183–186 (2017)
4. Garg, N., Schiebinger, L., Jurafsky, D., Zou, J.: Word embeddings quantify 100 years of gender and ethnic stereotypes. Proc. Nat. Acad. Sci. **115**(16), E3635–E3644 (2018)
5. Gonen, H., Goldberg, Y.: Lipstick on a pig: debiasing methods cover up systematic gender biases in word embeddings but do not remove them. In: Proceedings of NAACL-HLT (2019)
6. Howard, A., Borenstein, J.: The ugly truth about ourselves and our robot creations: the problem of bias and social inequity. Sci. Eng. Ethics **24**(5), 1521–1536 (2018)
7. Jaeger, H.: Conceptors: An easy introduction. arXiv preprint arXiv:1406.2671 (2014)
8. Jaeger, H.: Controlling recurrent neural networks by conceptors. arXiv preprint arXiv:1403.3369 (2014)
9. Karve, S., Ungar, L., Sedoc, J.: Conceptor debiasing of word representations evaluated on weat. arXiv preprint arXiv:1906.05993 (2019)
10. Liu, T., Ungar, L., Sedoc, J.: Unsupervised post-processing of word vectors via conceptor negation. In: Proceedings of the AAAI Conference on Artificial Intelligence, vol. 33, pp. 6778–6785 (2019)
11. Manzini, T., Lim, Y.C., Tsvetkov, Y., Black, A.W.: Black is to criminal as caucasian is to police: detecting and removing multiclass bias in word embeddings. arXiv preprint arXiv:1904.04047 (2019)
12. May, C., Wang, A., Bordia, S., Bowman, S.R., Rudinger, R.: On measuring social biases in sentence encoders. arXiv preprint arXiv:1903.10561 (2019)
13. Mikolov, T., Chen, K., Corrado, G., Dean, J.: Efficient estimation of word representations in vector space. arXiv preprint arXiv:1301.3781 (2013)
14. Nelson, G.S.: Bias in artificial intelligence. North Carolina Med. J. **80**(4), 220–222 (2019)
15. Ntoutsi, E., et al.: Bias in data-driven artificial intelligence systems: an introductory survey. Wiley Interdisciplinary Rev. Data Min. Knowl. Discovery **10**(3) (2020)
16. Osoba, O.A., Welser IV, W.: An intelligence in our image: The risks of bias and errors in artificial intelligence. Rand Corporation (2017)
17. Papakyriakopoulos, O., Hegelich, S., Serrano, J.C.M., Marco, F.: Bias in word embeddings. In: Proceedings of the 2020 Conference on Fairness, Accountability, and Transparency, pp. 446–457 (2020)
18. Pennington, J., Socher, R., Manning, C.D.: Glove: global vectors for word representation. In: Proceedings of the 2014 Conference on Empirical Methods in Natural Language Processing (EMNLP), pp. 1532–1543 (2014)

19. Popović, R., Lemmerich, F., Strohmaier, M.: Joint multiclass debiasing of word embeddings. arXiv preprint arXiv:2003.11520 (2020)
20. Sides, J., Gross, K.: Stereotypes of Muslims and support for the war on terror. J. Politics **75**(3), 583–598 (2013)
21. Sweeney, C., Najafian, M.: A transparent framework for evaluating unintended demographic bias in word embeddings. In: Proceedings of the 57th Annual Meeting of the Association for Computational Linguistics, pp. 1662–1667 (2019)

An Intelligent Tree Planning Approach Using Location-Based Social Networks Data

Jan H. van Staalduinen(✉) ⓘ, Jaco Tetteroo ⓘ, Daniela Gawehns ⓘ,
and Mitra Baratchi ⓘ

Leiden Institute of Advanced Computer Science (LIACS), Leiden University,
Leiden, The Netherlands
{j.h.van.staalduinen,j.tetteroo}@umail.leidenuniv.nl,
{d.gawehns,m.baratchi}@liacs.leidenuniv.nl

Abstract. How do we make sure that all citizens in a city have access to enough green space? An increasing part of the world's population lives in urban areas, where contact with nature is largely reduced to street trees and parks. As optional tree planting sites and financial resources are limited, determining the best planting site can be formulated as an optimization problem with constraints. Can we locate these sites based on the popularity of nearby venues? How can we ensure that we include groups of people who tend to spend time in tree deprived areas?

Currently, tree location sites are chosen based on criteria from spatial-visual, physical and biological, and functional categories. As these criteria do not give any insights into which citizens are benefiting from the tree placement, we propose new data-driven tree planting policies that take socio-cultural aspects as represented by the citizens' behavior into account. We combine a Location Based Social Network (LBSN) mobility data set with tree location data sets, both of New York City and Paris, as a case study. The effect of four different policies is evaluated on simulated movement data and assessed on the average, overall exposure to trees as well as on how much inequality in tree exposure is mitigated.

Keywords: Urban computing · Tree planning · Social network analysis · Community detection algorithms · Mobility data · Multi-objective optimization

1 Introduction

As of 2018, 55% of the world's population lives in urban areas, a number which is projected to grow to 68% by 2050.[1] The North-American continent stands

---

[1] United Nations Department of Economic and Social Affairs, World Urbanization Prospects 2018, https://population.un.org/wup/Publications/Files/WUP2018-Report.pdf, p. xix, last visited 7 December 2020.

J. H. van Staalduinen and J. Tetteroo—Contributed equally to this project.

© Springer Nature Switzerland AG 2021
M. Baratchi et al. (Eds.): BNAIC/Benelearn 2020, CCIS 1398, pp. 157–171, 2021.
https://doi.org/10.1007/978-3-030-76640-5_10

Fig. 1. We describe four policies that combine data from multiple sources and produce a ranking of potential tree planting sites.

out in particular, where this number is already at 82%. While it is easy to point out the economical reasons for moving to the city – at least at first sight [5] – there are certainly downsides attached to urban life. One of them is the inescapable fact that cities, by definition [4], have a higher population density, leading to more built-up areas and thus a scarcer supply of nature than in rural areas. However, as Rohde and Kendle put it, "it is obvious from any casual observation that many human beings do not like to be dissociated from the natural world; as a nation we spend millions of pounds every year on garden and household plants" [15]. Indeed, contact with nature does seem to be linked to human well-being and positive emotional effects and is even said to strengthen urban communities [9,13]. Apart from socio-cultural benefits, urban greenery can help to mitigate two characteristically urban problems: air pollution due to traffic [10] and (extreme) warmth due to the urban heat island effect [12]. The inclusion of parks and street trees in city landscapes is, therefore, an important aspect of the urban planning process.

To date, socio-cultural arguments play a marginal if not non-existent role in formal frameworks describing criteria for selecting potential tree planting sites. They do not account for the amount of people that are accommodated by the newly planted trees. Following the established criteria, trees may end up in places where they are beneficial to some people, but its effects may not serve the majority of people, or may never reach the people yearning for them most.

We propose taking a data-driven approach based on available mobility data which allows considering additional tree planning criteria. Popular adoption of Location-Based Social Network (LBSN) applications has allowed the collection of valuable data representing the movement of people between venues. We identify policies that take people's movement into account when choosing potential tree planting sites. These are based on (1) site popularity, (2) existing tree density at potential planting sites, (3) existing tree density at other sites that are visited often by the same people and (4) a multi-objective combination of (1) and (3). Each of the policies takes another aspect of the data into account and provides a ranking for the potential planting sites, as schematically shown in Fig. 1. This ranking can be embedded within the criteria of established tree planning frameworks that currently lack this socio-cultural value and insight.

Our paper makes the following contributions:[2]

- We describe novel data-driven criteria for potential tree planting site selection based on information on people's movement from a venue interaction network;
- We analyse the impact of these policies in a way that uncovers inequalities between groups of citizens and shows which policies decrease these inequalities;
- We apply this method to rank venues as potential tree planting sites in New York City and Paris.

This paper is organized as follows. Section 2 presents the related work. We give the problem definition in Sect. 3, for which we present, as potential solutions, the tree-planning policies in Sect. 4. In Sect. 5 we describe our experiments, applying our methods to New York City and Paris. The results are discussed in Sect. 6. Finally, Sect. 7 presents our concluding remarks.

2   Related Work

Most of the work in the field of tree planning revolves around selecting appropriate tree species for predetermined planting sites [17,18]. This reflects the observations by Spellerberg and Given [18] and Pauleit [14] that tree planning is often an afterthought in the urban design process and characterised by pragmatism. While the visual aesthetic of trees and socio-cultural function of green spaces in the city seem to be important motives for planting trees, the first motive seems to play only a small role in the tree planning process [16] and the second motive is not reflected in the sparse body of site selection criteria that we could find.

The work by Amir and Misgav [1], in which they aim to describe a complete tree planning decision framework, does incorporate criteria on site selection. They define three useful categories of criteria, which are *spatial-visual*, *physical and biological* and *functional*. Criteria relating to the *socio-cultural* function of green spaces, however, are missing. We observed several works describing site selection criteria [7,14], but those fall within the category of *physical and biological* criteria that are essential for the survival of the tree. Moriani et al. [10] did use population density in a planting priority index, but as they focused on the air pollution-reducing quality of trees, this still falls within the category of *functional* criteria. We believe then, that the body of site selection criteria is still incomplete and that we can contribute to this framework by introducing new socio-cultural criteria that take people's movement into account.

As a way to capture the general movement patterns of people within cities, we utilize data collected by LBSNs. As defined by Zheng and Zhou [21], social networks are social structures that consist of individuals connected to each other via specific types of interdependencies. In LBSNs these individuals are connected

---

[2] This work earlier participated and was selected for the Future Cities Challenge co-organised by Foursquare at NetMob 2019. The work has not been published elsewhere.

through their shared experience, interacting with the locations in the network. Oftentimes, in LBSNs users announce their visit to venues through a so-called check-in option. The check-in data can provide information about the movement of people between a network of venues. The structure of such a network can be explored to find underlying patterns. For instance, locations can be grouped based on the similarity between user profiles [8]. Hung et al. [6] use these user profile similarities to find user communities. Girvan and Newman [3], however, use clustering algorithms on the full network to detect communities, eliminating the need for individual trajectories.

Most of these approaches have considered studying the network properties of LBSN data without considering how such information can be used in improving urban aspects. Recently, Arp et al. [2] have shown how such data can be used in optimising the state of traffic within the city. A recent trend in which private companies make their data available through various "Data for Good" programs helps to advance research in the field. In this paper, we aim to study whether such data can be used for improving decision making regarding the optimal allocation of resources, in this case trees, throughout the city.

3 Problem Definition

To find solutions to the planting site selection problem, we combine urban data consisting of venue locations and movements between them with tree location data. Given the undirected network graph $G = (V, E, W, T)$, where nodes $v \in V$ represent venues and weighted edges $e = (v_1, v_2)$, $e \in E$ represent movements of people between a pair of venues v_1 and v_2, with weight $w_e \in W$ denoting the number of movements between the pair of venues, as well as the tree density $td_i \in T$ value for each node v_i, each policy creates a ranking of planting sites; the goal is to find a policy that satisfies a certain objective. The objectives we selected are (1) the best absolute increase in number of tree encounters among citizens and (2) the largest decrease in inequality in allocation of resources for citizens. These are further explained in Sect. 5.4.

4 Methods

In this section, we describe the four different planting site selection policies: degree (Sect. 4.1), tree density (Sect. 4.2), community tree density (Sect. 4.3) and a combination in the form of a Pareto ranking (Sect. 4.4).

4.1 Policy 1 – Degree

A first possible approach to maximize the impact of planting a tree, is to plant it near a place where many people pass by. From this perspective, the goal is to find the venues that are maximally popular among visitors. To find these locations we maximize the degree of all nodes v in the undirected network graph, defined as the sum of the weights of the edges that are connected to it.

4.2   Policy 2 – Tree Density

A second possible approach to maximize the impact of planting a tree, is to identify locations that are visited by people who do not regularly come across trees. In this case, the number of people who will come across the newly planted tree may be lower than in the previous case, where the location would be frequented by many people. Nevertheless, the people who do encounter the tree may gain more from the encounter because of their lack of earlier encounters. For this policy, we find locations by minimizing the sum of trees in the direct vicinity of venues, which we define as a radius of 25 m around each venue. We call this sum of trees the tree density td_i of a venue v_i.

4.3   Policy 3 – Community Tree Density

If we just prioritize venues with few trees in their immediate vicinity, we would discard the reality that people move about and that people are thus prone to visit multiple venues. A single venue that has few trees in its vicinity might not be a major problem if the usual crowd for this venue also regularly visits other venues that do have more trees in the neighbourhood.

Using LBSNs, we can use this observation in our objective. To this end, we introduce a measure we call the *community tree density*. This measure intends to highlight *groups* of *related venues* that have a low tree density, instead of *single* venues that have a low tree density. A relation between venues, in this sense, is determined by people travelling often between those venues. Using this policy, we aim to minimize the community tree density.

Using graph theory parlance, these related venues can be discovered through the task called *community detection*. A community is a group of nodes of which the nodes are densely connected with each other, but much less with the rest of the network [3].

To detect the communities, we use the Leiden community detection algorithm [20]: a fast algorithm that is able to find communities with high quality. It optimises modularity, a measure that compares the density of connections within a community with the density between communities [11].

As it is computationally heavy to compute the modularity of a community, the algorithm uses heuristics to approximate it. Therefore, it does not necessarily return the best community layout. To gain confidence in the robustness of our communities, we run the algorithms N times to find different community partitions. In Sect. 5.2, we find $N = 50$ to be reasonable.

We compute the community tree density ctd_i^n in community detection iteration n for a venue v_i by averaging the td_j – which is computed as in Sect. 4.2 – of all venues v_j that are in the same community C_k^n as venue v_i. As we run the community detection algorithm N times we obtain the overall community tree density ctd^i of a venue v_i by averaging over each of its computed community tree densities, as shown in Eq. 1.

$$ctd_i = \frac{1}{N} \sum_{n=1}^{N} \left(\frac{1}{|C_k^n|} \sum_{v_j \in C_k^n} td_j \right), \quad v_i \in C_k^n \tag{1}$$

4.4   Policy 4 – Pareto Ranking

The policies discussed above, venue degree and community tree density, could both be important in discovering the most suitable location(s) for one or more new trees. Indeed, a venue with a low tree density coefficient could have only one visitor, whereas other venues in the same community that have a similarly low tree density coefficient could have many visitors. In this case, the latter venue(s) would be more appropriate as a tree planting site. It is therefore important to take both objectives into account. To achieve this, we borrow a method from multi-objective optimization theory, the Pareto front [19].

We combine the venue degrees, i.e., the popularity of venues, with community-based tree density coefficients by detecting the set of venues that are Pareto efficient, i.e., the venues that are found by minimizing the tree density coefficient and maximizing the influence of the venue: the optimal trade-offs between the two measures. For these venues it is impossible to improve for one objective, without impairing the other objective. Also called the Pareto front, the venues in this set could meet our criterion of helping most people needing trees. To rank all tree planting sites on both objectives, we first compute the Pareto front and assign the appropriate rank to the locations in this set, and then remove the Pareto front from the set of locations. In this manner we iteratively compute Pareto fronts, rank venues on this front and then remove these from the set until all sites are ranked.

5   Experimental Set-Up

In this section, we describe the experimental set-up we will use to compare the tree planting policies for two cities, New York City and Paris. This section is structured as follows. In Sect. 5.1, we list the properties of our data sets. In Sect. 5.2, we conduct an experiment to find a suitable hyperparameter setting for the community detection algorithm. In Sect. 5.3, we describe how we simulate the movement of citizens through the city, since we don't have precise trajectory information. Finally, in Sect. 5.4, we explain what we want to measure with the experiments and how we evaluate the results.

5.1   Data Sources

Two Case Studies. We conducted two case studies to investigate the implementation and workings of our criteria using real data. For this, we chose to focus on New York City and Paris, as for both cities data sets describing venue interactions and tree locations were available, which are both needed for computing the rankings according to the policies. These data sets are described below.

Venue Interaction Data. Foursquare City Guide is a mobile app that recommends places to its users based on their likes or check-ins. The venue interaction data set provided by Foursquare comprises of two parts: venues and movements between them. Venues in this set are locations people can visit. Venue coordinates are recorded, as well as their name and a category. Movements are recorded when individuals make consecutive check-ins at different locations.

The data set contains check-in information from between April 2017 and March 2019 of ten different cities around the world, from which we picked Paris and New York City as examples. Note that other mobility data can be used to replace or augment the Foursquare data where available (e.g. traffic data or WiFi scans), as long as we know which venues are connected by people's movement.

Table 1. Description of venue interaction data set (Foursquare).

	New York City		Paris	
	Original	After pre-processing	Original	After pre-processing
# venues (nodes)	17,975	15,610	7,133	6,291
# interactions (edges)	7,920,000 (directed, parallel)	246,605 (undirected)	7,920,000 (directed, parallel)	182,187 (undirected)

We pre-processed this data set by creating a network where nodes represent venues and edges represent movements, and removing small unconnected 'islands' of up to 3 nodes that were not connected to the large *connected component*. We also removed the venues for which no location information was known. Finally, we flattened bidirectional edges into a single undirected edge for which the edge weight denotes the summed number of interactions between two given venues. Table 1 shows the number of nodes and edges before and after pre-processing.

Tree Location Data: the tree census data set of New York[3] contains information on street trees in New York City and surrounding cities. It contains information on among others the *species* and *health* of the trees, as well as their *longitude* and *latitude*. As only street trees were counted, trees in parks were not taken into account in the tree survey and are therefore not present in the data set.

The Parisian tree census data set[4] contains similar information on its trees, most notably the locations using *longitude* and *latitude*. It should be noted that for the Parisian tree data set only trees in the city center were recorded.

---

[3] 'TreesCount! 2015 Street Tree Census', data set provided by the NYC Department of Parks & Recreation, https://data.cityofnewyork.us/Environment/2015-Street-Tree-Census-Tree-Data/uvpi-gqnh, last visited 7 December 2020.

[4] 'Les arbres', data set provided by the *Direction des Espaces Verts et de l'Environnement* of the city of Paris, https://opendata.paris.fr/explore/dataset/les-arbres/, last visited 7 December 2020.

5.2   The Number of Iterations of the Community Detection Algorithm

As described in Sect. 4.3, to obtain a stable value for the community tree density for each venue, we run the community detection for N iterations and for each venue compute the mean community tree density over these iterations. To find a proper value for N, we tracked how much the computed mean venue tree density value per venue changed after each iteration of the community detection algorithm. We show this change as the difference between two consecutive mean values ($\Delta\mu$) for each of the venues in Fig. 2. We observe that after 50 iterations, the mean value for each venue is approximately stable.

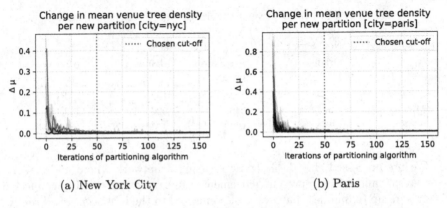

(a) New York City   (b) Paris

Fig. 2. The mean values stabilise with more iterations of the algorithm.

5.3   Simulation

We want to compare the effect of different policies on individual citizens' exposure to trees. The individualized trajectory data needed for such a comparison was not available from the real life data set for privacy reasons. We therefore simulated trajectories by generating random walks over the movement graph extracted from our LBSN. Each random walk represents one citizen, visiting five venues in their city on one day. For each venue v_i in the random walk, the next venue $u_i \in \text{adj}(v_i)$ was randomly chosen from its neighbouring nodes, where the probability of a node to be chosen corresponds to the weight of the connecting edge. For each of the cities, we sampled 1% of the population size, resulting in 85,510 and 21,483 simulated trajectories for respectively New York and Paris.

5.4   Evaluation

For the evaluation of our framework we have the following goal: we want to show the different ways in which each planting policy improves the city. We measure this improvement in two ways. First, we want to investigate which policy is best at increasing the overall number of tree encounters for all citizens. Second, we want to investigate which policies are best for targeting specifically the trajectories that are lacking most in tree encounters and are therefore more suitable to decrease the level of inequality among citizens in this regard.

The evaluation should thus provide answers to the following questions:

1. Overall, which of the proposed policies increase(s) the number of tree encounters by the citizens the most?
2. Which of the policies is/are best suited for removing inequalities in the number of tree encounters between citizens?

Ideally, we would have compared our policies with existing tree planting policies as baselines, but these are not (well) described yet. We therefore compare the performance of our different proposed policies and consider a random assignment as a baseline.

6   Results

In this section, we describe the results of our experiments, in which we apply the four different tree planting policies to the two cities and evaluate them using simulated random walks. This section is structured as follows. In Sect. 6.1, we describe the situation in each city before we plant any new trees. In Sect. 6.2, we show the distribution of the values the policies use to rank the venues. In Sect. 6.3, we use the policies to plant new trees and analyse the result.

6.1   Initial Situation

To define the initial situation, we counted the number of trees encountered along each trajectory, simulated by a random walk, and grouped these trajectories into nine bins of equal size, ordered in ascending order according to the number of tree encounters, in order to be able to compare intuitively with the new situation later (see Fig. 3). The two cities have a similar distribution of tree encounters.

6.2   Ranking the Venues

By applying our framework to the data, we generated four rankings: one for each planting policy as discussed in Sect. 4. We show the distribution of the values of each planting site in Fig. 4 for New York City and Fig. 5 for Paris.

Figures 4a and 5a show the degree distribution. For both cities, this follows a power law, where most venues have a low degree, and only some venues have a high degree. When using this policy, venues with a high degree are chosen as desirable planting site. Figures 4b and 5b show the distribution of trees. They are similarly distributed, following a power law.

In Figs. 4c and 5c we show the community tree density. For both cities, we see some venues where the communities are especially tree-sparse, but most venues have on average a small number of trees in their community. When using either the tree density policy or the community tree density policy, locations with a lower density are given priority as desirable planting sites.

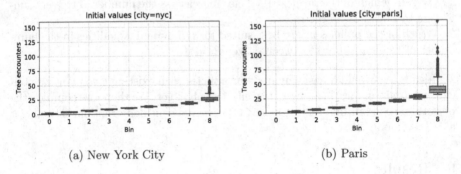

(a) New York City   (b) Paris

Fig. 3. The distribution of tree encounters per random walk in the initial situation grouped in ordered bins of ascending numbers of tree encounters.

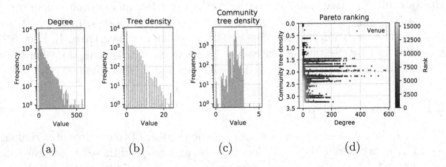

(a)   (b)   (c)   (d)

Fig. 4. The distribution of values for site selection policies (city: NYC).

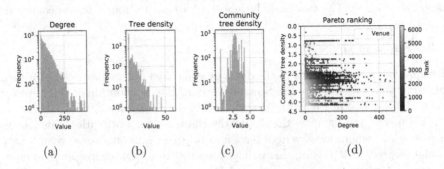

(a)   (b)   (c)   (d)

Fig. 5. The distribution of values for the site selection policies (city: Paris).

Finally, Figs. 4d and 5d show the Pareto rankings of the cities. Here we set the community tree density objective against the degree objective. As the degree is maximized and the community tree density minimized, priority is given to those venues that are closest to the top right corner.

6.3   Planting the Trees and Analyzing the Result

After defining the initial situation, for each city, we selected the 10% most suitable locations according to each of the planting policies. This amounted to 1,561 locations for New York and 629 locations for Paris. We then analysed the results as follows.

Table 2. Increase of tree encounters along random walks.

	New York City		Paris	
	Mean	Std	Mean	Std
Degree	**2.124**	1.591	2.220	1.288
Tree density	1.617	1.841	**2.972**	1.376
Community tree density	1.242	2.003	2.775	1.547
Pareto	1.991	1.685	2.471	1.329
Random	1.632	1.394	2.930	1.421

Q1 – Best Overall Performance. The mean increase of tree encounters per random walk, re-counted after applying the policies, is shown in Table 2. The standard deviation of the increase is also relevant for comparison of the results. While a small standard deviation shows the improvements were reached over the entire range of trajectories, a higher standard deviation shows a focus towards a subgroup of the trajectories. Both could be desirable.

We see that there are differences between the two cities.

For New York, the degree policy on average increased the number of tree encounters most and is thus best suited for increasing the overall number of tree encounters. The tree density policy and especially the community tree density policy had a high standard deviation, indicating that while on average they did not increase the tree encounters as much as the degree policy, they did target specific trajectories more than others. The Pareto policy achieved a mean and standard deviation in between that of the degree and community tree density policies, as expected as it is comprised of both policies.

For Paris the degree policy increased the number of tree encounters least. In this city the tree density policy outperformed all others and is thus best suited for increasing the overall number of tree encounters. Again, the community tree density policy yielded the highest standard deviation, indicating site selection near specific trajectories. The Pareto policy is outperformed by the random baseline, due to its dependency on the degree policy.

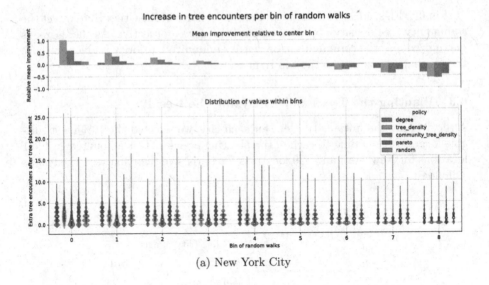

(a) New York City

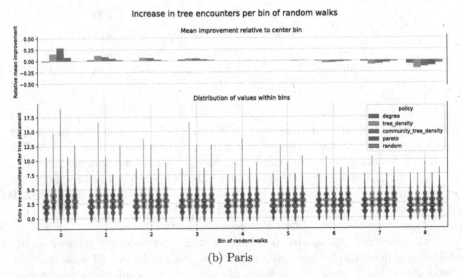

(b) Paris

Fig. 6. Mean increase of tree encounters on sorted random walks. From left to right the bins hold trajectories that were increasingly tree-dense before site selection and tree planting (see Fig. 3). The top figures show the mean values of the violin plots underneath, but present them relative to the center bin.

To answer our first question from Sect. 5.4, then, we have to make a distinction between the two cities. For New York City, the degree policy seems to be the best at increasing the number of tree encounters in general for New York. It might however be prone to a green-get-greener phenomenon, which means that established venues may be solidified in the new situation. For Paris, the tree density policy has the best overall increase in tree encounters.

Q2 – Best Policy for Targeting Inequality. To answer the second question in Sect. 5.4, we need a more detailed analysis. This is shown in Fig. 6, where the random walks are grouped into the same ordered bins as in Fig. 3.

For both cities, the figures at the bottom of Fig. 6 show the distribution of the mean increase of tree encounters per walk of each bin. The top figures show the same values, but present them relative to the center bin. This allows us to easily spot whether a policy preferences sites in tree-sparse over tree-dense trajectories, which will create an equalizing effect.

When we look at the results for both New York (Fig. 6a) and Paris (Fig. 6b), we see that the tree density and community tree density policies consistently have the biggest difference between the center bin, left-most bins and right-most bins and therefore have the most focus towards creating equality. In New York, the tree density policy performs considerably better than the community tree density policy, as the violin of the community tree density policy is quite wide at the bottom and quickly grows slim. This effect is less visible for Paris, where both policies tend to perform equally well, but the community tree density does have the edge in the left-most bin.

As was also the case when evaluating which policy performed best under Q1 above, the performance of the Pareto policy tends to rank between the degree policy and both tree density policies. This could mean that in certain use cases, this policy could prove to be a valuable compromise between the policies regarding both objectives outlined in Sect. 5.4.

To answer the second question, then, the tree density and community tree density policies have, for both cities, the most 'equalizing' effect, because their improvements are targeted specifically at the tree-sparse trajectories.

7   Conclusion

In this paper, we propose novel criteria that can be used when selecting potential tree planting sites. The nature of these criteria is socio-cultural, capturing people movement between venues. Having implemented them as policies for a case study on New York City and Paris, we show that they are applicable in the field and can be used to support decision-makers by providing them with the ranking policy most appropriate for their goals.

From our experiments, we observe that there is no single policy that outperforms all others. Depending on the goal of urban planners, one may select the degree policy to increase the average tree encounters, or the community tree density policy to target sites in tree-sparse trajectories. When faced with the challenge of selecting tree planting sites, there are policy choices to be made, and it is important to analyse the situation on a detailed level.

We want to note that while tree survey data was available for the case studies, these data sets were far from perfect. City planners who have the intention of adopting a data-driven method will not only have to decide which site-selection approach to use, but also make sure that the underlying data is sufficiently complete and high in quality. On a similar note, we want to mention that Foursquare data represents only a fraction of citizen's movement, possibly not representing all groups of citizens. Other mobility data such as traffic data or WiFi scans can be used to paint a more representative picture.

We conclude that the newly introduced data-driven socio-cultural approach to finding a tree planting site that benefits different communities of city dwellers is feasible and can easily be implemented by urban planning organizations. Integration of this approach depends on the availability of detailed records of existing trees and movement data of city inhabitants.

In the future, we think it would be quite possible to extend this work towards other site selection applications, such as communal waste bins. There is however also more work to be done in verifying the results, both by extending it to other cities, and also by implementing it with different data sources to enrich the analysis.

Acknowledgments. We thank Foursquare and the organisation of Netmob for organising the Future Cities Challenge and providing us with access to Foursquare's data set.

References

1. Amir, S., Misgav, A.: A framework for street tree planning in urban areas in Israel. Landscape Urban Plan. **19**(3), 203–212 (1990)
2. Arp, L., van Vreumingen, D., Gawehns, D., Baratchi, M.: Dynamic macro scale traffic flow optimisation using crowd-sourced urban movement data. In: 2020 21st IEEE International Conference on Mobile Data Management (MDM), pp. 168–177 (2020)
3. Girvan, M., Newman, M.E.: Community structure in social and biological networks. Proc. Natl. Acad. Sci. **99**(12), 7821–7826 (2002)
4. Hall, S.A., Kaufman, J.S., Ricketts, T.C.: Defining urban and rural areas in us epidemiologic studies. J. Urban Health **83**(2), 162–175 (2006)
5. Harris, J.R., Todaro, M.P.: Migration, unemployment and development: a two-sector analysis. Am. Econ. Rev. **60**(1), 126–142 (1970)
6. Hung, C.C., Chang, C.W., Peng, W.C.: Mining trajectory profiles for discovering user communities. In: Proceedings of the 2009 International Workshop on Location Based Social Networks, pp. 1–8. LBSN 2009 (2009). https://doi.org/10.1145/1629890.1629892
7. Jim, C.Y.: A planning strategy to augment the diversity and biomass of roadside trees in urban Hong Kong. Landscape Urban Plan. **44**(1), 13–32 (1999)
8. Li, Q., Zheng, Y., Xie, X., Chen, Y., Liu, W., Ma, W.Y.: Mining user similarity based on location history. In: Proceedings of the 16th ACM SIGSPATIAL International Conference on Advances in Geographic Information Systems. GIS 2008 (2008). https://doi.org/10.1145/1463434.1463477
9. Maller, C., Townsend, M., Pryor, A., Brown, P., St Leger, L.: Healthy nature healthy people: 'contact with nature' as an upstream health promotion intervention for populations. Health Promotion Int. **21**(1), 45–54 (2006)

10. Morani, A., Nowak, D.J., Hirabayashi, S., Calfapietra, C.: How to select the best tree planting locations to enhance air pollution removal in the MillionTreesNYC initiative. Environ. Pollut. **159**(5), 1040–1047 (2011)
11. Newman, M.E.J.: Analysis of weighted networks. Phys. Rev. E **705**, 056131 (2004). https://doi.org/10.1103/PhysRevE.70.056131
12. Norton, B.A., Coutts, A.M., Livesley, S.J., Harris, R.J., Hunter, A.M., Williams, N.S.: Planning for cooler cities: a framework to prioritise green infrastructure to mitigate high temperatures in urban landscapes. Landscape Urban Plan. **134**, 127–138 (2015)
13. Parry-Jones, W.L.: Natural landscape, psychological well-being and mental health. Landscape Res. **15**(2), 7–11 (1990)
14. Pauleit, S.: Urban street tree plantings: identifying the key requirements. In: Proceedings of the Institution of Civil Engineers-Municipal Engineer, vol. 156, pp. 43–50. Thomas Telford Ltd (2003)
15. Rohde, C.L.E., Kendle, A.D.: Human Well-being, natural landscapes and wildlife in urban areas: a review. English Nat. Sci. (1994)
16. Roy, S., Davison, A., Östberg, J.: Pragmatic factors outweigh ecosystem service goals in street tree selection and planting in South-East Queensland cities. Urban Forest. Urban Greening **21**, 166–174 (2017)
17. Sjöman, H., Nielsen, A.B.: Selecting trees for urban paved sites in Scandinavia. Urban Forest. Urban Greening **9**(4), 281–293 (2010)
18. Spellerberg, I.F., Given, D.R.: Trees in urban and city environments: a review of the selection criteria with particular reference to nature conservation in New Zealand cities. Landscape Rev. **12**(2), 19–31 (2008)
19. Stadler, W.: A survey of multicriteria optimization or the vector maximum problem, part I: 1776–1960. J. Optimization Theory Appl. **29**(1), 1–52 (1979)
20. Traag, V., Waltman, L., van Eck, N.J.: From Louvain to Leiden: guaranteeing well-connected communities. Sci. Rep. **9**, 5233 (2019). https://doi.org/10.1038/s41598-019-41695-z
21. Zheng, Y., Zhou, X.: Computing with Spatial Trajectories. Springer Publishing Company, Incorporated (2011)

Gaining Insight into Determinants of Physical Activity Using Bayesian Network Learning

Simone C. M. W. Tummers[1(✉)], Arjen Hommersom[2,3], Lilian Lechner[1], Catherine Bolman[1], and Roger Bemelmans[4]

[1] Faculty of Psychology, Open University of the Netherlands, Heerlen, The Netherlands
simone.tummers@ou.nl
[2] Faculty of Science, Open University of the Netherlands, Heerlen, The Netherlands
[3] Department of Computer Science, Radboud University, Nijmegen, The Netherlands
[4] Zuyd University of Applied Sciences, Heerlen, The Netherlands

Abstract. Bayesian network modelling is applied to health psychology data in order to obtain more insight into the determinants of physical activity. This preliminary study discusses some challenges to apply general machine learning methods to this application domain, and Bayesian networks in particular. We investigate several suitable methods for dealing with missing data, and determine which method obtains good results in terms of fitting the data. Furthermore, we present the learnt Bayesian network model for this e-health intervention case study, and conclusions are drawn about determinants of physical activity behaviour change and how the intervention affects physical activity behaviour and its determinants. We also evaluate the contributions of Bayesian network analysis compared to traditional statistical analyses in this field. Finally, possible extensions on the performed analyses are proposed.

Keywords: Machine learning · Bayesian network · E-health intervention · Structure learning · Physical activity

1 Introduction

Nowadays there are various e-health intervention platforms that employ integrated behaviour change techniques in order to change health-related-behaviour of participants, for example increasing physical activity. These interventions apply theoretical psychological methods to influence behavioural determinants, which are factors determining a certain behaviour. These general techniques are translated to behaviour change strategies by tailoring the theoretical method to the target population and intervention setting [1]. To measure the effects of such interventions, various research studies have been performed, assessing physical activity with tools such as questionnaires and activity trackers. While there is

The original version of the chapter was revised. The correction to this chapter is available at https://doi.org/10.1007/978-3-030-76640-5_13

M. Baratchi et al. (Eds.): BNAIC/Benelearn 2020, CCIS 1398, pp. 172–187, 2021.
https://doi.org/10.1007/978-3-030-76640-5_11

now a good understanding of what the most important determinants for increasing physical activity are, little is known about how these determinants interact. Improved understanding of these relationships could be used to improve existing e-health interventions.

Supervised machine learning techniques are used to identify relationships underlying data with labeled input and output, and predict output results for a given input. These techniques could for example be used to model relations between diseases and symptoms and give expectations about the presence of various diseases given symptoms. Bayesian networks [8] represent probabilistic relationships between a set of variables, where relationships between the input variables can also be investigated. Such networks can make probabilistic predictions and provide a visual insight in relations among all variables of interest, thereby providing a potential useful tool to exploratively investigate and better understand determinants of physical activity.

In this article, a Bayesian network model is learned from data from a single intervention study, i.e., the *Active Plus intervention* [12], aiming at influencing physical activity behaviour among older adults. We discuss ways to learn from these complex data containing a significant amount of missing values. Based on these initial findings, results from previous analyses are compared to results from applying the Bayesian network model to the same data, to examine the added value of this technique compared to traditional ones. We show that learning a Bayesian network model for measurement data from the Active Plus project indeed reveals conditional dependence and independence relations that provide new insights and explanations for previously found results.

This paper is organised as follows. Section 2 provides technical background about methods and algorithms. Section 3 provides a description of the data and intervention study at hand, and how the data has been pre-processed. Furthermore, the analysis based on the Bayesian network model is explained including a description of the applied learning strategy, and a missing data analysis to select appropriate methods for handling the missing data. Then, in Sect. 4, results are given about the comparison of evaluated methods, and the comparison of the results from the Bayesian network model, determined using the best method, and the results from previous analyses. Finally, Sect. 5 concludes this paper and Sect. 6 elaborates on possible extensions.

2 Preliminaries

This section gives an overview of the theoretical background relevant to perform the case study analyses, including a brief introduction of the modelling approach.

2.1 Bayesian Network Model

A Bayesian network [8] is a probabilistic graphical model represented as a directed acyclic graph $G = (V, E)$, where the set of nodes V represent random variables, and the set of arcs E represent probabilistic independencies among the variables. Associated with each node is a conditional probability distribution of that variable given its parents. The graphical structure implies conditional independence statements. Let $V = \{X_1, \ldots, X_n\}$ be an enumeration of the nodes in a Bayesian network such that each node appears after its children, and let Π_i be the set of parents of a node X_i. The local Markov property in the Bayesian network states that X_i is conditionally independent of all variables in $\{X_1, X_2, \ldots, X_{i-1}\}$ given Π_i for all $i \in \{1, \ldots, n\}$. These local independences imply conditional independence statements over arbitrary sets of variables.

The joint probability distribution over discrete variables follows from the conditional independence propositions and conditional probabilities:

$$\mathbb{P}(X_1, \ldots, X_n) = \prod_{i=1}^{n} \mathbb{P}(X_i \mid X_1, \ldots, X_{i-1}) = \prod_{i=1}^{n} \mathbb{P}(X_i \mid \Pi_i),$$

where the first equation follows from the usual chain rule in probability theory and the second from the local Markov property. Note that the conditional probabilities $\mathbb{P}(X_i \mid \Pi_i)$ correspond to the arcs in the Bayesian network specification. In continuous Bayesian networks, usually a linear Gaussian distribution is assumed, where the joint density is factorised where each $X_i \mid \Pi_i \sim \mathcal{N}(\beta \Pi_i + \alpha, \sigma^2)$.

A temporal Bayesian network is an extension to the static counterpart in that it is a Bayesian network model over time, where the nodes represent the random variables occurring at particular time slices. The temporal Bayesian network model is subject to the condition that arcs directed to variables in previous time slices cannot occur. In case the temporal Bayesian network is time-homogeneous (or time-invariant), these models are also called dynamic Bayesian networks [6]. Since in this case study there are only a few time slices and differences between these slices are not constant, we do not assume time-invariance in the remainder of this paper.

2.2   Learning Bayesian Networks

The following three common classes of algorithms are used to learn the structure of Bayesian networks from the data: constraint-based algorithms which employ conditional independence tests to learn the dependence structure of the data, score-based algorithms which use search algorithms to find a graph that maximises a goodness-of-fit scores as objective function, and hybrid algorithms which combine both approaches. Recent research has shown that constraint-based algorithms are often less accurate and seldom faster and hybrid algorithms are neither faster nor more accurate [11]. For this reason, we focus in the remainder of this paper on score-based structure learning algorithms, where local search methods are used to explore the space of directed acyclic graphs by single-arc addition, removal and reversal. In particular, we apply tabu search to the physical activity data in this case study as empirical evidence shows that this search method typically performs well for learning Bayesian networks [5, Chapter 13.7].

There are several model selection criteria that are used in the search-based structure learning algorithms , where in this paper we have chosen the commonly-used Bayesian Information Criterion (BIC) [9]. To fit the parameters we have chosen a uniform prior distribution over the model parameters [4].

Algorithm 1. Structural EM algorithm, given $(M_0, \mathbf{o})$:

---

for $n = 0, 1, \ldots$ **until** convergence **or until** predefined maximum number of iterations is reached **do**
    Compute Θ^{M_n} using a parameter learning algorithm.
    Expectation-step:
    compute $\mathbf{h}^* = \arg\max_{\mathbf{h}} \mathbb{P}(\mathbf{h} \mid \mathbf{o}, M_n)$
    Maximization-step: apply structure learning to determine M_n using data $\mathbf{h}^* \cup \mathbf{o}$
    if $M_n = M_{n+1}$ **or if** stopping criterion is met **then**
        return M_n
    end if
end for

2.3 Handling Missing Data

Learning Bayesian networks with missing data is significantly harder as the log-likelihood does not admit a closed-form solution if values are missing. In this paper, we assume that data are missing at random, for which commonly used methods are listwise deletion, pair-wise deletion, single imputation, multiple imputation [7]. The deletion approaches omit (observed) values from analyses. In the listwise deletion approach on the one hand, all observations with missing values at any measurement are omitted completely. On the other hand, the pair-wise deletion method does not require complete data on all variables in the model, and mean and covariance estimations are here based on the full number of observations with complete data for each (pair of) variable(s). Imputation methods involve replacing missing values by estimates such as by the mean of observed values in the attribute, called mean imputation. Single imputation imputes a single value treating it as known, whereas multiple imputation replaces missing values by two or more values representing a distribution of possibilities. In multiple imputation, missing data are filled in an arbitrary number of times to generate different complete datasets to be analysed, and results are combined for inference. Finally, in Bayesian network learning, the Expectation Maximization (EM) algorithm [2] is often applied, which iteratively optimises parameters in order to find the maximum likelihood estimate, assuming the missing data is missing at random (MAR). The Structural EM algorithm (SEM) [3] combines this standard EM algorithm with structure search for model selection.

The variant of the structural EM algorithm that is used in this case study can be described as follows (see Algorithm 1 for an overview). Let $\mathbf{d}$ be a dataset over the set of random variables $\mathbf{V}$. Assume that $\mathbf{o}$ is part of the dataset that is actually observed, i.e., $\mathbf{o} \subseteq \mathbf{d}$. Furthermore, we denote the missing data by $\mathbf{h}$, i.e., $\mathbf{d} = \mathbf{o} \cup \mathbf{h}$, and $\mathbf{o} \cap \mathbf{h} = \varnothing$. The SEM algorithm aims to find a model from the space of Bayesian network models over $\mathbf{V}$, denoted by $\mathcal{M}$, such that each model $M \in \mathcal{M}$ is parametrised by a vector Θ^M defining a probability distribution $\mathbb{P}(\mathbf{V} : M, \Theta^M)$. To find a model in case of missing values, the complete data likelihood $\mathbb{P}(\mathbf{H}, \mathbf{O} \mid M)$ is estimated. The algorithm iteratively maximises the expected Bayesian network model score optimised by the score-based algorithm. First the posterior parameter distributions, given the currently best model structure and observed data, are computed. In the expectation step, these distributions are used to compute the expected complete dataset, imputing missing values with their most probable values, also sometimes called *hard EM*. During the maximization, the currently best model structure is updated using a tabu structure learning algorithm, using the imputed data from the expectation step. Then parameter learning gives new distributions to be used as input for the next expectation step. To perform the first expectation, an initial network structure is given as input to the algorithm. In case a maximum number of iterations is reached or in case of convergence, the Bayesian network model is returned.

3   Description of the Data and Methodology

The experiments in this intervention case study aim to analyse performance of different methods to handle missing values and to learn the Bayesian network model for given intervention data in order to compare its results to previous analyses. This section describes the data, preprocessing phase, magnitude of the missing data problem and the approach to determine a suitable method in order to analyse the data by Bayesian network learning. The raw research data that has been collected during the Active Plus intervention was provided to the authors and is described in the first subsection.

3.1   Data Acquisition and Description

The raw research data has mostly been collected via questionnaires and consists of determinants, external factors, measurements of physical activity and intervention-related information at different time-slots, starting with a baseline measurement before the participant receives the intervention [14]. For example, the validated self-administered Dutch Short Questionnaire to Assess Health Enhancing Physical Activity (SQUASH) is included in the questionnaires as subjective measurement of physical activity [16]. Figure 1 illustrates the intervention outline including moments of receiving intervention content and of measurement in time [12]. There is a distinction between control, intervention basic and intervention-plus groups, representing the intervention condition. This condition determines whether a participant receives an intervention or not and if environmental content is included in the intervention with additional information such as opportunities to be physically active in the own environment. Within these main groups, content is further personalised based on characteristics of participants, for example state of behaviour change (stage) measured at baseline or age. Since in the analyses in this article intervention content is proxied

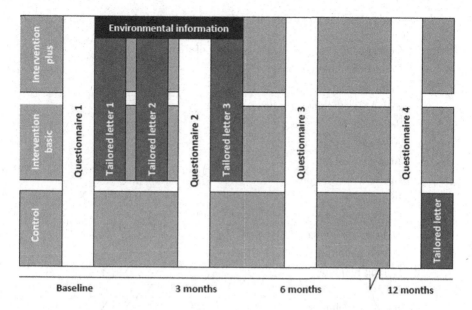

Fig. 1. Outline intervention program including moments of measurement [12].

by a few main characteristics, this personalisation is beyond the focus of this article [12].

As depicted in Fig. 1, data has been collected at 4 time-slots; at the baseline (before receiving the intervention, T0) and, to measure intervention effects, 3 (T1), 6 (T2) and 12 (T3) months after the baseline. About 1258 variables have been measured for a sub-population being a random sample of 1976 adults aged 50 and older. Measurements are at item-level of detail, where an item is a specific measurement, for example a question in the questionnaire. In preprocessing rules, it is described how concepts are calculated from item data in order to perform analyses at a higher level of abstraction.

3.2   Data Preprocessing and Concept Design

The raw data is preprocessed, according to rules to integrate data from different studies and to aggregate, by calculating concepts from the raw data at item-level of detail, as mentioned in the previous subsection. This subsection describes assumptions and decisions made during the data preprocessing phase and rules to calculate the concepts included in analyses in this article.

In general, concepts are calculated by the mean or sum of items taking into account a maximum percentage of items allowed to be missing, except from a few concepts calculated using predefined formulas. In particular, the SQUASH-outcome measure, which is the number of minutes per week of moderate to intensive physical activity, is calculated in a standardised way [12]. In case more than 25% of the items are missing, the concept value is assumed to be missing. Besides

Table 1. Overview of concept-level variables included in case study.

Concept	Number of items	T0	T1	T2	T3
Condition: intervention	1	X			
Condition: environment	1	X			
SQUASH outcome measure	–	X	X	X	X
Self-efficacy	10	X	X		
Attitude(-pros)	9	X	X		
Attitude(-cons)	7	X	X		
Intrinsic motivation	6	X	X		
Intention	3	X	X	X	X
Commitment	3	X	X	X	
Strategic planning	10	X	X	X	X
Action planning	6	X	X	X	
Coping planning	5	X	X	X	
Habit	12	X		X	X
Social modelling	1	X	X	X	
Social support	1	X	X		

these aggregation rules, preprocessing rules contain decisions about recalculation of raw data values to unipolar scale.

This article focuses on a selection of the data measured in the Active Plus intervention and, as already mentioned, analyses are performed at concept-level. The selection consists of data about the main determinants of physical activity behaviour, including some social-related determinants, the main outcome measure from the SQUASH questionnaire and some variables indicating the intervention content the participant receives. As described, the intervention content that an individual participant has received is personalised and proxied in the analyses. The proxy of the intervention content is represented in the data by intervention condition variables, which thus play a central role in analyses. Table 1 gives an overview of these and all other concepts included in this article's analyses, indicating the number of item-level variables the concept variable aggregates and at which moments in time the concept is measured. Note that the number of items for the SQUASH outcome measure is not indicated since it is calculated by standard rules.

3.3   Missing Data Analysis

A significant part of this case study consists of the evaluation of several ways to handle missing data values. This subsection illustrates the magnitude of the missing data problem in the case study and determines which methods are appropriate to be evaluated.

Table 2. Overview of number of missing values in included concepts (out of 1976). If the value is '–', then this concept was not recorded at that time point.

Concept	T0	T1	T2	T3
Condition: intervention	8	–	–	–
Condition: environment	8	–	–	–
SQUASH outcome measure	3	518	565	628
Self-efficacy	229	638	–	–
Attitude(-pros)	149	587	–	–
Attitude(-cons)	167	597	–	–
Intrinsic motivation	325	690	–	–
Intention	141	571	654	748
Commitment	31	531	573	–
Strategic planning	156	601	652	661
Action planning	182	604	686	–
Coping planning	192	621	668	–
Habit	136	–	633	662
Social modelling	532	915	952	–
Social support	68	561	–	–

A total of 39 variables being concepts at certain moments in time are selected as subset for analyses. Table 2 demonstrates the number of missing values out of 1976 observations for each of the included concept-level variable. Since the time dimension is crucial to analyse intervention effects and, as can be seen in Table 2, more than a fourth of the values are missing for measurements after the baseline, applying pairwise deletion would result in an immense loss of information. Furthermore, the number of complete observations is for the selection of concepts 360 out of 1976 in total, meaning that applying list-wise deletion would neglect a large part of the dataset. Since deletion methods are not appropriate to deal with the missing data in this case study, we resort to the remaining methods for dealing with missing data, i.e., mean imputation, multiple imputation and the SEM algorithm described in Sect. 2.3, are applied and results are compared.

3.4 Approach

This subsection discusses how a suitable method for handling missing data is determined in order to model the intervention data. To perform experiments, the bnlearn package in R is used for Bayesian network learning [10]. Source code has been made publicly available[1].

In the comparison of the methods to handle missing data values evaluated in this article, we apply discrete dynamic Bayesian networks for preprocessed data

---

[1] https://github.com/SCMWTUM/Active4life-datascience.git

that is discretised by manually creating intervals meaningful in the health psychology field. The models are learnt by the tabu search algorithm optimising the BIC score (see Sect. 2.2). Model parameters are learnt by the Bayesian method, where the imaginary sample size setting prevents zero probabilities in the conditional probability tables while keeping parameter estimates close to maximum likelihood estimates. In the intervention study at hand only system missing values occur, for example, in case a participant has not answered a specific question in the questionnaire or if the maximum amount of items allowed to be missing is exceeded. The methods evaluated apply imputation where missing values are substituted by (maximum likelihood) estimators during the structure learning phase, namely mean imputation, multiple imputation and the structural EM algorithm, introduced in Sect. 3.3. Different variants of multiple imputation are evaluated, imputing $m = 3$, $m = 10$ or $m = 20$ datasets, where each variable in each dataset is imputed using a classification tree. The parameter m has been chosen to evaluate its effect on the performance of multiple imputation within acceptable bounds for evaluation running time. The m datasets are analysed by creating a fully directed averaged Bayesian network model. These methods are compared by means of comparing the mean test-set log-likelihood using k-fold cross-validation (with $k = 10$).

Finally, a linear Gaussian temporal Bayesian network model for the Active Plus intervention data is constructed from the preprocessed selection of data by learning the network structure using SEM. The model is learnt by the tabu search algorithm, optimising the BIC score, and maximum likelihood parameters are learnt in the continuous case. It was chosen to learn a continuous network rather than a discrete one to prevent possible loss of information from the discretisation process. In order to evaluate significance of edges, a bootstrap analysis is applied. Edges that are identified in most bootstrap samples and in the original network are considered stable findings in the following.

4   Results

This section describes the performance comparison of the methods applied to handle missing values. Furthermore, the learnt Bayesian network to model the Active Plus data is presented and results are compared to previous analyses of relations between determinants in the study by Van Stralen et al. [13].

4.1   Comparison Bayesian Network Missing Data Strategy

Table 3 demonstrates the mean log-likelihood over the folds resulting from applying the implemented cross-validation algorithm to the selected methods for handling missing data.

The cross-validation analysis shows that the structural EM algorithm significantly outperforms mean imputation and multiple imputation to handle missing data, because of significant difference of the mean log-likelihoods over the folds at 5% confidence level. Note that increasing the number of imputed datasets

Table 3. Results of cross-validation analysis for missing data methods.

Handling missing data	Mean log-likelihood	95% Confidence Interval
Mean imputation	-4779	$[-4832; -4726]$
Multiple imputation ($m = 3$)	-4528	$[-4623; -4433]$
Multiple imputation ($m = 10$)	-4344	$[-4397; -4292]$
Multiple imputation ($m = 20$)	-4327	$[-4399; -4254]$
SEM algorithm	-4127	$[-4183; -4071]$

in multiple imputation significantly improves the performance of this method, which significantly outperforms mean imputation, though only minor improvements are observed between $m = 10$ and $m = 20$, which suggests that it is close to convergence.

Based on these performance results of the evaluated methods, the structural EM algorithm is chosen to be applied in learning the Bayesian network model in this case study. In the next subsection, the learnt model is presented and results are compared to those from previous analyses.

4.2 Comparison of Bayesian Network Model to Previous Analyses

Figure 2 shows the union of the temporal Bayesian network model learnt by the tabu search algorithm and the result of bootstrapping (which we call *averaged model*). Note that the edges represent probabilistic dependencies that not necessarily imply causal relationships. Table 4 gives the summary statistics of the temporal Bayesian network model learnt and its averaged counterpart, indicating that model complexity is decreased in the averaged model. A comparison of these models shows that in the original temporal Bayesian network model learnt, 20.74% of the edges that occur are not present in the averaged model, represented by blue edges in Fig. 2. Besides, 12.35% of the edges appearing in the averaged model have not been selected in the original model learnt, which are represented by red edges in Fig. 2. These unstable edges should be analysed further in the future.

Compared to previous analyses, the Bayesian network model provides a more complete insight in the complexity of mechanisms influencing physical activity behaviour. Previously, mediation analyses by Van Stralen et al. [13] have shown that factors such as social modelling, self-efficacy and intention are significant mediators of the intervention influencing physical activity behaviour. In Fig. 3, a fragment of the stable part of the averaged model (Fig. 2) is shown that includes these previously proven significant determinants, intervention effects, and effects on physical activity. It also includes coefficients, which represent the maximum likelihood estimators of parameters of the Gaussian conditional density distribution of variables given their parents. This part of the network suggests that the intervention effect on physical activity levels is mainly mediated by influencing habit and intention. Since the concept of habit has not been included in

Table 4. Statistics Bayesian network model versus averaged counterpart.

Model	Statistics	
Optimal Bayesian network	#nodes	39
	# arcs	188
	# undirected arcs	0
	Average Markov blanket size	19.90
	Average neighbourhood size	9.64
	Average branching factor	4.82
Averaged Bayesian network	#nodes	39
	# arcs	170
	# undirected arcs	0
	Average Markov blanket size	17.54
	Average neighbourhood size	8.72
	Average branching factor	4.36

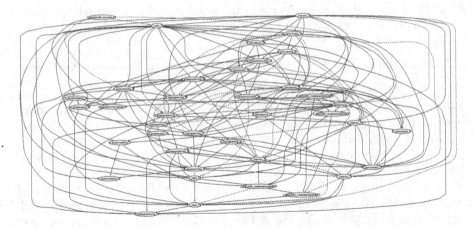

Fig. 2. Averaged model learnt by bootstrapping, which includes unstable edges (in blue and red), from the model learnt for the original dataset. (Color figure online)

analyses by Van Stralen et al. [13], no comparison can be made with respect to results about this concept. Note that results from the Bayesian network model in general would probably have been more comparable to those from previous analyses if this concept would have been included in both previous and this papers researches. Previous results with respect to the intention concept are confirmed. However, although the network confirms significant effects of social modelling and self-efficacy on physical activity, this model does not find a direct effect of the intervention on social modelling nor on self-efficacy. The direct influence of the intervention on these concepts previously found is thus not confirmed by the network model. This difference can be explained by looking at the whole

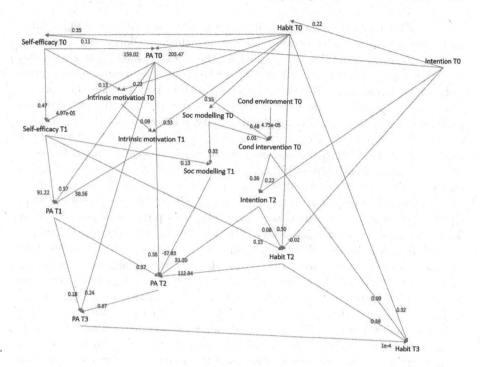

Fig. 3. Selected subgraph of the averaged model.

Bayesian network model, where longer paths can be found from the intervention variable to these concepts via several other determinants. For example, the intervention influences intention, which is correlated with action planning that is again correlated with social modelling. The network thus indicates that important mediators of physical activity are rather indirectly influenced by the intervention.

The submodel in Fig. 3 further shows that the extension in which environmental components are added to the intervention does not significantly influence physical activity nor its determinants. This differs from results from previous analyses by Van Stralen et al. [13], where differences have been found between effects in groups of participants having received environmental content and those who did not receive this extension. The previously found significant influence of the environmental extension on physical activity and determinants is thus not confirmed by the Bayesian network, in case of focusing on stable edges. Taking into account unstable edges some correlations are found between the environmental extension variable and for example the commitment concept. The difference in results from the network model compared to previous findings with respect to the influence of environmental components might be explained in future analyses by exploring these unstable findings.

Furthermore, the submodel shows that a clear distinction can be made between determinants of physical activity in the short (T1) and in the long

(T2 and T3) run. In the short run, effects on physical activity are mainly determined by self-efficacy and intrinsic motivation, which mediates effects of habit and self-efficacy measured at T0. In the long-run, social modelling, intention and habit are important, where habit at T2 has the strongest correlation with physical activity levels at T2. Recall that findings with respect to the habit concept cannot be compared to previous findings by Van Stralen et al. [13]. Previous analyses on mediator effects on physical activity, do have shown the significance of the other determinants of physical activity levels indicated by the network model, except for the intrinsic motivation concept that appears in the Bayesian network to significantly directly influence physical activity. The network model shows that the effect of self-efficacy on physical activity at T1 is both direct and mediated by intrinsic motivation, since self-efficacy at T0 influences intrinsic motivation at T0, which subsequently influences physical activity levels at T1 via intrinsic motivation levels at T1. In this way, the network model explores the mechanism in which self-efficacy influences physical activity. It shows, that intrinsic motivation emerges as mediator, since intrinsic motivation mediates effects of other determinants on physical activity, in this case self-efficacy. This result of intrinsic motivation being a significant determinant of physical activity in the short run is thus new, compared to results from previously performed classic mediator analyses. This new short run determinant is found by the network by revealing the structure in which other determinants, that have already been found in previous analyses, effect physical activity. This structure reveals concepts that mediate effects of previously found determinants.

5   Discussion and Conclusions

In this article, the Bayesian network modelling technique has been applied to an e-health intervention case study to achieve better understanding of relations between determinants of physical activity. The reason for that was that this technique has not been applied often in this field and traditional analyses are not sufficient to reveal the dependence structure between determinants.

One particular challenge has been the magnitude of the missing data problem, which is examined for this case study and shown to be of such size that conventional methods to handle it cannot be used. The performance of several suitable methods, i.e., mean imputation, multiple imputation applying classification trees and the structural EM algorithm, has therefor been evaluated. Results show that applying the structural EM algorithm leads to the best results in terms of goodness of fit when learning a Bayesian network model for intervention data. In particular, by evaluating different numbers of imputed datasets as parameter setting in the multiple imputation method, the results suggest that the multiple imputation method does not outperform the structural EM algorithm even if the number of imputed datasets is increased to a large number. Note that we have compared these methods using a single cross validation run. Repeated cross validation is often suggested to increase confidence in the estimates, though it has been shown [15] that applying repeated cross-validation does not necessarily give more precise estimates of model accuracy. Furthermore, since the differences are quite large, further investigation does not appear to be necessary.

Since the modelling technique of Bayesian networks has not yet often been applied in this research field, its added value compared to more classic analyses in health psychology is evaluated. The model learnt for the case study data, applying the, in cross-validation evaluated, best performing algorithm to handle missing values, shows that the intervention does influence physical activity behaviour. The model also confirms previously-found important mediators of these intervention effects. However, there is some room for improvement to increase confidence in relations in the model, due to some unstable edges found. These should be explored in future analyses and would hopefully clarify the added value of the environmental extension on intervention effects. In a submodel, including significant edges only, some differences with respect to intervention effects on determinants and mediation effects on physical activity have been found compared to previous analyses. The network model shows that some determinants are rather indirectly influenced by the intervention and reveals a new significant mediator of intervention effects on physical activity, as it mediates effects of another determinant.

By the design of the study, the extent to which the intervention aims to influence different determinants in content received at different moments in time, varies across the participants. Each participant receives a unique focus in content fitted to their personal characteristics. Since the (personalised) content of the intervention is not included in the dataset, i.e., it is a latent variable, some care should be taken in the interpretation of the results. In particular, when a certain concept appears in the Bayesian network to be a significant determinant of physical activity, then this suggests that it is important in determining this behaviour. However, we cannot exclude the possibility that the effect of this determinant on physical activity is only mediated by the (personalised) contents of the intervention. Therefore, for designing new interventions, care should be taken in interpreting the present results.

In conclusion, the network has provided a more in-depth view in the dependencies and the complex structure in which determinants and physical activity are influenced by the intervention. In this way, the added value of applying the Bayesian network model compared to traditional analyses has been shown as the model provides new information relevant to understand the working mechanisms of the intervention, though care should be taken in the interpretation of the results. Nonetheless, the results show that Bayesian networks provide a useful technique to better understand dependence mechanisms of determinants of behaviour change.

6 Future Work

In future work, analyses in this article could be extended for example by evaluating other imputation methods to be implemented in the structural EM algorithm, such as a distribution over values instead of imputing the value with highest probability (*soft EM*). Also, although imputation using classification trees in multiple imputation has been an informed choice, evaluating alternative methods would be interesting. From a technical perspective, we will also consider exploring constraint-based structure learning algorithms, other score-based algorithms, alternative parameter learning algorithms or alternative model selection criteria. From the application perspective, future research could further elaborate on the structure, in which determinants are related to each other and physical activity, and on the differences found in the Bayesian network model compared to previous (regression) analyses.

A combined model could in future be designed for an integrated dataset including measurements from several different e-health intervention studies. Data on different sub-populations could be combined in order to examine if a general model yields different or additional results compared to the submodels for a smaller amount of data from single studies. It would also be interesting to perform analyses on an integrated dataset in more detail by using item variables in order to clarify correlations between concepts in a network model learnt for concept variables.

Even with data from a single study, this paper already shows that the Bayesian network model provides a more complete and in-depth insight in dependency structures, by exploring differences between its results and those from previous analyses. More specifically, the network reveals relations between variables where a variable influences another via a third one. In previous analyses, only some of the hypothetical mediator effects are explored by regression analyses. Hence, our results provide new opportunities to analyse and confirm our findings using traditional statistical methods.

Acknowledgements. This work is part of the research programme Active4Life with project number 546003005, which is financed by ZonMw.

References

1. Brug, J., van Assema, P., Lechner, L.: Gezondheidsvoorlichting en gedragsverandering, 9th edn. Koninklijke Van Gorcum, Assen (2017)
2. Dempster, A.P., Laird, N.M., Rubin, D.B.: Maximum likelihood from incomplete data via the EM algorithm. J. R. Stat. Soc. B (Method.) **39**(1), 1–22 (1977)
3. Friedman, N.: The Bayesian structural EM algorithm. In: Proceedings of the Fourteenth Conference on Uncertainty in Artificial Intelligence, pp. 129–138 (1998)
4. Ji, Z., Xia, Q., Meng, G.: A review of parameter learning methods in Bayesian network. In: Huang, D.-S., Han, K. (eds.) ICIC 2015. LNCS (LNAI), vol. 9227, pp. 3–12. Springer, Cham (2015). https://doi.org/10.1007/978-3-319-22053-6_1
5. Koller, D., Friedman, N.: Probabilistic Graphical Models: Principles and Techniques. MIT press, Cambridge (2009)
6. Murphy, K.: Dynamic Bayesian networks: representation, inference and learning. Ph.D. thesis, UC Berkeley (2002)
7. Nakai, M., Ke, W.: Review of the methods for handling missing data in longitudinal data analysis. Int. J. Math. Anal. **5**(1), 1–13 (2011)

8. Pearl, J.: Probabilistic Reasoning in Intelligent Systems: Networks of Plausible Inference. Morgan Kaufmann, Burlington (1988)
9. Schwarz, G.: Estimating the dimension of a model. Ann. Stat. **6**(2), 461–464 (1978)
10. Scutari, M.: Package 'bnlearn'. Bayesian network structure learning, parameter learning and inference, R package version 4.4 1 (2019)
11. Scutari, M., Graafland, C.E., Gutiérrez, J.M.: Who learns better Bayesian network structures: accuracy and speed of structure learning algorithms. Int. J. Approximate Reasoning **115**, 235–253 (2019)
12. van Stralen, M.M., Kok, G., de Vries, H., Mudde, A.N., Bolman, C., Lechner, L.: The active plus protocol: systematic development of two tailored physical activity interventions for older adults. BMC Public Health **8**, 399 (2008)
13. van Stralen, M.M., de Vries, H., Bolman, C., Mudde, A.N., Lechner, L.: Exploring the efficacy and moderators of two computer-tailored physical activity interventions for older adults: a randomized controlled trial. Ann. Behav. Med. **39**(2), 139–150 (2010)
14. van Stralen, M.M., de Vries, H., Mudde, A.N., Bolman, C., Lechner, L.: Determinants of initiation and maintenance of physical activity among older adults: a literature review. Health Psychol. Rev. **3**, 147–207 (2009)
15. Vanwinckelen, G., Blockeel, H.: On estimating model accuracy with repeated cross-validation. In: Proceedings of the 21st Belgian-Dutch Conference on Machine Learning, pp. 39–44 (2012)
16. Wendel-Vos, G.C., Schuit, A.J., Saris, W.H., Kromhout, D.: Reproducibility and relative validity of the short questionnaire to assess health-enhancing physical activity. J. Clin. Epidemiol. **56**, 1163–1169 (2003)

Swarm Construction Coordinated Through the Building Material

Yating Zheng[1,2], Michael Allwright[2(✉)], Weixu Zhu[2], Majd Kassawat[3], Zhangang Han[1], and Marco Dorigo[2]

[1] School of Systems Science, Beijing Normal University, Beijing, China
zhengyating@mail.bnu.edu.cn, zhan@bnu.edu.cn
[2] IRIDIA, Université Libre de Bruxelles, Brussels, Belgium
{michael.allwright,weixu.zhu,marco.dorigo}@ulb.ac.be
[3] Universidad Jaume I, Castellon, Spain
majd@uji.es

Abstract. This paper demonstrates a swarm robotics construction system where the intelligence that coordinates construction has been moved from the robots to an advanced building material. This building material, that we call Stigmergic Blocks, is capable of computation and local communication. Using comprehensive simulation models based on real hardware, we investigate approaches to improving the efficiency and flexibility of a swarm robotics construction system.

Keywords: Swarm robotics · Stigmergy · Swarm construction · Stigmergic material

1 Introduction

In swarm robotics, groups of robots coordinate their actions by communicating with their neighbors and by sensing and modifying the surrounding environment [5,7]. These interactions between the robots and their environment can result in the emergence of useful collective behaviors. It is the goal of swarm robotics researchers to understand how the individual robots in these swarms can be programmed so that these collective behaviors not only perform a useful task but do so in a way that is generalizable, scalable, and robust to disturbances such as robot failures. If these characteristics can be realized in robot swarms, this approach to robotics may be well suited to automating construction in hostile environments. As an example, environments with excessive radiation are too dangerous for human workers and may result in high failure rates of robots and their supporting positioning and communication infrastructure.

From an abstract perspective, the goal of construction is to arrange materials in an environment into one or more structures with respect to a set of constraints. For example, an ordering that ensures that the structure remains stable during the entire building process. In the case of swarm robotics, these constraints can

M. Baratchi et al. (Eds.): BNAIC/Benelearn 2020, CCIS 1398, pp. 188–202, 2021.
https://doi.org/10.1007/978-3-030-76640-5_12

be realized in terms of reactive rules that instruct robots to perform construction actions in response to environmental stimuli. If these stimuli are defined in terms of the results of previous construction actions by other robots, we say that the robots are coordinating a construction task through stigmergic communication [6,16]. This approach to construction has been used by Jones and Matarić to build 2D structures from colored blocks [8,9] and by Allwright et al. to build a staircase using a single robot and a stepped pyramid using four robots [1,2]. A significant challenge in this approach, however, is finding a set of rules that unambiguously map all intermediate construction states to construction actions. The complexity of these sets of rules increases with the size of the structure and has necessitated the use of offline algorithms to generate rule sets in similar research [11]. Moreover, if we want to take advantage of the potential scalability of swarm robotics systems by building in parallel, this complexity is exacerbated since building in parallel imposes additional constraints on a rule set to guarantee that the structure is always in a valid state [4,15].

To work around these limitations, researchers have supplemented stigmergic communication in a variety of ways. For example, Werfel et al. [17,19] use the concept of extended stigmergy in their work on multi-robot construction. This approach leverages a robot's or a block's ability to localize itself to simplify the construction rules. The work by Sugawara and Doi [13,14] takes another approach and instead has the building materials guide the robots to where building material should be added. In this paper, we extend the work of Sugawara and Doi by further investigating the potential advantages of having a building material coordinate construction in a more capable multi-robot construction system, namely, the one designed by Allwright et al. [3]. This construction system consists of two components, a robot called the BuilderBot and a building material, called the Stigmergic Blocks, which the BuilderBot assembles into structures using its manipulator (see Fig. 1). We have developed plugins that provide comprehensive models of the BuilderBot and the Stigmergic Block for the ARGoS simulator [12] and used them in the experimental work presented in this paper.

The general setup of our construction system involves having the robots use computer vision to identify the configuration of a structure by observing the location of its blocks and the colors of the LEDs on those blocks. The robots then perform construction actions such as attaching another block in response to certain configurations of the structure. In the experiments where we extend the work of Sugawara and Doi, we use the building material's peer-to-peer near-field communication to allow messages to be exchanged between adjacent blocks. By enabling the routing of messages through intermediate blocks, we enable one block to monitor the structure and to communicate directly with the robots by changing the colors of the LEDs on one or more blocks.

The remainder of this paper is organized as follows. In the following section, we describe two classes of construction algorithms that we use to coordinate construction. In Sect. 3, we present three experiments that demonstrate how the efficiency and flexibility of the building process can be improved and how the need to find complex sets of construction rules can be eliminated by enabling the

Fig. 1. The Swarm Robotics Construction System (SRoCS) consists of two components, the BuilderBot robot and the Stigmergic Block building material.

building material to coordinate its own assembly. Where possible, we compare this approach with a standard approach where the construction is coordinated exclusively by the robots. In Sect. 4, we discuss the tolerance of our system to faults and the trade-offs that are made by moving the intelligence into the blocks. We conclude the paper in Sect. 5 by suggesting several directions for future work. The results presented in this paper and the tools required to reproduce those results are open source and available as an OSF project [20].

2 Construction Algorithms

In this paper, we use two classes of algorithms for coordinating construction. The first class of algorithms, referred to as the *standard algorithms*, is a generalization of the approach used by Allwright et al. [1] and is used for comparison with the second class of algorithms. This second class of algorithms is called *block algorithms* and represents the approach where the intelligence that coordinates construction has been moved into the building material.

2.1 Standard Algorithms

In the standard algorithms, construction is coordinated exclusively through stigmergic communication. The robots perform a random walk in their environment, avoiding obstacles and searching for building material to attach to a structure. The robots perform construction actions as a response to their observations of the results of previous construction actions. In a standard algorithm, the robots are provided with a look-up table that associates intermediate construction states with construction actions. We assume here that the robots do not have access to global information and are not able to sense the complete state of larger structures. Therefore, an entry in this look-up table often does not contain the entire intermediate construction state, but rather only a partial representation of that state. This partial representation corresponds to a configuration of blocks that can be reliably detected by a robot's camera. The robots use this look-up table and their sensor readings to detect patterns of blocks in their environment and to execute the construction actions associated with them.

In our experiments with the standard algorithm, we allow robots to change the colors of the LEDs on the Stigmergic Blocks just before attaching them to a structure. Changing the LED colors on a Stigmergic Block enables a BuilderBot to detect more complex patterns of blocks with its computer vision system more reliably. After a BuilderBot has attached a Stigmergic Block to the structure, however, the block's LED colors are fixed.

2.2   Block Algorithms

In a block algorithm, the intelligence that coordinates construction is mainly in the building material. Similar to the standard algorithms, the robots perform a random walk in the environment, avoiding obstacles and searching for building material that can be added to an incomplete structure. In a block algorithm, however, the robots do not have any internal representation of the structure being built and rely on the building material for coordination.

In our system, construction starts with a single *root* Stigmergic Block in the environment. While in our experiments we assign the role of the root block statically, it would also be possible to have one or more robots assign this role to one or more blocks dynamically as a result of environmental stimuli. The root block in our current implementation of a block algorithm contains the entire target structure encoded as a rooted tree. The root block decomposes this rooted tree and sends only the required branches to its children using peer-to-peer near-field communication (NFC). This process continues until all blocks currently in the structure have received instructions from the root block. The non-root blocks in the structure continuously send data back to their parents who then forward the received data back to their parents as a single message until the root block has been reached.

Upon receiving the messages from its children, the root block can monitor construction progress, can detect incorrectly placed blocks, and can update the colors of the LEDs on the Stigmergic Blocks in the structure, triggering further construction actions by the BuilderBots. By controlling these LEDs, the root block is able to coordinate the construction of the structure by telling nearby robots where further blocks can be attached or should be removed.

Although this paper focuses primarily on results from simulation, we have successfully implemented a block algorithm using the Stigmergic Blocks, whose hardware is described in [3]. A video of this algorithm working on the hardware (with blocks being attached and detached by hand) is available online as part of the OSF project[1]. In the following section, we describe our experiments in simulation.

3   Experiments

In this section, we present three experiments that we have completed using the models of the BuilderBot and Stigmergic Block in the ARGoS simulator. We model the behavior of the Stigmergic Block firmware in ARGoS using a Lua controller that allows callbacks to be executed while messages are being exchanged. This model reflects the actual hardware with the exception that the firmware for the real block is written in C++ and is interrupt-driven, while the code used in simulation is written in Lua and uses polling to detect if a neighboring block is attempting to exchange messages. The control software for the BuilderBot robot is also written in Lua and uses a behavior tree architecture. An API for the BuilderBot has been developed, which provides a library of behavior trees for obstacle avoidance, picking up unused blocks, and attaching them to structures following rules that have been defined in terms of patterns of blocks that can be detected by the robot's computer vision system.

Our first experiment demonstrates a concept called dynamic construction paths, where the root block is able to adjust the target structure as it is being built. In the second experiment, we show how the blocks can be used to guide a robot towards a vacant construction site. Finally, the third experiment demonstrates how using a block algorithm allows for a more flexible construction process where robots can attach blocks to any vacant construction site in any order. These experiments aim to demonstrate the potential advantages of moving the intelligence that coordinates construction from the robots to the blocks.

3.1   Dynamic Construction Paths

In the standard algorithms, the Stigmergic Blocks are unable to communicate with each other, they can only have their LEDs configured by a robot to display a certain color before they are attached to a structure. The robots change the color of the blocks as part of executing a construction action. The set of rules that maps the intermediate construction states to these construction actions is prepared offline and is loaded into the memory of the robots before an experiment is started. In contrast, the block algorithms only require the root block to have the internal representation of the structure, which can also be modified during construction. This capability enables a feature called dynamic construction paths. The concept of dynamic construction paths is realized when two or more sequences of construction actions can be selected during construction according to a condition that can be detected by the root block (or one of the blocks with which it is in communication).

In this section, we set up an experiment with a structure that can be completed by following one of four different construction paths. This structure is

---

[1] Video: `hardware-demo.mp4` at https://osf.io/ve3za/.

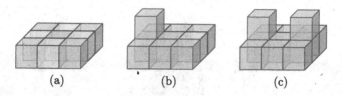

Fig. 2. Structure for demonstrating the use of a block algorithm to dynamically select construction paths. The root block in the structure indicates to nearby robots when and where a block can be attached to the structure by setting the color of a valid construction site to yellow. (Color figure online)

shown in Fig. 2. If we ignore the orientation of the structure, there are four construction paths that advance the state of the structure from what is shown in Fig. 2a to Fig. 2c. That is, we can attach blocks (i) left and then right, (ii) right and then left, (iii) front and then back, or (iv) back and then front.

In this experiment, the root block decides which path to follow by initially indicating that a block can be attached to the top face of either the left, right, front, or back block (Fig. 2a). Once a block has been attached to one of these sites (and this information has propagated back to the root block), the root block updates the illumination pattern of the structure to show nearby robots that there is one valid construction site remaining (Fig. 2b). Following the attachment of a block to this site, the root block updates the illumination pattern of the structure one last time to indicate to nearby robots that the structure is complete (Fig. 2c).

Results from Simulation. The image on the left of Fig. 3 shows a robot approaching the partially built structure. At this point, all four construction paths are possible. After the robot has placed the block on the right-hand side of the structure, the root block disables the LEDs on the right, front, and back blocks to indicate that a block can now only be added on the left. The structure is completed when the robot adds this last block to the structure, as shown on the right of Fig. 3.

To investigate the impact of using more robots, we repeated this experiment with two and four robots. Each of these configurations was repeated 25 times, with the blocks and the robots starting in random positions. Each experiment was automatically terminated when all required blocks have been deposited at the building sites. The videos and the source code for these experiments are available as part of the OSF project for this paper[2].

---

[2] Videos: `dcp-single-robot.mp4` and `dcp-multiple-robots.mp4` at https://osf.io/9562j/ and https://osf.io/4cpyh/.
Source code: `dcp-single-robot.zip` and `dcp-multiple-robots.zip` at https://osf.io/j2pqh/ and https://osf.io/nasf6/.

Fig. 3. Illustration of the dynamic construction paths experiment in simulation. From left to right: (i) a robot approaches a partially built structure and places a block on top of one of the orange faces, (ii) the root block responds by selecting a construction path, changing the illumination pattern, (iii) the robot places the final block in the correct location to complete the structure.

Figure 4 shows the distribution of the total experiment time with one, two, and four BuilderBots. While there is a decrease in the time taken between one and two robots, the decrease between two and four robots is not statistically significant. This diminishing return when increasing the number of robots is commonly observed in swarm robotics systems since adding more robots to a system increases the likelihood of interference between those robots. From this data, we may conclude that the use of two robots is optimal for this particular construction task in this particular environment.

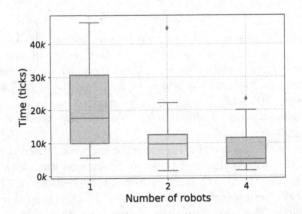

Fig. 4. Time to complete the task in simulation with different numbers of BuilderBots. Each configuration was run 25 times. Each box consists of observations ranging from the first to the third quartile. The median is indicated by a horizontal bar, dividing the box into the upper and lower parts. The whiskers extend to the farthest data points that are within 1.5 times the interquartile range. Outliers are shown as dots.

3.2   Guided Construction

In this experiment, we show how a block algorithm can be used to guide a robot towards a construction site. This configuration involves using the illumination pattern on the blocks to communicate the direction in which a robot should go to reach a construction site. The motivation behind implementing this mechanism is that, in the standard algorithms, the robots tend to spend a lot of time performing a random walk before locating a construction site where they can attach a block. The idea of using the building material to guide robots towards a construction site is sometimes referred to as *gradient following* and has been demonstrated before in a more abstract simulation by Werfel et al. [18].

For example, consider the partially built structure consisting of six blocks arranged in a line in Fig. 5a. To complete this structure, a robot must place one block on top of the left block and one block on top of the right block (Fig. 5b). However, since the perspective of the robot is limited, it must discover these attachment sites either through random walk or through gradient following.

In a standard algorithm, the colors of the LEDs on the blocks can not be updated once they have been attached to a structure. For this reason, the robot must rely on random walk to discover the possible attachment sites. Figure 6 shows how this construction may take place. The robots' rule set in this case is that a green block is to be attached to the top of a yellow block (unless a green block has already been attached).

The construction speed for this structure can be increased using a block algorithm that implements gradient following. In this case, the illumination pattern of the structure is under the control of the root block and can be updated in response to changes in the structure. Moreover, the robots now follow three rules: (i) when a yellow block is detected, the robot attaches a block to the top of it, (ii) if red blocks are detected, the robot biases its random walk behavior to the right, (iii) if blue blocks are detected, the robot biases its random walk behavior to the left. Figure 7 shows an example of how this construction may take place. In this example, a block is attached on top of the leftmost block, which is detected by the root block. The root block updates the illumination pattern so that a robot approaching the structure will turn to the right and find the remaining construction site.

Results from Simulation. To test our hypothesis that guided construction with a block algorithm reduces the overall construction time with respect to what is possible with a standard algorithm, we run experiments with two structures: a short line composed of six blocks and a long line composed of thirteen blocks. We run each experiment for the two structures 25 times using both the standard algorithm and the block algorithm. Figure 8 contains three screenshots of the construction of the short structure with a block algorithm in the ARGoS simulator.

The box plot in Fig. 9 shows for the shorter structure that the approach based on the block algorithm has similar performance to the approach based on the standard algorithm. However, for the longer structure, the block algorithm shows

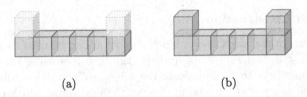

(a)   (b)

Fig. 5. Structure for demonstrating guided construction. (a) The initial state of the structure is a line consisting of six blocks. (b) The structure is completed by placing a block at each end of the structure. (Color figure online)

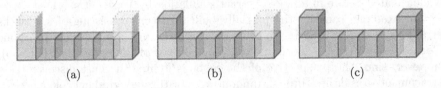

(a)   (b)   (c)

Fig. 6. Construction of the structure in Fig. 5 using a standard algorithm. (Color figure online)

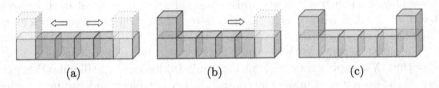

(a)   (b)   (c)

Fig. 7. Construction of the structure in Fig. 5 using a block algorithm to indicate which way a robot should turn to reach a valid construction site. (Color figure online)

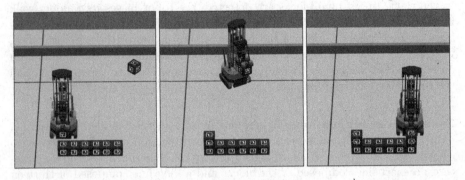

Fig. 8. Illustration of the construction of the structure in Fig. 5 with a block algorithm in the ARGoS simulator. (a) The robot attaches a block to the top of the leftmost block. (b) The illumination pattern is updated by the root block and the robot searches to the right for possible construction sites. (c) The robot attaches the last block to the top of the rightmost block.

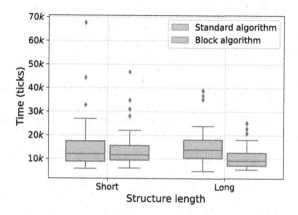

Fig. 9. Time taken to build the short and long structures in simulation using a standard algorithm and a block algorithm. Each structure was built 25 times. Each box consists of observations ranging from the first to the third quartile. The median is indicated by a horizontal bar, dividing the box into the upper and lower part. The whiskers extend to the farthest data points that are within 1.5 times the interquartile range. Outliers are shown as dots.

marginally better performance than the standard algorithm. From comparing the results for the two structures, it appears that the decrease in construction time is related to the size of the structure, however, further experiments with different types of structures and varying numbers of robots are needed to get a proper insight into this relationship. The videos and the source code for reproducing these experiments are available as part of the OSF project.[3]

3.3   Flexible Construction

Implementing construction in a swarm robotics system using a standard algorithm puts a heavy burden on the designer to come up with a set of rules that unambiguously maps each intermediate state of a structure to a construction action. This burden is only made worse when we want to design rules that facilitate flexible construction. For example, consider the structure in Fig. 10. If we wanted to build this structure using the standard algorithm, we could constrain the building process so that there is only one construction path that can be followed, that is, there is exactly one construction action associated with each intermediate state (Fig. 11). This constrained approach, however, may be inefficient, since a robot could approach a possible construction site but be prohibited to attach a block due to the constraints of the rule set. In contrast to the constrained approach, if we allow a building process where a robot can attach

---

[3] Videos: `gc-standard-algorithm.mp4` and `gc-block-algorithm.mp4` at https://osf. io/5h9cs/ and https://osf.io/cdvty/.
Source code: `gc-standard-algorithm.zip` and `gc-block-algorithm.zip` at https://osf.io/we754/ and https://osf.io/3znua/.

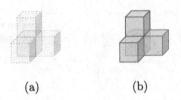

Fig. 10. Candidate structure for flexible construction. (a) initial state of the structure, (b) target state of the structure.

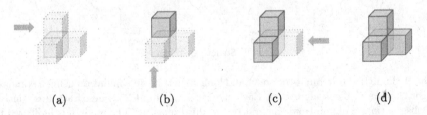

(a)   (b)   (c)   (d)

Fig. 11. The structure in Fig. 10, can be built sequentially using a standard algorithm to map the possible intermediate states of the structure (configurations of blocks) to construction actions.

a block to any possible construction site at any time, the number of possible intermediate states would increase significantly. Even for the simple structure in Fig. 10, the number of intermediate states increases from three to seven. Finding the unambiguous mappings between all of these intermediate states and the possible construction actions that advance the building process while keeping the structure in a valid state is at least difficult and may in many cases be infeasible.

A block algorithm can solve this problem since the root block can detect when and where one or more blocks have been added to (or removed from) a structure and can update the illumination pattern on the blocks accordingly. Furthermore, in the case of a block being attached to an incorrect site, the root block can detect the incorrectly placed block and update the illumination pattern so that nearby robots remove it, restoring the structure to a valid intermediate state. In the final experiment for this paper, we demonstrate the construction of the structure in Fig. 10 using the ARGoS simulator.

Results from Simulation. We have implemented the construction of the structure in Fig. 10 using a standard algorithm for sequential construction with a single robot (Fig. 12) and with a block algorithm for construction of the same structure with three robots in parallel. Videos of these experiments and the related source code are available online as part of our OSF project for this research[4].

---

[4] Videos: `fc-standard-algorithm.mp4` and `fc-block-algorithm.mp4` at https://osf. io/ycxes/ and https://osf.io/tvhs2/.

Source code: `fc-standard-algorithm.zip` and `fc-block-algorithm.zip` at https://osf.io/gf94r/ and https://osf.io/kjhu7/.

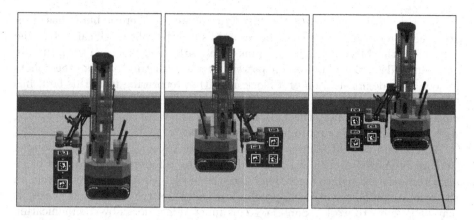

Fig. 12. Construction of the structure in Fig. 10 using a standard algorithm with a single robot in simulation.

4   Discussion

In this section, we compare the ability of the standard algorithms and the block algorithms to recover from faults during construction. Furthermore, we consider the trade-offs that we have made as a result of introducing a degree of centralization into our system and as a result of requiring more capable building materials.

4.1   Fault Tolerance

For this part of our discussion, we consider two types of faults and how the standard and block algorithms can recover from them. The first type of fault is when a robot attaches a block to an incorrect site. This fault can be caused by a sensor error on the behalf of the robot or can be due to unfortunate timing. For example, when two or more robots attach blocks to valid attachment sites but where the combination of those attachments puts the structure into an incorrect state. The second type of fault is when a block stops working correctly. This fault may be the result of a bad power source, corrupted firmware, or damaged hardware.

The standard algorithms can handle the first type of fault, where a block has been incorrectly attached to a structure, at the cost of increasing the complexity of the rule set. That is, in addition to the rules necessary to advance the construction, it would be possible to add rules that match the structure when it is in an incorrect state and that trigger the removal of one or more blocks until the structure is back in a state from which the construction can continue. The second type of fault is difficult to solve with the standard algorithm and relies on the robots being able to infer that a block is faulty, e.g., the LEDs are displaying the wrong color. If the robots detect a faulty block in the structure, it can be ignored or removed if it is disruptive to the building process.

For the block algorithms, the first type of fault, where a block has been attached to an incorrect site, can be resolved since the root block can detect the presence of this block by exchanging messages with other blocks in the structure and can update the illumination pattern of the structure so that the robots remove it. A demonstration of a block algorithm recovering from this fault has been implemented for the dynamic construction paths discussed in Sect. 3.1. A video of the recovery from this fault is available as part of the OSF project along with the source code to reproduce the experiment[5].

The second type of failure, that is, if the block has (i) a bad power source, (ii) corrupted firmware, or (iii) damaged hardware, is more problematic for block algorithms than standard algorithms since the block algorithms currently rely on the accurate propagation of information through the structure. In some cases, it may be possible to work around these malfunctioning blocks by communicating through other blocks; however, thin sections of the structure where there is only a single path through which information can flow remain problematic and will require further research.

4.2   Trade-Offs

Although the experiments in this paper show that the block algorithms can make construction more flexible and efficient and can put less of a burden on the system designer, there are some important trade-offs that must be addressed. The first trade-off is the increase in complexity of the building materials, which can no longer be passive but now have to be capable of computation and local communication, which increases the cost and necessitates a source of power. This trade-off, however, is not so unreasonable considering recent developments in smart label technology where NFC communication, small micro-controllers, and lithium batteries can be combined into cheap flexible tags that could be attached to building materials in an automated construction system.

The second trade-off that must be considered is that a block algorithm uses a root block in the structure to coordinate its construction, introducing a form of centralized control which may be undesirable since (i) it is a potential bottleneck in terms of computational and communication throughput and (ii) it creates a single point of failure in the system. We believe, however, that it is feasible to use centralized control in a swarm robotics construction system without negating the benefits of decentralized control as long as the following conditions can be met: (i) the role of the centralized controller can be transferred to another unit in the case of hardware failure, and (ii) the centralized controller can partially delegate its authority to other units so that it is not a computational/communication bottleneck in the system (see [10] for recent research in these directions).

---

[5] Video: `dcp-fault-tolerance.mp4` at https://osf.io/mvhk6/.
   Source code: `dcp-fault-tolerance.zip` at https://osf.io/scm7q/.

5 Conclusion

In this paper, we demonstrated the advantages of moving the intelligence that coordinates a building process in a swarm robotics construction system from the robots and into the building material. We referred to these algorithms as block algorithms and compared them against solutions where the intelligence that coordinates construction was in the robots, namely the standard algorithms.

In future work, we intend to investigate the scalability and fault tolerance of the block algorithms and to validate the experiments presented in this paper using real robots.

Acknowledgments. This work is partially supported by the Program of Concerted Research Actions (ARC) of the Université libre de Bruxelles, by a Research Credit (CDR – Crédit de Recherche) grant from the Belgian F.R.S.-FNRS, and by the European Union's Horizon 2020 research and innovation programme under the Marie Skłodowska-Curie grant agreement No 846009. Yating Zheng and Weixu Zhu would like to acknowledge their support from the China Scholarship Council (grant numbers 201806040106 and 201706270186). The research in this paper was partly undertaken at the UJI Robotic Intelligence Laboratory. Support for this laboratory is provided in part by Ministerio de Economía y Competitividad (DPI2015-69041-R) and by Universitat Jaume I (UJI-B2018-74). Marco Dorigo acknowledges support from the Belgian F.R.S.-FNRS, of which he is a Research Director.

References

1. Allwright, M., Bhalla, N., Dorigo, M.: Structure and markings as stimuli for autonomous construction. In: Proceedings of the Eighteenth International Conference on Advanced Robotics, pp. 296–302. IEEE (2017). https://doi.org/10.1109/icar.2017.8023623
2. Allwright, M., Bhalla, N., Pinciroli, C., Dorigo, M.: Simulating multi-robot construction in ARGoS. In: Dorigo, M., Birattari, M., Blum, C., Christensen, A.L., Reina, A., Trianni, V. (eds.) ANTS 2018. LNCS, vol. 11172, pp. 188–200. Springer, Cham (2018). https://doi.org/10.1007/978-3-030-00533-7_15
3. Allwright, M., Zhu, W., Dorigo, M.: An open-source multi-robot construction system. HardwareX **5**, e00050 (2019). https://doi.org/10.1016/j.ohx.2018.e00050
4. Bonabeau, E., Guérin, S., Snyers, D., Kuntz, P., Theraulaz, G.: Three-dimensional architectures grown by simple 'stigmergic' agents. BioSystems **56**(1), 13–32 (2000). https://doi.org/10.1016/s0303-2647(00)00067-8
5. Brambilla, M., Ferrante, E., Birattari, M., Dorigo, M.: Swarm robotics: a review from the swarm engineering perspective. Swarm Intell. **7**(1), 1–41 (2013). https://doi.org/10.1007/s11721-012-0075-2
6. Grassé, P.P.: Reconstruction of the nest and coordination between individuals in terms. Bellicositermes Natalensis and Cubitermes sp. the theory of stigmergy: Test interpretation of termite constructions. Insectes Sociaux **6**(1), 41–80 (1959). https://doi.org/10.1007/bf02223791
7. Hamann, H.: Swarm Robotics: A Formal Approach. Springer, Cham (2018). https://doi.org/10.1007/978-3-319-74528-2

8. Jones, C., Matarić, M.J.: From local to global behavior in intelligent self-assembly. In: 2003 IEEE International Conference on Robotics and Automation, pp. 721–726. IEEE (2002). https://doi.org/10.1109/robot.2003.1241679

9. Jones, C., Matarić, M.J.: Automatic synthesis of communication-based coordinated multi-robot systems. In: 2004 IEEE/RSJ International Conference on Intelligent Robots and Systems, pp. 381–387. IEEE (2004). https://doi.org/10.1109/iros.2004.1389382

10. Mathews, N., Christensen, A.L., O'Grady, R., Mondada, F., Dorigo, M.: Mergeable nervous systems for robots. Nat. Commun. 8(439), 1–7 (2017). https://doi.org/10.1038/s41467-017-00109-2

11. Petersen, K., Nagpal, R., Werfel, J.: TERMES: An autonomous robotic system for three-dimensional collective construction. In: Proceedings of Robotics: Science and Systems, pp. 257–264. RSS Foundation (2011). https://doi.org/10.15607/rss.2011.vii.035

12. Pinciroli, C., et al.: ARGoS: a modular, parallel, multi-engine simulator for multi-robot systems. Swarm Intell. 6(4), 271–295 (2012). https://doi.org/10.1007/s11721-012-0072-5

13. Sugawara, K., Doi, Y.: Collective construction by cooperation of simple robots and intelligent blocks. In: Kubota, N., Kiguchi, K., Liu, H., Obo, T. (eds.) ICIRA 2016. LNCS (LNAI), vol. 9834, pp. 452–461. Springer, Cham (2016). https://doi.org/10.1007/978-3-319-43506-0_40

14. Sugawara, K., Doi, Y.: Collective construction of dynamic equilibrium structure through interaction of simple robots with semi-active blocks. In: Chong, N.-Y., Cho, Y.-J. (eds.) Distributed Autonomous Robotic Systems. STAR, vol. 112, pp. 165–176. Springer, Tokyo (2016). https://doi.org/10.1007/978-4-431-55879-8_12

15. Theraulaz, G., Bonabeau, E.: Coordination in distributed building. Science 269(5224), 686–688 (1995). https://doi.org/10.1126/science.269.5224.686

16. Theraulaz, G., Bonabeau, E.: A brief history of stigmergy. Artif. Life 5(2), 97–116 (1999). https://doi.org/10.1162/106454699568700

17. Werfel, J., Nagpal, R.: Extended stigmergy in collective construction. IEEE Intell. Syst. 21(2), 20–28 (2006). https://doi.org/10.1109/mis.2006.25

18. Werfel, J., Nagpal, R.: Three-dimensional construction with mobile robots and modular blocks. Int. J. Robot. Res. 27(3–4), 463–479 (2008). https://doi.org/10.1177/0278364907084984

19. Werfel, J., Petersen, K., Nagpal, R.: Designing collective behavior in a termite-inspired robot construction team. Science 343(6172), 754–758 (2014). https://doi.org/10.1126/science.1245842

20. Zheng, Y., Allwright, M., Zhu, W., Kassawat, M., Han, Z., Dorigo, M.: Hybrid coordination for swarm construction (2020). https://doi.org/10.17605/osf.io/vh2k6

Correction to: Gaining Insight into Determinants of Physical Activity Using Bayesian Network Learning

Simone C. M. W. Tummers, Arjen Hommersom, Lilian Lechner,
Catherine Bolman, and Roger Bemelmans

Correction to:
Chapter "Gaining Insight into Determinants of Physical
Activity Using Bayesian Network Learning"
in: M. Baratchi et al. (Eds.): *Artificial Intelligence*
and Machine Learning, **CCIS 1398,**
https://doi.org/10.1007/978-3-030-76640-5_11

"Gaining Insight into Determinants of Physical Activity Using Bayesian Network Learning" was previously published non-open access. It has now been changed to open access under a CC BY 4.0 license and the copyright holder updated to 'The Author(s)'. The book has also been updated with this change.

The updated version of this chapter can be found at
https://doi.org/10.1007/978-3-030-76640-5_11

M. Baratchi et al. (Eds.): BNAIC/Benelearn 2020, CCIS 1398, p. C1, 2021.
https://doi.org/10.1007/978-3-030-76640-5_13

Author Index